Both Jenny Randles [and Peter Hough are] writers who have speci[alized in paranormal] phenomena. They hav[e collaborated on investi]gations and magazine [articles, as well as books] together.

Jenny Randles has had numerous books on the paranormal published and has written and presented radio programmes for both the BBC and IBA. She has appeared on or been consulted by radio and TV programmes around the world and is the paranormal consultant for ITV Teletext. She has also lectured and organized seminars with several universities in Britain and America.

Peter Hough has written over one hundred features for a variety of journals and magazines all over the world. He has also made a number of radio and television broadcasts, and lectured to the presitigious Institute of Physics and Royal Air Force personnel. Recently he advised and helped plan a two-hour TV documentary with NIPPON Television on UFOs.

SCARY STORIES

A Supernatural Yearbook

———— ◆ ————

Jenny Randles and Peter Hough

Futura

A Futura Book

First published in Great Britain in 1991 by Futura Publications
a Division of Macdonald & Co (Publishers) Ltd
London & Sydney

Printed and bound in Great Britain by
BPCC Hazell Books
Aylesbury, Bucks, England
Member of BPCC Ltd.

ISBN 0 7088 4484 7

Futura Publications
A Division of
Macdonald & Co (Publishers) Ltd
Orbit House
1 New Fetter Lane
London EC4A 1AR
A member of Maxwell Macmillan Pergamon Publishing Corporation

Authors' Note:

◆

In some of the stories which follow, names have been changed. The real identities of these witnesses are known to the authors, who are satisfied by the basic authenticity of the claims.

Where a name *has* been altered it has been done to avoid embarrassment to the percipient or his or her family – and was often a decision taken by the authors rather than by the witness. This change should not in any way detract from your acceptance of their story.

We would like to dedicate this book to those people within its pages who have had the courage to speak out about their strange experiences.

Life is full of little mysteries – and life itself is an even bigger mystery. We are feeling our way in the dark towards an understanding of reality and our path is illuminated by the brave souls willing to face prejudice and scepticism in order to say precisely what took place.

One day we may all owe them a debt.

Jenny Randles and Peter Hough, September 1990

CONTENTS

INTRODUCTION

Every story in this book is true. A couple may seem like old chestnuts, others have been culled from the pages of small journals, but most have never been published at all, until now. They are from our own files, and are the results of our investigations and personal interviews with the percipients.

To make these intriguing – and often frightening – accounts more digestible, we have presented them here in short-story form. But nothing has been changed which alters or conflicts with the basic facts of each case. Indeed, we believe it is wrong to sensationalize a subject which is intrinsically sensational by its very nature. But what this format has allowed us to do, is emphasize the emotional impact on a person who suddenly comes face to face with the Unknown. This natural component of the *super*natural is necessarily underplayed in the dry pages of academic reports which lie in the filing cabinets of psychical societies. Ironically, the emotional factor may be one of the keys to our understanding of events which are currently beyond scientific comprehension.

How would you react upon being confronted by a friend whom you had seen blown to pieces by a landmine twelve years before? A friend who was solid and warm to the touch? That is what professional artist Henry Thomson claims in *A Bonfire Story*.

How would you feel if a disembodied voice told you your stepfather was about to die – a man who had mistreated and abused you? That was what happened to fourteen-year-old Caroline Howe in *January's Deadly Voices*.

1

WHAT IF THAT PROMISE CAME TRUE?

Would you feel helpless if *your* family was suddenly plagued by a sinister nocturnal noise and your house invaded by small beings? In *The August Story, Terror in the House of Dolls*, you will find out how it feels.

To make this collection more interesting we have selected accounts which tie in with certain months and special dates of the year. There are also Birth, Marriage, and Death stories. Everyone remembers certain dates because of the emotional impact of particular incidents.

Did *you* attend a wedding on Saturday, 19 September 1987? Larry Mayer did, and it's a wedding he will never forget. On his way home through the dark South Yorkshire countryside, he lost a period of time after seeing something very strange hovering in a wood. Read about it in *After the Wedding*.

Do you celebrate St Valentine's Day with a loved one? On St Valentine's Day, 1981, Lee Fields was rushing back home to England from Germany, for a date with Death. It's all there in *St Valentine's Day – Warning From The Heart*.

Easter is a time of religious celebration, but there was something ungodly in the cellar of the Bull's Head that weekend during 1985, as two men were to find out. In *The Easter Monday Poltergeist*, one of them was left with more than just mental scars.

At the beginning of this introduction, we stated that 'every story in this book is true'. Perhaps this needs some qualification. Certainly those involved in these bizarre experiences are not *lying*. Many carry the mental, and sometimes the physical, scars which seem to indicate that *something* out of the ordinary has occurred. But what the exact nature of that 'something' is, is an evolving debate.

What we have presented here is mainly the raw data of a person's *experience*, without the in-depth investigation and inquest which often take place afterwards. If your interest takes you beyond this basic narrative, then we try to help by directing you to many sources which cover the subject more deeply. You will find a comprehensive section at the back of this book, together with the names of leading researchers.

While it is 'true' that people have out-of-body experiences, are confronted by apparitions and have close encounters with UFOs, this does not necessarily mean that the essence of a person has actually left the body, or that apparitions are spirits of the dead, any more than UFOs are extraterrestrial spacecraft. While we may accept the sincerity of a witness, we make no presumptions about precisely *what* they have witnessed.

We have collated a list of useful addresses which you will find at the end of this book. If you think you have had an anomalous experience, the organizations listed there will be pleased to hear from you. We can be contacted by writing to the address for NUFON given in that section. But if you would like a reply try not to forget return postage.

Now read on, and enjoy . . .

BIRTH

Alone and Defenceless

◆

This was her greatest joy: Margaret was pregnant.

She had been married for only six months when they got the news. Her husband, Bill, was working a horrible schedule in the Maryland office, trying to make ends meet and keep up the payments that would let them cope with their newfound togetherness.

But now this. He would have to keep to that terrible days on, days off, nights on, nights off programme. She would see far less of him than she might choose, but wasn't this the way for most newlywed couples who had started out together?

Her thoughts drifted back to her own childhood. It had been a strange time. Things were so different in America in those postwar years. But the most different thing of all had been that strange ability she had possessed as a youngster. Then it simply faded – as she grew up.

For years she had *floated*. That was the only word that described what took place. She drifted free of the moorings of her body and sailed into the air, hovering in a pleasant kind of buoyancy by a corner of the ceiling.

These bizarre nocturnal expeditions happened frequently. Sometimes she would be sent to bed early and this floating would be a good way to ease the tensions. So what if she had been chided for some slightly naughty deed? Her parents did not know her secret.

They could not fly.

It was so peaceful there, over by the corner resting against the wall. If she practised she could bump up and touch it. That felt good. How pretty all the lights looked too. From up here you had a whole new perspective on the world.

But then when she was fourteen it just stopped. She could no longer float. All she was left with was a terrible fear of heights, like some psychic legacy that was scarring her memories.

Would Margaret's child have this strange ability, which perhaps was something peculiar to certain children? Maybe adults lost it, just like in *Peter Pan*. Of course, that was a fairy tale, but what a delightful thought ... Romantic childish nonsense *might* be TRUE!

Others had told her not to be so silly. People did not fly – *could* not fly. It was all just imagination or a dream. After all, hadn't it stopped at about the same time that her father died? The emotional shock of losing him while still a teenager must have preyed heavily on her mind. A psychologist would explain it all in a trice.

That would be it. That was what had caused her delusions.

But then hadn't she also had that weird dream the very night before her father died? The one where she seemed to know that he was passing away from her and she might never see him again.

Was that coincidence, or more akin to those poems she used to conjure up magically out of thin air. Was there something special about the young mind that vanished with the passage of the years?

What a terrible and rather awful prospect. A kind of psychic senility.

Alone in the apartment, she smiled at the reality. She was pregnant as can be. The night stretched ahead, with her husband having just left for work. The clock ticked ponderously onward, past 11.30 p.m. Bill did not start work until midnight, but he always liked to be early. That was just his way.

Margaret was careful. Precautions had to be taken in an age where burglars doubled as gunmen and life came all too cheap. Who could know what danger might snap unexpectedly at your heels?

She made the door fast, locking it and putting on the heavy safety chain that was a fact of life in many American homes. Then she went to the bed, closed the door and pretended that Bill was still in the adjacent living room, maybe reading a book. Her conscious mind knew the lie, but it was one she told herself often. Somehow it seemed to help as the lonely night drew on and she fought her battles against insomnia and tiredness.

Suddenly there was a sound. For a moment her heart leapt as she thought of all those TV images and her nightmares about someone breaking in while she was all alone. The key in the front door was turning. Then the chain rattled, as if being cast aside.

It was only Bill. He had returned. What on earth had he forgotten this time?

She could hear his footsteps pounding about in the living room. Then he entered the kitchen and opened cupboard doors. What was going on? Had he left his packed meal behind? He never did that. Soon it would be obvious. He was approaching the bedroom door and would tell her what was going on.

The handle turned. The door did not open.

Fear crawled up Margaret's throat ... 'Bill – What are you doing?' she forced herself to say. The footsteps retreated. The front door opened and the chain clanked. Then there was silence.

She remained in the stillness and isolation for some moments. Her breathing was heavy. Her heart pounded. She rushed to the window, determined to call out to Bill as he left the front of the building and demand to know why he had scared her so.

The car was not in the parking lot. The area was

deserted. No movement. Nothing. How could Bill get into the car and drive away in the few seconds before she had reached this vantage point? How could anyone?

It was impossible, and she knew it. But knowing it made the truth only harder to bear.

She went to the kitchen. The cupboard doors were loosely ajar as if someone might have looked in them. But nothing was missing. It could not have been a thief, because there was no sign that anything which came easily to hand had been snatched. Besides, wasn't the door still on its chain?

No – it *had* to be Bill. What other explanation could there be? She cast aside all question of how the chain could be fastened again, once he was back outside.

Sleep was impossible. She gave it a few more minutes, enough time for Bill to return to work after his hasty exit.

It was now after midnight. He had to be back there now.

She dialled the number. Bill answered. What was all the fuss about? he asked. He had been at work, as usual, since 11.30 p.m. Of course, he had not come back and scared her half to death. What did she take him for?

'No,' she kept saying. 'That's not possible.'

Bill put his boss on the line. 'Sure, Bill has been here all the while. He didn't leave. I should know.'

Margaret went crazy about someone or some *thing* getting in, and so Bill insisted on going straight home. He even made his boss talk to her all the time until he finally *did* open the front door. After that he refused to work another night shift.

Bill and Margaret never did find out who the mysterious intruder was. Slowly the clinging terror disappeared. For there were too many other things to think about more worthy. The baby was on its way.

The great day came and Margaret went into hospital for the exhilarating, if exhausting, experience of childbirth. As is natural in such situations, she made friends with the woman in the next bed whose child was born just a few hours later.

8

This peculiar emotional bond linked them together in a curious way. Still groggy from the light anaesthetic Margaret heard the woman, Pat, ask what her new friend was called. She smiled back, murmuring her name, but it came out slurred, as if she was drunk. 'Margaret' ended up sounding like 'Margie'. Nobody had ever called her this before, but it was pleasant enough and so she never corrected it.

During the next few days preparations continued for both women to take their new arrivals home. They exchanged phone numbers, as they both lived in Maryland, although miles apart. In truth neither really expected the friendship to survive beyond the hospital walls.

Yet it was a strong relationship. It did survive. For some weeks they would call each other occasionally and swap stories about the progress of their respective offspring. Motherhood was new to them both and full of excitement and strange experiences. To have someone sharing the joys and the worries somehow heightened the moment.

The only sad part was that the large distance separating their homes prevented any reasonable prospect of a friendly meeting. So they made the most of the few odd moments on the telephone.

That would probably have been the way of things, with these sporadic conversations continuing for a little while until, very likely, the two women would have grown further apart and 'Margie' and Pat would gradually return to living their separate lives.

It was four months after the birth of the two babies. Bill had to go away on a course to New York where he was to learn all about a new computer system they were installing at work. Margaret was reluctant to be left alone, especially for six weeks. Although, of course, she was not alone. Not any longer. Besides, the memory of that nocturnal intruder was months in the past. It was fast disappearing and no longer caused any real distress. Whoever, or whatever, it had been could not harm her now.

Many miles away Pat did not know that her friend

Margie was alone. But she was suddenly plunged into a weird situation of her own.

The first phone call came early that morning. It was a man and Pat did not recognize his voice. Yet she could tell that he had the very distinctive accent of a native of the state of Pennsylvania. He seemed worried and said: 'Your friend Margaret is in danger. You must warn her.'

Then he hung up the phone.

Obviously this was a crank, Pat thought. She had no friend called Margaret. It was just some fool trying to frighten her or playing what he considered to be a practical joke.

Well it wasn't funny. Not to her. But it was the sort of thing you had to expect from time to time. It was one of the disadvantages of having a telephone.

That afternoon it became even less funny. The man rang again. 'You must tell your friend, Margaret Brendan. She is in great danger and only you can warn her.'

'Look, I don't know anyone called Margaret Brendan,' Pat insisted. But the distinctive click and tone indicated that the caller had hung up.

This was sick, Pat thought. As soon as her husband got home that evening she told him about the odd calls. Did he know a Margaret Brendan? No, he didn't. It was obviously a psycho and she had done the right thing by ignoring his pleas. He would not call again.

But at eight o'clock that night the phone gave a trill and there was the same richly accented voice saying: 'You haven't called her.'

Pat tried to explain that she did not know any Margaret Brendan. But the man, now irate, almost shouted down the phone: 'Margaret Evelyn Brendan. She is in very grave danger. You haven't even *tried* to contact her. Do it now!'

It sounded like an order. She sat by the phone stunned into silence, as the line beeped again to indicate that the caller had put down the receiver.

Jim, her husband, had immediately recognized that it was the spooky caller. He had rushed into the other room and picked up the extension. Just as he was about to say his piece the line had cleared.

'Did you hear it?' Pat asked him.

He nodded sombrely, rather shocked by the ferocity of the speaker.

This is nuts, they both thought, desperately trying to rack their brains to think of someone whose name began with 'M'. Whether the call was genuine or not they could take no risks.

Then it struck Pat. 'You know that woman I met in hospital. Her name is Margie. Do you think it might be her?'

Jim was not convinced. She was practically a stranger. Who would know of their bond? But it was the only lead they had. The only possible connection they could think of.

Pat called the number immediately, to find Margaret Brendan on her own.

Pat tried to sound calm, but could not avoid the strange feel of her peculiar question, 'What's your other name, Margie?'

'Brendan, why?'

'Oh God.' She related the story.

'Actually my name *is* Margaret, not Margie,' came the hushed response. 'And my middle name is Evelyn too.'

'But who ... What ...?' Pat said. The questions asked themselves.

The two women had no mutual friends. It made no sense at all. Who would go to all the trouble of calling Pat, such a distant acquaintance, with this repeated life or death message, when he could have just as easily called Margaret direct?

'You said this man had an accent?' Margaret enquired.

'Yes, Pennsylvanian.'

'You're sure?'

'Absolutely ... why?'

'My father came from Pennsylvania.'

'*Came* from?'

'He died when I was fourteen.'

The two friends exchanged pleasantries in a stunned manner, then Margaret said that she was going to call her husband in New York. She reassured her friend that she would be all right and would get a neighbour to come round immediately.

Margaret called Bill at the training course. He was naturally disturbed and insisted on driving right over to collect her. 'There is no way I will let you two stay there on your own.'

As she packed her bags, the neighbour stayed with her, house lights blazing deep into the night. At last Bill arrived, thanked their friend for such kindness, and bundled Margaret and the child into the car. Almost without a second look they set off for the long drive to New York.

They stayed away for three weeks and as soon as they returned home Margaret called Pat. Her number was unobtainable and the operator advised that she had changed it, become unlisted and was no longer contactable.

Afraid, but she knew not why, Margaret persuaded Bill that they must do the same.

It is now several years later and Margaret has never heard from her friend again.

What was this all about? There is no clear answer. The voice never explained to Pat what the danger was and, most fortunately, no such danger ever befell the Brendans. But the thought still haunted tiny corners of Margaret's mind. What if she had stayed in that building on her own? The idea that somehow she had been spared from a terrible destiny was hard to push aside.

We have our suspicions. Perhaps no more than hints, but they suggest that the night-time visitor of some months before *might* have been more than just a figment of Margaret's imagination.

Margaret seems to have been what we call psychic. Did she receive a preview of what was to be – *if she dared to stay alone in that room*?

Was this a warning – screaming in silence through some

inexplicable process, telling Margaret that she was vulnerable to attack? A cry from some part of the mind that could see into the future and show her what might come to be? For surely, such an attack would have had devastating consequences for a young mother and her baby.

Yet the warning, if it was a warning, had not been heeded. It failed to impress upon the Brendans the extreme danger of the situation. And so a second, desperate plea from somewhere beyond may have become a necessity.

The only thing we know for sure is that during those three weeks while Margaret was away in New York a spate of break-ins took place at the local apartments.

Was the Brendan household already targeted for attack? And – if it had been selected by some callous thief – then almost certainly Margaret would have been in there, standing in the intruder's way, without her husband or protection for herself and her baby.

She would have been alone ... Alone and defenceless.

JANUARY

3rd Edgar Cayce, a famous American psychic healer, died this day 1945, after successfully predicting his own funeral three days before!

6th Twelfth Night. Superstition says it is now safe to take down Christmas decorations.

10th An entity which had manifested in a house on the Isle of Man, calling itself 'Gef', successfully predicted the winner of the Grand National, in 1932. The entity, which said it was a talking mongoose, spoke to many journalists and psychic investigators. The case was either an elaborate joke, or a further example of the bizarreness of poltergeist phenomena.

16th In 1958, a Brazilian survey ship, the *Almirante Saldanha*, packed with scientists, was anchored off the island of Trindade, when a bright object was observed moving across the sky. Saturn-shaped, it was silent, dark grey, and covered in a greenish mist. Several photographs were taken of the object, and because of the calibre of the witnesses, it is judged that this case is impressive.

18th In 1979, the House of Lords debated the UFO phenomenon.

23rd Loud unexplained explosions were heard in the mountains near Llandrillo, Clywd, in 1974.

25th Betty Andreasson, of South Ashburnham, Massachusetts, in 1967 was allegedly abducted from her home by UFO entities, while her family were rendered paralysed.

The entities had pear-shaped heads and almond-shaped eyes. She was subjected to a frightening and painful physical examination by these entities before being released.

28th A young girl student at college in Widnes, Cheshire, burst into flames in front of eye-witnesses and later died, an alleged victim of spontaneous human combustion. The 1985 inquest ruled otherwise and the coroner advised the jury to reject such paranormal sensationalism.

Deadly Voices

———————— ◆ ————————

Life was never easy for Caroline Howe. At fourteen and already facing an uncertain future without her father, she was growing into an unruly teenager with a stepfather who would sometimes beat her senseless.

Christmas 1964 had offered a brief respite in the haven of their Lincolnshire home, but as the New Year began she saw more long months of torture ahead. The situation was desperate. Holiday revelry, and drink, brought added danger.

On New Year's Day she slept fitfully. Something was eating away at her, deep inside. The feeling persisted over the weekend, but it had no clear origin. She spent the nights tossing and turning, casting blankets hither and thither. How far away was the dawn? How long before she could get up and be free of her fears?

Suddenly, as Caroline lay prone, a sound teased her mind. It was a woman's voice, calling softly 'Caroline – Caroline.'

She ignored it. This had to be a dream.

But the dream was a nightmare that went on and on. In the end she had to answer the spectral call.

The soothing voice was like nobody the young girl

15

remembered and it asked some very strange questions.

'How would you feel if I were to say that your stepfather is going to die?'

Caroline pondered. 'We all die.'

'I mean soon.'

Memories of the maltreatment suffered at his hands swept across the teenager in a deluge. 'I would clap my hands and jump for joy.'

There was no response from the voice. But immediately she had said these words, Caroline felt a twinge of guilt.

After a moment the stranger continued: 'Caroline, I would like you to promise me something.'

'Yes.'

'Will you look after your mother?'

'Of course.'

As if satisfied, the weird floating voice that tickled inside her head said finally, 'You must not get up and look at me. I want you to lie there on your stomach for twenty minutes. Then you may get up.'

The voice trailed away. Not for a second did Caroline think of disobeying. She knew what she must do.

Time passed and the terrified girl lay face down with her head pressed into the sheets. What would she see if she dared to look up? Could she peek now? Were the twenty minutes up?

With eyes half closed she cast the bedclothes aside. Making a wild grab for her daywear, the girl fled the room. Clattering down the stairs, still half naked, her breath coming in spasms, she plunged from the darkness and through into the kitchen.

It was just after 6 a.m. Her mother was making porridge for breakfast.

The poor girl stood there, looking helpless and visibly shaken. Her mother, never having seen her daughter in such a state, demanded to know what was wrong. Caroline blurted out the whole story.

Shock filled her mother's face. 'That's ridiculous. It was just a dream.'

Caroline shook her head.

'Yes it was. Now get dressed and ready for school.'

Dream or not, the memory haunted Caroline. A new term was beginning that Monday and much work had to be done. But the sound of the strange voice and its terrible warning would not go away. It gripped her tight with invisible claws.

For a week Caroline struggled through. Nothing further happened and the bedroom became more welcoming again. Night after night of expecting something, anything, followed by nothing except darkness and sleep.

At school, work progressed normally. But the next Monday morning, when Caroline was in history class, the terror struck again. They were copying some notes from the board and the teacher was passing from desk to desk, peering over the shoulders of each pupil in turn to check on the results of their work.

The woman hovered by Caroline, staring down at her exercise book. 'Howe, I thought I told you to copy that out.' She glanced back at the board and gestured.

Caroline was baffled. She was a swift writer, having had much practice, and she had already finished the notes.

'I have copied it, Miss,' she insisted.

The teacher then did a very strange thing. She grabbed the girl by her long hair and pulled her head up until it was facing her own.

'You have not,' the woman claimed.

Caroline was suddenly overcome by a wave of revulsion. It was something that she had never experienced before. Anger and hatred boiled up inside, brewing a maelstrom, and she exploded into an uncontrollable rage.

As the rest of the class looked on in astonishment, Caroline grabbed the teacher's hair and smashed her fist into the startled woman's face. Her spectacles tumbled to the floor, damaged beyond repair. The hefty blows brought out the first traces of two black eyes in the bemused tutor.

Stunned into defensive action, the teacher stood back,

pulling the maniacal-pupil with her. Caroline was ripping and tearing at the woman's clothing, as the turmoil inside her continued to bubble in an inexplicable fashion.

Barking instructions to the class, the shocked teacher led the girl to the front of the class. Caroline was calming a little, but the anger still seethed within.

'You will go straight to the head. This appalling behaviour will not be tolerated.'

In a peculiar state of half-consciousness, Caroline crept along the corridor to the office of the headmistress. She knocked softly on the door and was invited to enter and then to explain why she was there.

Caroline replied, 'The teacher said I was to come. She pulled my hair, so I pulled hers back. She said I hadn't done the work. But I had done it. Then I hit her.'

The headmistress reflected on the situation and reached out for the most immediate remedy.

'Hold out your hand!' she ordered, brandishing the thin wooden cane with which severe punishment was meted out.

'But, miss . . .'

'Do as I say. Now!'

Caroline held out her hand, but as the cane came rushing towards her palm with a swish of displaced air, the girl grabbed it and yanked it from the unprepared head-mistress.

Still unaware of what she was doing, Caroline raised the cane and thrashed it against the cheek of the headmistress, then brought it down on the other side of the middle-aged woman's face.

Heart racing and in a state of fury, the girl dropped the cane to the floor with a clatter. The headmistress could hardly grasp what had taken place, for her assailant had already burst from the room and was running down the corridor as if demented.

Within seconds Caroline was out of the building and heading home in a crazy and unrelentless flight.

As she reached the house, Caroline's mind had cleared

somewhat. The rage had dissipated, like a punctured balloon. She now understood what had just transpired, but not how or why.

Knowing full well that she must tell the truth and explain why she was home from school in the middle of the morning, she was very much aware of what would follow.

Excuse or no excuse, justification or not, her stepfather would react with venom. He would behave exactly as she had just behaved, beating his stepdaughter for her gross misdemeanour. There was no escape. The result was inevitable.

As she stood by the back door, Caroline was puzzled by the silence which enveloped the house. She called out: 'Mum?' But there was no answer. Bursting in through the kitchen and dining room, she found nobody there. The house appeared empty.

Then came a noise which sounded like laughter. Her four-year-old sister, Lorraine, was chuckling. At least, that was who it seemed to be.

'Lorraine?' the girl called. Again there was no answer.

Entering the sitting room, from whence the chuckling sound had emerged, Caroline saw Lorraine playing on the floor over in the corner. She seemed happy enough.

'Lorraine – where are Mum and Dad?' Caroline enquired.

Her sister pointed, amidst a giggle, directing Caroline to the fireplace.

A settee obscured the full view. As she walked around it, Caroline's mind was still confused and she was not anticipating what lay in wait.

On the floor in front of the fireplace lay her stepfather, a broad smile beaming across his face. He was silent and still, as if enjoying a game. Caroline was sure that was what it was. He was playing a game with Lorraine.

Yet, spreadeagled across the top of him was their mother. She was clearly unconscious.

Caroline tried to wake them both. But only her mother

stirred. Her stepfather was rigid and was certainly not playing a game.

He was dead.

Much later, after the ambulance had taken both her parents away, Caroline began to wonder what had happened.

She never found out. Her mother was in deep shock and could not bring herself to speak, or think, about the terrible events that had occurred in that room. Lorraine grew up with a blank in her mind, knowing nothing of the tragedy that had unfolded about her.

But had her stepfather been aggressive? Was this what Caroline had picked up, like a distress flare, at the emotional level? Was that why she had suddenly behaved in such a bizarre manner?

The questions continued, but there was still no explanation.

It took many months of hospital treatment before Caroline's mother showed signs of improvement, undergoing electro-convulsive therapy to try to bring her out of her stupor. It appeared that the stepfather had in fact suffered a heart attack and so there were actually no suspicious circumstances surrounding his death. And yet . . .

Caroline knew there was more to this affair than anybody else realized.

For why had she suddenly gone beserk at school and then rushed home at precisely the appropriate moment? And whose was that voice that had told her about the catastrophe days before it happened and who had seemingly foreseen the need for somebody to look after her mother?

Caroline took great care of her surviving parent as they both battled to recover from the tragedy. After a while they could bring themselves to speak about the voice that had come in the night.

'I believe you now,' her mother said reassuringly.

'I told you it was not a dream.'

'No. But do you know who it was?'

Caroline said she did not.

'I think it was your gran. She would have wanted to look after me.'

Caroline had never known her mother's mother. The woman had died several years before her first grandchild was born.

Some years later Caroline's mother made an almost complete recovery and there was a new man in her life. She married him and had two more children. Her eldest daughter, having lived up to the promise given to that phantom voice, married at the age of just eighteen and moved away to a village in South Humberside.

After a while she found herself awakening in the night with a strange sensation. It was like pins and needles all over her body. Caroline consulted a doctor and he said she was not getting enough oxygen during the night and the best way to handle these attacks was to breathe deeply into a paper bag. But this remedy did not really help.

Then one night Caroline awoke and found herself floating about eight feet above the bed, but she could see her own body down below on the bed. She was absolutely petrified.

I don't want to die, she kept thinking. *I have my children to live for, and my mother.*

In 1970 Caroline's first daughter had been born. Soon after the child learned to speak, she began to wake up in the middle of the night screaming. Sleeping potions did nothing to help and Caroline would try desperately to placate the child. The toddler said that a woman wearing black clothing was standing silently by the end of the bed and was frightening her night after night.

Naturally, Caroline thought about her own experiences. Could this be her grandmother returning again? But why appear to the child and why frighten her in this way? Why did she not speak?

Caroline delved into the history of the house – part of a

new estate – and discovered it had been built on the site of a very old farmhouse. She tracked down an elderly man who had lived in the village when the farm still existed. Did he remember anything odd about it?

'Oh, yes,' he told her. 'It was very sad. There was this woman who looked after her father. She always used to wear black. One day she fell in love with a man and wanted to marry him, but the father said no. In those days the way of the country was that a woman obeyed her father. She had no choice. But her love was intense. She strung herself up from the rafters and hung herself.'

'Which room?' Caroline asked urgently.

'I'm not sure,' she was told.

But it turned out to be below the area which was now in use as their nursery.

The family packed up and moved out.

As the years rolled by the memories of these events have faded, but they remain as a symbol of how the supernatural can invade your life.

Caroline has since had another fright. One night she woke up to feel a strange sensation, a feeling that she knew only too well from her past experiences, a feeling that something was amiss, but not knowing exactly what.

Opening her eyes, in trepidation, she observed a dark form bending over the bed.

Desperately she tried to shake her husband awake, as he slumbered beside her. It was as if he were deeply unconscious. Nothing would make him budge.

Meanwhile the figure continued to look at her. It was a man, but she could not see who it was. *If only it would speak*, she thought to herself. But the man continued to stare at her and remained silent.

Caroline dived under the covers and did not dare to surface until the morning.

Was this another warning? The thought buzzed around her head, but she said nothing. Then, some while later, an image flashed into her mind in the middle of the day. It would not go away. It was sharp and very clear and featured an envelope with the name and address of her mother-in-law written upon it.

This time there was nothing else to do but tell her husband. He was baffled, but recognized her fear and sincerity. Immediately they set out for his parents' home.

On arrival, they were greeted with sombre faces and the words: 'You had better sit down. There is something you have to know.'

Caroline's brother-in-law stared at them both, and said: 'It's mother. She has taken an overdose. They've taken her to Lincoln Hospital.'

On this occasion, there was a happy ending. Caroline's mother-in-law pulled through. But there remains with Caroline a terrible dread that one day the dark figure will wake her from her sleep or speak those strange, soft words into her mind.

If it does, then Caroline knows one thing. Ghosts do not bring good news.

The Bi-centennial Terror

---- ◆ ----

January 1988 was an exciting time for every Australian. The bi-centennial of the nation was due to be celebrated in grand and most extravagant style, with royal visitors, huge spectaculars and a TV show that would be beamed around the world.

But, less than a week before the great day dawned, came events that were outside the control of any TV producer. They would shape the destiny of one family and for a time replace the celebrations on the front pages of newspapers from the southern to the northern hemisphere.

The party was about to be gatecrashed by a terror from the skies.

On 19 January, seven days before the anniversary, the Knowles family had been driving from Perth on the mammoth, several-day journey from west to east in order to reach Melbourne: a two-thousand-mile drive. It was the sort of expedition that you dream about and normally plan with great care.

This was to be something very special. They were to visit Mrs Knowles' own family, separated in that distant city. It was going to be a surprise. They did not know what was coming.

But neither did Mrs Faye Knowles and her three sons. They were about to face the surprise of *their* lives.

The coastal highway sweeps some miles inland between Eyre and the South Australian state border. To the north rise mountain ridges, guarding the hinterland which stretches on and on through thousands of miles of aborigine reservations and is one of the least populated yet enormous spaces on this earth. To the south lies the Great Australian Bight, an ocean filled with fishing vessels and nothing else, until you reach the frozen wastes of Antarctica, thousands of miles away.

The highway is like a ribbon of life bisecting two completely different environments. A few cars and a few more trucks owned by transport conglomerates rumble along, providing the connection between Australia's scattered and isolated pockets of habitation out to the west and the narrow coastal strip of modern civilization which grows and thrives far to the east.

With Faye Knowles on that expedition were her sons Patrick, aged twenty-four, Sean, twenty-one, and Wayne, just eighteen. They were driving a blue Ford Telstar sedan that was four years old. As with most trips through arid climates in the summer they were taking advantage of the cooler night air and making up as much ground as they could in the dark.

As Wednesday, 20 January began, the Knowles family were skirting the edge of the notorious Nullarbor Plain. It was a beautiful night, with many stars, a clear black sky and little in the way of wind. They were simply enjoying the experience.

Unknown to any of the occupants in the sedan a truck driven by Graham Henley was several miles ahead of them proceeding in the same direction. It was one of two, travelling as companions, both heading for Adelaide. The second truck was a similar distance behind the Knowles' car and contained John 'Porky' De Jong, the truck driver, and his girlfriend, Anne.

The trio of vehicles was sufficiently spread out on the unlit roadway that they were not aware of the location of any of the others during the dramatic events which were about to unfold.

At the Madura Pass, Porky stopped his truck to take a rest. He was only stationary for a few minutes but this stopover allowed Graham Henley to pull further ahead, with the Knowles' car in between the two trucks.

At about 4.15 a.m. Graham Henley observed a bright light in the sky through his rear-view mirror. It appeared above the highway to the west and looked like a brilliant star. It was unusual, not seeming to be car headlights coming up behind. He tried to use the CB radio to call back to Porky and suggest that he look out, since the light would probably be in front of the other truck. However, he could not raise his friend, who was not listening. Graham Henley also had no idea that the other truck was now about twenty miles further back and possibly out of range of the radio.

Graham Henley merely noted the incident, especially when the light eventually disappeared. He proceeded towards the next rest point, which would be the small township of Mundrabilla.

Meanwhile, some seven or eight miles behind Henley's truck, Sean Knowles spotted what was presumably the same light. It was white with a yellowish tinge and roughly kite-shaped. His immediate thought was that it was a truck on the highway ahead. Had he known about Henley's presence he would certainly have written it off as that vehicle's lights.

Sean Knowles dismissed the matter from his mind and continued with his driving. Patrick was in the seat next to him and his mother and Wayne were resting in the rear passenger seats. Their two dogs were with them in the car, passing the journey in silence and dozing away.

After a few moments Sean realized that the light in front of him was moving. In fact it was heading in their direction, low along the road surface on a virtual collision course. It seemed to jink from side to side, then it suddenly disappeared from view. By now he was very puzzled and debated its presence with the others.

As they continued the journey, the brilliant glow appeared again, this time brighter and again moving towards them. It seemed to be several feet wide and spanned the road. There was no obvious route of escape for the sedan.

Inside the car the tension rose to a sudden peak, as the glow swept down the road in their path. In the still night air its silence was eerie.

Now it was just feet away from the car and there was only one thing to do. Sean turned the wheel and swerved rapidly away from the left-hand kerb, swinging out towards the centre of the highway in a desperate ploy to get away from the 'thing'. But Sean had not seen the vehicle that was coming down the road in the opposite direction. It was a car towing a caravan, heading back towards Perth – the driver apparently unaware of the glowing object that was rapidly approaching from behind.

Sean swerved back into his lane, missing the car and caravan by inches. The latter vehicle continued on, the occupants presumably unperturbed – or possibly in desperate haste to escape from the pursuing glow. For the 'thing' in the sky had now apparently shunned the Knowleses and, to their great relief, was out of sight and behind them – moving off towards Perth and tailing the unfortunate car and caravan outfit.

Breathing more easily the Knowles had little time to discuss the termination of their ordeal, for the glow was suddenly back ahead of them, once more moving in their direction. How it had got there they did not know.

This time Sean was taking no chances. Checking that the road ahead was clear, he screeched the car into a U-turn, and charged off down the Eyre Highway heading back the way they had come. Somewhere, out of sight in the east, was that persistent glow.

Inside the car there was now pandemonium. The dogs were in turmoil. The passengers were not much calmer and Sean was desperately pushing the car to the limit of its speed in a frantic flight away from the 'thing'.

On top of all this a weird noise was now building up, seemingly above them. It was like a whirring or rotating hum. They had never heard anything like it before. As if in response to this terrifying 'music' the car was dancing up and down and shaking. Awful vibrations threatened to tear it apart.

Faye Knowles wound down the window and stuck out her hand. The whole family were certain the 'thing' was right above them, but they could not see anything except the blackness of night. Mrs Knowles felt something smooth and textured like rubber, and warm. It seemed as if the 'thing' was now on the roof of their car!

Meanwhile, just a few miles down the highway to the west, Anne and Porky were continuing their drive in the direction of the Knowles sedan. Each party did not know that they were careering straight towards the other, with the Knowles family convinced that a glowing nightmare was sitting on the roof of their Ford.

Anne had the CB and UHF radios switched on. There was distant background chatter, but the volume was purposely turned down as she was listening to a cassette to pass the time. Ahead of her the road stretched into night. Occasional cars buzzed by, but there was nothing at all strange about the drive. She could see no unusual lights at any point.

The Knowles could not see the glow now, either. But they knew it was there. Patrick had opened his window and stuck out his hand like his mother had done. When he drew it in, a fine layer of black dust was splattered over his palm. The dust came into the car, momentarily suspended like a grey mist, then settling all over the interior. Hastily all windows were sealed.

The car was still jerking and shaking as they rattled on as fast as Sean could drive, hitting bumps on the road and the tyres taking a battering. Suddenly they all became convinced that the car was rising into the air. The 'thing' above them was sucking them skywards, as if ready to devour them within its unseen mass!

A sickly odour was pervading the car. 'Like dead bodies' they agreed. They were all at screaming pitch. 'Oh God – we're going to die,' somebody said. But it seemed as if their speech was strangely slowed. A vacuum effect was taking air from the car and doing strange things to the pitch of their voices.

Then the car seemed to drop. Had they been floating? Nobody had dared look outside to see if they had left the ground, but now they were definitely back on the road. Then the car was swerving wildly. One of the tyres had burst and Sean was struggling to regain control.

Amazingly he whisked them off the edge of the highway and they came safely to a dead stop at the edge of the bush.

Heavy breathing punctured the silence. There seemed to be nothing outside. But they took some moments to assure themselves of that. Then Sean jumped out to inspect the damage. They rummaged through the boot, scattering clothing about, and found the spare tyre. A hasty repair was effected.

Having decided to return to their original route, they were just about to set off again when the light appeared once more some distance away. They immediately forsook the roadway and drove the car behind some bushes, then fled the vehicle to hide behind cover for some minutes. Finally, they satisfied themselves that the glow had definitely gone at last and they decided to drive back east towards Mundrabilla.

At some point during this enforced stop, Porky's truck drove right past the Knowles. Anne recalled seeing two figures standing by the darkened roadside, apparently gesticulating. A few hundred yards further on was a car, facing back towards Perth and clearly immobile.

It is a common rule of the road in remoter parts of Australia that you do not ignore someone who may be in trouble. After all, you could be the only ones to pass them for hours. Yet there was no obvious sign of trouble here – certainly no glow in the sky. And other traffic was occasionally passing.

As they passed the sedan Anne asked Porky if they should stop. However, surveying the scene, he said 'No', and they continued with their journey.

Some minutes later Anne recalls a car shooting past her at speed, heading towards Mundrabilla and in an obvious hurry. It could have been the same vehicle. It had no lights on, even though it was still dark.

Sean Knowles confirms they did drive on without lights for a brief period; although he switched them on later. For the time being, they had no desire to attract the 'thing' again. Indeed, in their haste and with the semi-dark surrounding them, they struck a glancing blow on a kangaroo that was bounding across the road. This did some superficial damage, including a smashed wing mirror.

At about 4.45 to 5 a.m., soon after the car sped by, Anne and Porky arrived at Mundrabilla – which is some 30 miles ease of the point where the Knowles' close encounter took place. The dawn was now lightening the sky enough for them to confront a strange scene on the main street.

They found Graham Henley and his truck and a group of other people all gathered around a Ford Telstar. They soon discovered this *was* the car they had first passed stationary by the roadside and then seen streak past them heading towards Mundrabilla.

Mrs Knowles was still in great distress and the three young men were obviously very upset. Anne and Porky were convinced that something terrible had happened to them. They were spouting incredible tales about a UFO which had landed on the roof of their car and sucked them up into the air.

Mrs Knowles displayed her left hand and kept saying 'Someone has got to do something ... Someone is going to get hurt' The hand seemed to have a peculiar red blotch upon it, a sort of a rash.

Anne, Graham and Porky asked them many questions, and Graham described his own very limited observation of a light.

'Could the whirring noise have been a helicopter that came too low?' Graham posed.

'No way,' he was told. 'It was completely different.'

They all looked over the Knowles' Ford. A strange smell rather like Bakelite seemed to be inside. No black ash was readily visible; although the vehicle was naturally rather dusty, having travelled hundreds of miles through very grim conditions.

They examined the damaged tyre, which had shredded very substantially. There seemed to be no sign of any suitcases or clothing in the boot, whose contents were tossed about all over the place.

On the roof of the sedan were four small marks. These were at each corner and were not cuts, but looked like very small depressions. The sort of relatively small and shallow dent you might cause if you were to thump the roof fairly hard with your fist.

Having calmed down somewhat, the Knowles family insisted that they wanted to continue their journey, driving eastwards towards the Western Australia/South Australia state border.

However, the truckers were greatly intrigued. They offered to drive the Knowles family back to the location of the incident and inspect the ground in daylight. 'Absolutely not!' was the very firm reply; although they were given details of more or less where to look for themselves.

After the Knowles family had left between 5.30 and 6 a.m., the intrepid trio went into a roadside hostelry and Shirley Lundron, who was manager, phoned the police at Eucla, the nearest main town some miles further east down the highway.

Borrowing a car from Mrs Lundron, Graham, Porky and Anne all set off back down the highway to find the spot where the terror had struck out of the night. They cruised slowly down the route, but found no trace of rubber suggesting a tyre blow-out nor the clothing which the Knowles said they left at the scene.

At around 6.15 a.m. the brave investigators thoroughly inspected the place where the Knowles family had hidden in the bush. They found a good deal of proof that the family *were* telling the truth; including four fresh sets of prints heading away from the road towards the west and into the scrub. There were dog tracks in the sand, marks left by a jack, a set of skids about 50 feet long and traces suggesting that a vehicle had made a U-turn to head off the roadside back towards Mundrabilla – and that when it had first driven *off* the road *after* the skid there was one flat tyre, but that when driving back *onto* the road the tyre was once more quite normal.

Yet despite a meticulous search, the allegedly discarded jack and clothing were still not found.

Driving back into Mundrabilla, the truck drivers reported their findings to the Eucla police. The Knowles sedan had now passed straight through and had not stopped at the town. This information was conveyed to the police at Penong, just across the state border. But the Knowles did not stop at that station either.

Around lunchtime the truck drivers finally left Mundrabilla, still bemused, to continue their journey towards Adelaide.

At 1 p.m. that afternoon Sean and Patrick Knowles finally walked into the police station at Ceduna, South Australia. This was over three hundred miles east of

Mundrabilla, although the next major town after Penong (at which the Knowles claim they did not see a police station).

According to the report filed that day by Officer Trebilcock of the Port Lincoln Crime Scene Department they put the time of the close encounter as around 5.30 a.m. (more than an hour later than the truck drivers suggest). The confrontation had lasted approximately twenty minutes.

Nippon TV later arranged for Mrs Knowles to be hypnotized; this strange experiment brought no new memories.

The Victorian UFO Society stated that several hours had been 'stolen' from the family by the glow, as found in popular American alien 'kidnaps'.

Officer Trebilcock, whilst unmoved by this, did remark: 'They displayed great anxiety and were visibly shaken by their ordeal.'

The policeman inspected the car and saw what he called the 'superficial dents' and grey ash 'similar to a road film left on a vehicle in need of washing'. This covered both the outside and the upholstery.

The Ford was then thoroughly inspected at the police station, whilst first Faye and Sean Knowles, then finally Patrick, were interrogated separately. They gave closely similar descriptions of what had taken place.

At 2.30 p.m., with the Knowles family still at Ceduna police station, the police contacted Ray Brooke, an investigator with UFO Research (South Australia). They advised him of the Knowles' experience and the fact that they were investigating. Ray Brooke arranged to meet the Knowles upon their arrival in Adelaide and there interview them and inspect the car, recovering samples of the dust traces for analysis. Ceduna police confirmed that they had secured a sample themselves and had written accounts from the witnesses, which were forwarded to the investigators.

However, during the still lengthy journey to Adelaide

(several hundred more miles from Ceduna) the media somehow heard of the story and intercepted the Knowles family en route, making a financial offer that few could refuse. In this way Channel 7 Television purchased the rights to have first bite at the story which they had gambled would be a classic, given the fast approaching bi-centennial celebrations.

By that Thursday, 21 January, with the Knowles family safely in the confines of the TV station at Adelaide, the raw details of the case were being flashed around the world as the story was whipped up into fantastic proportions.

By that evening, as Channel 7 recorded their exclusive interviews, the Knowles family were already beginning to fill lead pages of newspapers in almost every country of the world. Headlines varied from the banal 'Close Encounter of the Spongy Kind' (*Today*) to the presumptive 'The Pong From Outer Space' (*Daily Mirror*) and the just a little far fetched version in one West German newspaper, stating with 'mild' exaggeration: 'Egg from Outer Space Destroys Car'!

Several potentially confirmatory stories emerged, the most interesting of which was reported by a man and his girlfriend driving on the Eyre Highway between Ceduna and Penong about one and a half hours before the Knowles met the 'thing' from out of the sky. They said that a series of flashing white lights were seen coming from the air towards the ground over a quarter-hour period and mysterious 'gale force winds' hit the car from out of nowhere and blew them all over the road for about an hour. The radio aerial was bent by the force. No storm system was known to be in the area.

This may be accounted for by the explanation quickly put forward by Professor Peter Schwerdtfergger, a meteor-ologist from Flinders University in Adelaide, who specu-lated that the Knowles had run straight into the midst of a rare type of weather system – a clear-sky electric storm. The tumultuous but highly localized winds would account for the damage suffered. The intense ionization introduced into the atmosphere could create physical effects, produce ash particles by electrostatic attraction and also perhaps lead to the glowing form that was seen.

There are many similarities with the research of British meteorologist, Dr Terrence Meaden, who for several years has proposed a similar phenomenon to explain the numerous circles found in cornfields throughout southern England during the summer months. These are especially prevalent in July, January being an equivalent month in Australia.

Several analyses of the ash samples took place, by the police forensic team, by US aviation scientist Dr Richard Haines, and the Australian Mineral Development Laboratory, on behalf of Channel 7. All these concurred with one another, and with the UFOR investigation by Ray Brooke and Keith Basterfield, when they studied the Ford on 2 February. Nothing unusual was found within the sample by any of these. It had similar composition to that of worn brake linings.

However, the Victorian UFO society disputed this finding, claiming that an extreme proportion of chlorine was found in ash they vacuumed out of the Ford twelve days after the encounter. A Melbourne University report on this said the chlorine was so strong that it was almost as if the ash had come out of a swimming pool. Why this result differs so markedly from all the others remains unexplained.

All experts, however, remain convinced that the Knowles family did have a terrifying close encounter with *something* on that January night. But the probability seems to be that it was a rare and unusual natural phenomenon.

Not that this stopped the car being purchased for display by an entrepreneur, or reports that TV producer Aaron Spelling, fresh from his mega-soap empire, was interested in making the movie about the bi-centennial terror.

Nor has the confusion over the physical evidence

prevented a small-scale tourist boom taking place within the Nullarbor plains.

Near Mundrabilla you can now find a sign that says 'Beware! UFOs next 111 km'.

FEBRUARY

2nd This date in 1980 was when a diesel engine called *Nimbus* was dismantled at Doncaster after over seventeen years' service. Yet seven months later, two train spotters claimed to have seen the *same* engine, shrouded in mist, disappearing into Hadley Wood South tunnel. One of them recorded its number: 55020, which was correct for the *Nimbus*. Recently it has been claimed this story is a hoax.

5th Jeane Dixon, an American prophetess, claimed that on this day, in 1962, the antichrist was born in the Middle East.

9th The 'Devil's hoofprints' were discovered on this date in 1855 in fresh snow all over south-west England. The prints had appeared overnight covering a distance of 200 miles, travelling in straight lines over fields, hedges *and buildings.*

13th The *Lady Luvibund* set sail on this date in 1748, and made its way down the Kentish coast. There was a party onboard, celebrating the captain's wedding, when one of the crew, John Rivers, decided to wreck the ship. Best man at Captain Reed's wedding, Rivers was privately jealous, and drove the vessel onto the Goodwin Sands, causing much death and destruction. Since then, other mariners have claimed to have sighted the *Lady Luvibund* every fifty years, on the anniversary of its destruction.

15th In 1955 a mysterious fall of snow occurred around Clwyd, North Wales. The sky was clear blue and cloudless at the time.

18th A man calling himself Cedric Allingham claimed he was bird watching on this date in 1954, when he photographed a flying saucer. He then met its Martian pilot. The result was a book called *Flying Saucer From Mars*. However, modern research has proven that this story was in fact a hoax.

19th UFO author Brad Steiger was born at 6 a.m. at Fort Dode, Iowa, on this date. Steiger is thought by some to have extreme views on his subject, writing about 'star people' who *look* like humans, *think* they are humans but come from an alien world.

24th In 1979 a fiery orange ball was seen from all over Lancashire. It allegedly damaged a caravan park near Southport, shook the pier at Blackpool, was chased by police cars and taxis and reportedly landed in a quarry at Bacup. Sightings were between 2 and 2.45 a.m. Questions were asked in Parliament by Robert Kilroy-Silk – then an MP and now a TV presenter.

The February Fire

It was deathly quiet in the suburban house, except for the rustle and crackle of a fire burning in the open grate of the drawing room. Outside, the trees and shrubs bent unwillingly to a chill northerly wind. Inside, the radio, with its nut brown Bakelite casing, was silent for once.

In the middle of the room sat a small table. On it rested a strange apparatus. It consisted of a large flat board with a sheet of blank paper covering it. Sitting on that was a heart-shaped piece of wood mounted on small castors. Attached to this was a pencil. This was a planchette, a device which allegedly allowed contact with the dead.

There were two young people in the room – a brother

and sister – who eyed each other nervously before dropping their gaze to the planchette for a moment. When they were satisfied the house was quiet, they sat down at opposite sides of the table. Each placed a single finger on the heart. They were ready to begin.

'Does anyone want to speak to us?'

The girl's voice was firm, hardly betraying her nervousness at all. Then, without any pressure being put on the planchette by either of them, *the pencil began to move.*

Yes . . . it wrote.

'Who are you?' And this time there was a slight tremor in the girl's voice. The pencil went wild.

Sunex Amures and one of his men . . . mean to burn the Rectory tonight at nine o'clock end of the haunting go to the Rectory and you will be able to see us enter into our own and under the ruins you will find bone of murdered . . . wardens . . . under the ruins mean you to have proof of haunting of the Rectory of Borley . . . the understanding of which gamenl . . . game tells the story of murder which happened there.

The couple studied the paper feverishly. Much of it did not make sense, some of it was indecipherable, but overall the message was clear. Borley Rectory, 'the most haunted house in England', was to be destroyed by fire, and beneath its ruins would be found the source of many of the happenings – the remains of a murder victim. They wanted to know more.

'In which room will the fire start?'

Over the hall. Yes, yes, you must go if you want proof.

'Why cannot you give us proof here?'

We will . . .

The séance took place in Streatham, on March 27 1938. But there was no fire that night. Was this because the sitters did not go out to the Rectory as ordered? The burning was to come exactly eleven months later on 27 February 1939, and it *did* start over the hall, and human remains *were* discovered 'under the ruins'.

The couple, Miss Helen Glanville and her brother,

Squadron-Leader Roger Glanville, were part of a large and diverse number of investigators attempting through orthodox and unorthodox means to shed light on the strange phenomena and mystery of Borley Rectory.

Borley is about two miles from Long Melford on the Sussex/Essex border. The place is so small it is not even worthy of mention on a modern road map. Much of the land was owned by a family of parsons called the Bulls. Henry Bull built the rectory in 1863, on the site of a much older rectory belonging to the Herringham family. There was also some indication – although not much proof – that that building had in turn supplanted a Benedictine abbey.

Opposite stands Borley Church, dating from Saxon times, itself the source of many strange occurrences. Objects had been displaced, and at the time of the Rev. Henry Bull, heavy coffins in the crypt were discovered to have been moved about.

Henry Bull was succeeded by his son, Harry, who became Rector. He died in 1927, and many people afterwards said they had seen his ghost walking the corridors of the cold damp Rectory. For the next six months about a dozen clergy and their wives visited the house, but all declined to take up residence. The Rectory was a large rambling ugly building built of red brick. It had neither gas nor electricity, and water was provided by a hand pump. The cellar was so damp that many frogs and newts had made their home there. On top of these physical discomforts, the place also had a 'reputation'.

Then, in the autumn of 1928, the Reverend Eric Smith and his wife moved in. Their stay lasted just nine months. The doorbell would ring furiously of its own accord. One night, all the door keys fell out of their locks then later vanished. Slippered footsteps were heard about the house, small pebbles were thrown, lights were switched on, voices were heard, and Mrs Smith saw a phantom horse-drawn carriage standing on the drive . . .

When the publicity became too much, the Smiths later

tried to deny much of it. But it was through them that the controversial psychic investigator, Harry Price, became involved. Although Price had his critics, without him the alleged phenomena at Borley would not have been so intensely investigated.

Just when had the hauntings started?

It is difficult to state exactly when the phenomena were initially noticed, but the first recorded incidents were made in 1885, when during the following twelve months, there were many accounts of an invisible coach and horses being heard on the road outside. A Mrs Byford, a nurse, was driven from the Rectory on account of ghostly footsteps. Apart from this, the building had been plagued by a myriad of anomalous phenomena, including the padding of a dog, apparitions, amorphous shapes, the appearance of messages, apports, teleportation of objects, destruction of objects, and the many sightings of a nun . . .

Who was the nun?

One of the earliest and best accounts of the ghostly lady was a sighting in broad daylight by the three sisters of the Reverend Henry Bull.

Ethel, Freda and Mabel were in a happy and gay mood on the afternoon of 28 July 1900. They were returning from a garden party, and chatting amicably as they entered the grounds of Borley Rectory. Suddenly all thoughts of the pleasant afternoon were forgotten, as they noticed the figure of a young woman dressed as a nun. With bowed head, she was telling her beads as she walked – half glided – along the path between the trees and bushes.

The young women were fear-stricken. They stood by the summer house watching the strangely garbed figure of what looked like a normal flesh-and-blood human being . . . One of the girls ran and fetched another sister, Elsie. Now there were four witnesses to this amazing sight. Was it someone who had just dressed up as a prank? Elsie was determined to find out. She ran across the lawn towards the nun. Every step seemed to take for ever. She was conscious of the others behind her, and of this unknown *thing* in her path. Her heart thudded in her breast and her mouth went dry.

The nun seemed to sense someone was coming after her. She stopped and turned her face towards Elsie. There was such an expression of intense grief written across it, that Elsie came to an abrupt halt. At that moment, the nun *vanished.*

The sisters had several other strange experiences. Ethel was confronted one night by a tall dark man in one of the passageways, upon which he vanished in front of her. Several of the sisters one day watched a girl dressed in white, walking towards the nearby River Stour where she disappeared. This same apparition was apparently sighted nearly half a century later, in 1951, by one of the members of the Ealing Psychical Research Society, as described by psychic researcher, Andrew Green:

One of the Society members grabbed my arm and, although obviously terrified, proceeded to describe a phantom that he could see some thirty feet in front of him, standing at the end of the 'Nun's Walk'. It was a woman in a long white gown, and moved slowly towards the end of the neglected garden ... the witness was perspiring profusely with fear and later with annoyance that I had failed to see the ghost.

The Reverend Harry Bull also had his share of inexplicable happenings. One evening he was in the garden with his retriever, Juvenal, when the animal began howling, and 'pointing' at some fruit trees. The Rector moved closer and saw a pair of legs behind the foliage. Thinking he had disturbed a poacher, Bull skirted around to surprise the man. But as he rounded the trees, he discovered the perplexing truth. It was *just* a pair of legs, and legs which could pass through a closed gate ...

Harry Bull also saw a wizened old man standing on the lawn, whom he recognized from old family portraits as a family retainer who had died some two centuries before.

A Mr Edward Cooper and his wife had many strange tales to tell during their long employment with the Bull family. Almost every night from April 1916 for some three years, they heard a sound coming from the kitchen like a large dog padding about the room. The last occurrence of this phenomenon was accompanied by a terrific crash like the breaking of china. Jolted out of sleep, the couple raced to the kitchen only to discover nothing out of place at all. But the 'dog' never returned.

A Mrs Newman had been employed as a cook for three and a half years from 1924 until the death of the Reverend Harry Bull. She habitually locked her bedroom door every night before retiring. Because her room was so large, a fine curtain was suspended down the middle to divide the apartment into two halves. She slept in the portion which did not contain a window. The other side – the window side – had some pegs fixed to the wall from which she hung her clothes.

On several occasions, just as it was getting light, she was awakened by *something* – she never discovered what – which was examining her clothes. She could see, through the thin material of the curtain, her clothing being disturbed. As the light from the window increased, it was plain that *something* was moving between the curtain and the closed window. The young woman was too terrified to do anything but clutch fearfully at her bed sheets, hoping that whatever it was, it would remain there, on the other side of the curtain.

That Borley Rectory and its grounds were haunted cannot be denied. But at least up until the vacation of the premises by the Reverend Smith, in 1929, that haunting had been *benign*. With the arrival of the Reverend L.A. Foyster, his much younger wife, Marrianne, their little boy and their adopted daughter, a wickedness crept into the haunting which was not there previously.

Harry Price was at the house on one occasion, near the study, when suddenly an empty claret bottle came rattling down the stairwell and smashed at his feet. Some bells in the kitchen went beserk, and the bottle was followed by a shower of small pebbles. No one was upstairs at the time. A little later, Mrs Foyster called out in alarm. She had been taking a nap in the bedroom, and although the door key had previously 'disappeared', she discovered she was locked in. Price and the Reverend Foyster rushed upstairs. Apparently, the vicar was used to this little problem. With the aid of a religious relic and much prayer, the lock mechanism was heard to snap back and the door opened!

Guy L'Estrange, a Justice of the Peace, visited the Foysters early in 1932.

I arrived at the Rectory in the early darkness of a January afternoon and was immediately struck by its gloomy appearance. It was exactly the sort of place one associates with ghosts. It had barred windows set in its red-brick walls, and a pinnacled tower stood over the main doorway. The house was approached by a gravel drive, bordered with trees and shrubs, and I remembered that (according to reports) a phantom coach had been seen and heard in the grounds at various times.

I was getting out of the car which had brought me from Colchester, when I noticed a tall figure standing quite still in the angle between the wall and the porch. It did not seem to be a shadow, though it was rather dim, and I called the driver's attention to the form.

'Wait a minute!' I said, and strode towards the wall, but the figure vanished when I was within a few feet of it.

A few minutes later I was enjoying a cup of tea in the Rector's drawing room, while he and his wife told me about their experiences. 'I never believed in ghosts until I came here,' said my host, 'and used to laugh at the stories people told about this house. Since then I have discovered it is anything but a subject for laughter. One day while I was in my study,' he declared, 'I saw a pencil rise from my desk, and scrawl words on the wall. No hand was visible.'

Then the Rector related how the earthenware ewer from the toilet set in his bedroom had been thrown at him while he was sleeping. 'It hit me on the head, and I woke up to find it lying beside me,' he said. Two or three times, I was informed, rooms had been set on fire and the doors locked in some unaccountable way.

While I was listening to these almost incredible stories we were all startled by a loud crash in the hall. 'They're at it again!' groaned the Rector. Jumping up, I hurried to the door, and found the floor outside littered with broken crockery. The Rector, who had come to my side, looked miserably down at the wreckage. 'These things come from the kitchen dresser,' he sighed. 'You can see how impossible it would have been for anybody to fling them down here and get out of sight so quickly.'

He was quite right, but I was not yet convinced that trickery was out of the question.

We went back to our seats after the mess had been cleared away, but an appalling series of crashes soon took us back to the doorway. The sight we witnessed made me wonder for a moment if I were dreaming.

Bottles were being hurled about in all directions in the hall, though nobody could be seen throwing them. Appearing suddenly in mid-air, they would hurtle through space and smash to pieces on the floor or against the wall. One large wine bottle missed my left ear by about an inch.

'Where on earth are they coming from?' I gasped.

The Rector explained that they had been stored in a shed outside, but could not tell me how they got into the house. 'You see,' he said, 'the doors are locked, and every window is bolted.' All the same, two or three dozen bottles lay on the floor, mingling with broken china and earthenware, before there was a lull in the commotion. My host's face was careworn as he turned to me: 'You haven't seen half!' he announced.

Then we made a tour of the whole house, the Rector pausing in many of the rooms to tell me about the strange things which had occurred there.

As we went onto the landing there was a loud ringing of bells downstairs. The Rector beckoned me to the banisters, and, leaning over, I could see all the bells in the kitchen passage below were clanging wildly at the same time, while my hostess and the one maid who had not refused to remain in the house looked on helplessly. There were about thirty of these bells, so the din can be imagined, and I had to shout the question I put to the Rector.

'We cannot explain it,' he replied. 'The wires of all but three have been cut.' We returned to the hall.

The bellringing continued for some time. At my hostess's suggestion, I tried to communicate with the unseen entity responsible. 'If,' I cried, looking up at the bells, high above our heads, 'some invisible person is present and can hear my words, please stop those bells ringing for a moment.' Instantly, every bell became still. I do not mean that they gradually slowed down, as one would expect. It was as though each had been seized and held by a hidden hand.

Previously, an attempt at exorcism had only intensified the phenomena. During one night, Mrs Foyster was thrown out of bed by *something* three times.

During this period, Marrianne Foyster became more and more the centre of attention for the strange unbelievable power that seemed to have Borley Rectory in its grip. Messages appeared on the walls addressed to 'Marrianne', asking for 'light', 'mass' and 'prayers'. An earthbound soul asking for deliverance? The words were written in a scrawl, unintelligible at times. Underneath, Mrs Foyster would reply in block letters: TELL ME MORE, I

CANNOT UNDERSTAND. Later, more writing would appear beneath this. On one occasion, Mrs. Foyster and a visiting priest, Dom Richard Whitehouse, knelt down and asked where the mass should be offered. The word *here* appeared on the wall.

As the investigation proceeded, many of those involved began to formulate the idea that the messenger was the same entity who had been sighted around the grounds dressed as a nun. Was that why the messages were addressed to a woman?

Back in the autumn of 1927, when the house was empty, a carpenter called Fred Cartwright, from nearby Sudbury, passed the house on his way to work just as it was getting light. He saw what he took to be a 'Sister of Mercy' standing by the first drive gate of the Rectory. She looked quite normal but did not speak. Next Friday, at exactly the same time and place he saw her again. Her eyes were closed as if she were tired. On the following Wednesday things came to a head.

As usual, Fred was walking to work. It was a crisp autumnal day, the milky amorphous light of the newly risen sun bringing the skeletal trees out of shadow. The nun was there again – exactly as before. As he walked up towards her, Fred had no reason to believe this was anything other than a normal flesh-and-blood human being. Again, her eyes were closed, and the carpenter received the impression that not only was she tired, but also ill. He walked past and then stopped. Was there anything he could do? He turned – the nun had vanished ... But had she, somehow, noiselessly, slipped past the gate and into the unoccupied Rectory? Fred was not sure.

Friday arrived again, and he was on his usual route to Borley village. The nun was there again ... As he drew nearer, he was about to voice a cheery 'good morning' when he saw that she was gone. He did not actually *see* her vanish, but in the blink of an eye she was *gone*.

But could the apparition of the nun be linked with the more violent goings-on in the Rectory itself? Apart from the smashing of crockery and wine bottles, there were the personal physical attacks. Mrs Foyster was walking along the passage outside the bathroom when something struck her a terrific blow under the eye, cutting the skin and causing a lot of bleeding. The damaged eye was black for several days. On another occasion she was struck on the back by a piece of pottery which drew blood.

The Foysters came to the conclusion there were two types of entities operating in the Rectory. Benevolent ones and ones which were cruel. But which sort were leaving the cryptic messages, or was it really the nun?

Scraps of paper bearing scrawled messages began to appear and the writing on the walls became more intense. Yet it was difficult to find a priest to conduct a Catholic mass, because the Rectory was Anglican. It was the Glanville family, experimenting first with a small table, then with the planchette, who seemed to tighten the connection between the nun and the paranormal messages. Through the séances a story began to emerge, along with much contradictory and nonsensical information.

The 'nun' stated she was unhappy but would be content once a Christian burial had been made of her remains. But where were the remains? The sitters were given a variety of locations. She was buried in the garden, 'near the house', near a path, under some trees, buried *not* in a coffin, and *not* under a stone. They were then informed she *was* buried under a stone let into the garden path. All of this information was gleaned during two séances held on 23 and 25 October 1937.

It was several days later that Helen Glanville decided to try the planchette – a device she had never used before. The results were so numerous that they were recorded on rolls of wallpaper! An examination of the yards and yards of writing indicated that the nun's name was 'Lairre' and she had come over from a nunnery situated somewhere near 'Havre' in France. The entity also made mention of 'Marianne'. She asked for a mass to be held, and communicated the date of her death – 17 May 1667 ...

Three days later, the séance was repeated, in the presence of Helen's father, brother, and a family friend. The four placed one finger each gently on the planchette, and Helen Glanville called out:

'Who is there?'

The planchette began to move, and the name 'Mary' and then 'Mary Lairre' appeared on the paper beneath. The 'entity' also conveyed that she was nineteen years old when she died, and was buried 'at the end of the wall'. The reason for her unhappiness was because someone called 'Waldegrave' had strangled her after enticing her away from her native France ...

The Waldegraves did in fact exist! They were an old family who had at one time owned Borley and the surrounding area for centuries. Had these events really taken place at Borley, only to be revealed nearly three hundred years later in the drawing room of a London home?

There was a lot of 'information' given by 'Mary Lairre' which turned out to be factually inaccurate or blatantly contradictory. Yet through the smoke-screens and confusing waves of white noise, emerged a pattern – a thread of uniformity.

A young Waldegrave had enticed the young novice away and installed her at Borley as his mistress. Something had gone drastically wrong with the relationship, and Waldegrave had strangled the girl, burying her body somewhere in the grounds or beneath the house. There were several references to a blocked-up well in the cellar.

Harry Price saw much of the poltergeist activity as clues, or pointers to the real source of the mystery. Things which emerged from these alleged paranormal sources were often half true and half false.

Were the details which emerged during the séance in March 1938 half true and half false? Yes and no ...

According to the communication, the Rectory was to be burned down that night by 'Sunex Amures and one of his men'. As Harry Price noted: 'Miss Glanville and her

48

brother did *not* go to the Rectory that evening at nine o'clock, as instructed, and that is, perhaps, why the place was not burnt down on that night "as promised"! But "Sunex" eventually kept his word.'

He did indeed! Exactly eleven months later, to the day, on the night of 27 February, Borley Rectory *burned*. And, as notified at the séance, the fire *did* start over the hall.

Someone – or something – knocked over an oil lamp, and the flames, once released, ravished the first floor and roof of 'the most haunted house in England'. Many people gathered to watch the destruction, and some of them, including a policeman, claimed to have seen strange figures moving amongst the flames.

But did the events of that February night put paid to the strange goings-on at Borley Rectory – events which had been reputedly witnessed by over two hundred people since the place was built in 1863?

It is true that strange things continued to be recorded in the ruins of this once gaunt and ugly Victorian building, but not on the scale of previous years. What the fire failed to achieve, subsequent winter gales succeeded in doing, toppling down the upper walls and chimney stacks in ignoble victory.

But even in defeat, the house offered up one more tantalizing mystery. With its now dilapidated state, Harry Price and his colleagues found little trouble in gaining permission to excavate the cellar floor.

As the entities had promised, 'at the end of the wall', in the old well, were discovered some human remains. They belonged to a young woman.

St Valentine's Day: A Warning from the Heart

◆

Lee Fields was driving down a familiar road back in England.

She could not actually drive and yet this paradox was somehow lost to her mind amidst the strangeness of this gloomy night. Taking such things in her stride the young woman happily chugged along in her new husband's car.

The scene was fraught with sexual innuendo. Wasn't that what they said about driving a car? Yet why – in this weird sideshow – was she passing by one of her four brothers standing on the pavement dressed in an awful black suit. He was gazing up at her as if this were a funeral cortège.

And who was it that stood next to him? It seemed to be her father. He was wearing a plain grey suit and stood firm, as if to attention, sporting a deadpan expression. Both men gave nothing away.

Lee drove on past, musing over this peculiar sight. It had to mean something. It was not the sort of thing she expected to be confronting. And anyway – wasn't she in Germany?

In a moment of determination, Lee swung the car around, marvelling at how effortlessly this untried task was performed. She pulled it up beside the men. They were still standing there, holding the same position as before, and looked rather like solemn statues.

Opening the car door, Lee walked over to them. She faced her brother, mustering composure. 'James? What is wrong with Dad?'

James continued to watch her with a vaguely wistful look in his eyes, but his lips remained silent.

'Dad?' Lee pleaded, facing him squarely.

To her horror and astonishment, the elderly man suddenly crumpled to his knees and put both arms around the waist of his youngest child and only daughter. He was clinging to her, hugging her tight and sobbing, with the tears streaming down his cheeks.

'Please, Lee – don't go over there. Stay here with us.'

The intensity of the emotion hit her hard. What else could she do but respond to it? Her tear ducts filled with salty fluid. She too was crying.

'Oh, Dad,' she sobbed.

Lee's eyes opened to the piercing sunlight of a fresh February morning. It had all been a dream, of course.

That explained so many things. Why she had been back in England. Why she was driving down that familiar Liverpool street. And the odd behaviour of her father and brother.

She shook the images from her mind and got up. That would teach her for changing her routine.

It was over a week now since they had moved to Germany, in early February 1981. That date she would remember for a very long time.

She had married an army man just a month ago, knowing only too well what the consequences would be. He was serving in this borderland nation, where East and West postured before one another in a visible battle of wills and an invisible stalemate of horrible and deadly missiles.

But there were compensations. This was a pleasant town and there were many English wives around her. She did not feel quite so isolated as she might have expected and probably she would see through this tour of duty.

It could have been worse. The posting might have been to Northern Ireland, where the dangers were rather more real than theoretical. There you did not face a future nuclear holocaust – if and when it ever came. Instead you had to constantly guard against the terrorist bullet which saw a young man, sent there with no real say in things and simply doing the job he had been taught, as nonetheless fair game for murder.

Normally she got up with her husband as he rose at the

unearthly hour decreed for soldiers. But the move had involved a lot of hard domestic work and today she had chosen to lie in. Perhaps that had been a mistake.

Her thoughts returned to the dream. It was not proving quite so easy to dismiss as she had imagined. But, of course, dreams were just dreams. Nobody was supposed to take them very seriously. They were games that your mind played when the brain was fast asleep – juggling with pictures inside the head and piece by piece assembling jigsaws that were not significant in any way.

And yet . . . And yet.

Two days before they had departed from Liverpool to fly to this strange and foreign land there had been that very peculiar experience in the bedroom.

Lee thought back over the past two weeks.

Her husband had already been out in Germany doing his stint and preparing the way. But he had returned that weekend to say goodbye to his family and to carry his bride back across the threshold of the English Channel.

The household arrangements at the Fields' homestead were somewhat cramped. But being married they had naturally decided that they must sleep together as man and wife. In order to do so there was no alternative to squeezing in side by side in Lee's tiny single bed.

It would certainly prove very cosy.

Making the bed that Sunday evening she noticed, as if for the very first time, the mirror that hung on the wall above.

It was old and heavy-framed and ponderously large. Yet it had been in the room for a very long time. She had not had the heart to move it. Besides it had its own peculiar sort of charm.

Yet, with the bed pushed right up against the wall as it was, it did present a threat that she had never perceived before. It might fall off.

The idea was frankly absurd. It had never budged in years, so why should it do so on this particular night? It looked almost a part of the wall – solid and attached.

However, the thought would not go away. It niggled at the back of her mind so much that she could not resist it. She struggled and tugged the bed almost a foot away from the wall. Now – if the wretched glass should crash down – it would hit the floor beside the blankets, harmless and inoffensive.

Later she chided herself for such a silly thought. It seemed a ridiculous sacrifice of objectivity to the quirks that the human imagination can pull.

But when, in the early hours of the morning, they were both awoken by a fearful crash, the silliness evaporated very quickly. Her impulsive act now looked like a lifesaver.

Seeing the shattered remains of the mirror on the floor, Lee could not help thinking that but for her woman's intuition, or gut reaction, or stupid little foible – whichever it was – then the descending mass of wood and glass would have come down right on top of their heads and at best have cut very badly.

The experience was receding into the past as the days went by. At the time it had seemed to be important. Now there was absolutely no reason to anticipate that it was anything other than sheer coincidence, the sort of thing that happened all the time. Although normal people did not go around looking for coincidences and so never noticed them when they actually happened.

But she still felt uneasy about the dream. A call back to England would not go amiss. It could be justified on their bank account in return for her peace of mind.

Lee was very fond of her father. There is a special bond when you are the only daughter and the fact that he had struggled for many years now with gradually failing health had done nothing to diminish that sense of care and concern.

Perhaps the dream was only her guilty conscience, telling herself that she should not have gone away to a foreign country, leaving him on his own.

Except, of course, he was not alone. Nor did she have any choice in the matter. Her father would understand all that.

She put off the call, telling herself that it was pointless worrying. If there was anything wrong then she would have heard. But when she did eventually hear from home, the news was terrible.

Her father had been taken dreadfully ill, on the very morning after her nightmare. He was currently in hospital where he was being well cared for, but nobody knew what the outcome would be. The situation could not be kept from Lee, her family decreed.

As she made hasty preparations to fly for the second time in as many weeks, only now in the reverse direction, her mind kept replaying the dream and the mirror incident. Maybe there was more to that event as well. Perhaps the falling of the mirror had been an omen – a warning. Just like the dream it was trying to tell her something. Perhaps to keep her in England and stop her from flying so many hundreds of miles away from home and her father.

And there had been those other little incidents back in her past. She had tried to dismiss them too. But possibly that had been a mistake.

That time when she was idling away the moments putting on her makeup, staring at her reflection, as if the glass were a crystal ball and with her thoughts many light-years away.

For no reason, into her head fluttered the impression about the actor in the TV soap – *Dallas* – who was unexpectedly dead. Again, like a butterfly, the thought floated away. But two days later the actor *was* dead.

Then there was the day of her twenty-first birthday party. Readying herself for the grand occasion she was thinking about the arrival of a friend whom she had not seen for many years. Into her head came another stray image – oh so clearly – of the young girl coming up to her, saying hello, and asking 'Did you know that my gran has died?'

An hour or so later the party began. In came her friend – just as she had done in the quick thought flashing across Lee's idling mind. In the real world the girl came over to

Lee, smiled and said: 'Did you know that my gran has died?'

Coincidences one and all. But where did coincidence end and premonition begin?

Lee flew back to England, and rushed to the hospital. But as she did so, on the night of St Valentine's Day – the patron saint of true love, her father passed away. She was just too late to see him. Her brother's stoney face greeted her as it had done in the dream.

Lee Fields returned to her husband and her new life, pondering the meaning of these strange images and frightening messages.

Were they warnings? Or, perhaps, goodbyes?

MARCH

2nd In 1951 a London Transport Engineer working on a platform at Ickenham Station, Uxbridge, observed a middle-aged woman wearing a red scarf beckoning him. She indicated that he should follow her down a flight of stairs, but then she vanished. It is thought that she might have been the ghost of a woman who had fallen onto the live electric rail some years earlier.

5th A bright cloud of yellow-orange vapour spread out across the skies above the Canary Islands in 1979 and was seen by many witnesses. Several sets of photographs were taken.

9th On this day in 1977 two mill workers encountered a dark object descending out of clouds above Pendle Hill, famous for its association with the Lancashire witches. It stalled their car engine and put out lights in the deserted streets of the town of Nelson and beamed down radiation that affected them both afterwards.

15th In 1978 a woman reported seeing an apparition of herself! The figure was stooped, wearing an expression of grief, over the end of a bed in her house. She realized that the dress worn by the spectre was one she herself had not worn for some time – the last occasion being three months earlier, when one of her young children had died.

19th In 1963 ball lightning invaded the fuselage of an Eastern Airlines aircraft over the USA, giving a close encounter to a scientist on board as it travelled along the aisle. For the first time this rare and little-understood natural phenomenon became scientifically acceptable.

23rd A mysterious airship was seen above Peterborough in Cambridgeshire in 1909. It was one of the best of a large number of reports during that year. The spate of sightings was never adequately explained, although speculation raged about a German invasion.

25th Paranormal researcher and leading author of books about the mysterious, John Keel, was born in New York in 1930. Keel's books include *Operation Trojan Horse* and take the line that a race of ultraterrestrials, or superior beings in another dimension, might lie behind many strange phenomena. Keel's real name is Kiehle.

Storm Warning

◆

The Canadian skies teemed with danger and threatened imminent death. Evil-looking clouds spat jagged lightning bolts viciously towards the ground as the rain hissed at the sodden earth.

Storms such as these often bombarded the small Nova Scotian town. Sitting as it did on the confluence of two rivers, the static would build up in the atmosphere and rush along the water courses, ultimately combining forces in one almighty tempest. The village suffered more than any village ought to suffer as a consequence of this geographical misfortune.

Ellen Taylor hated these times. Having lived there all her life she knew that major destruction often came in the wake of these encounters.

Once, long ago, she had seen power surge through all the wiring in their house after one horrendous strike and then continue on its path at the speed of light. A fraction of a second later the house next door erupted into flames as the mindless energy chose this place to be its next victim.

Ellen had always counted her blessings at that escape.

But the mental legacy was a real one. Whenever a storm brewed above the twin rivers her panic rose like bile throughout her system. A prickly, intuitive terror filled her senses and she prayed for the moment when it would all be over.

This night was worse, much worse. The storm was a particularly nasty example and her husband was working away. She was at home with two young children and an elderly father and grandmother to contend with. They posed many problems through their immobility.

If the need arose, then how could she get them out of here in time?

As the thunder crashed and the lightning tore at the earth, warning of the arrival of the heart of this tumult, Ellen roused the children, dressed them and prepared for the worst. Her grandmother was deaf and seemed unaware of what was happening. So be it, that was probably for the best. Father was dimly conscious of the dangers, sleeping fitfully. How would she prise him away, given his severe near-total paralysis?

For hours the nightmare endured. It seemed as if the world were coming to an end and the entire village would cave in beneath the weight of heavy air and crazed electricity.

Suddenly, around 5.30 a.m. an enormous bang came almost simultaneously with a surge of light. Ellen jumped. The bolt had hit somewhere very near. But didn't they say that if you saw the lightning and heard the thunder then you were safe? You would simply never know about any bolt that was going to hit you, because your nerves could not respond as fast as the killer energy would be able to strike.

Breathing heavily she desperately wanted some respite from this dreadful chaos. She would love to call her neighbours, some distance away and surely too far for immediate rescue. Just to talk to them would help bring reassurance. But she could not do such a foolhardy thing. In such conditions telephones were potentially lethal. She had known people who had been electrocuted whilst calling for assistance and phones that had literally exploded off the wall as lightning struck the vulnerable poles and raced along the wiring.

No. She must not go near that telephone . . . Yet it was so tempting.

As she pondered, relief came in such an unexpected manner.

A wave of calmness swept over Ellen. It was so rapid and soothing that it was strangely inexplicable. A voice probed into her mind, saying: 'It will be all right. There is someone watching out for you and help will arrive if you need it.'

Somehow this was all the comfort the besieged woman required. It gave her the confidence to ride out the storm, sit calmly in the living room and wait for it to pass.

Finally, the tempest died away and the wonderful coolness and freshness that follows such atmospheric dementia filled the air around their village. The relieved inhabitants could now step out and assess the damage.

In the aftermath Ellen met with her neighbours, who had a clear sight of the Taylor property, although from about half a mile away. They consoled one another and were thankful that no serious destruction had affected either of them in any personal way. But they knew it was a close-run thing.

The neighbour approached Ellen, saying: 'That was quite a storm. Normally I sleep right through them, but this was so bad that I got up and got dressed.'

She told him how she had dressed the children, but had been petrified with worry about her elderly relatives.

'Well, I saw every bolt of lightning. I was watching your house. Nothing came near it,' her neighbour mused. Then added: 'If it had I would have been right over to see what I could do.'

She smiled in understanding, but he continued. 'I could not help worrying about you. I was thinking all the time that I wished I dare phone you up, but I knew it was too dangerous. I just wanted you to know that it would be all right, someone was watching out for you and help would arrive if you needed it.'

Ellen eyed him curiously, then nodded. 'When would that be?'

'Oh – you know when that big bolt struck. It hit the tree in the park. About 5.30 wasn't it?'

'Yes,' she confirmed. Then whispered, 'Don't worry, I think I got your message. I just wasn't sure who was sending it.'

She told him the story, but was unable to be sure if he fully understood what she was talking about.

This was the sort of thing that had happened to Ellen all through her life.

Once she had been asked to help out as organist in the church. She usually took appropriate music to blend in with the sermon, but that Sunday the parson was having trouble working out his theme and Ellen had not been told in advance what it might be. As she left to go to the church she picked on impulse one of her own music books. It was in no way full of church songs and she would never usually take such a thing on such an occasion. Why had she felt so compelled today?

The parson began a long discourse on the theme of Exodus, citing passages from that book of the Bible. Opening her music before her, Ellen played the 'Theme from Exodus' – which was ready and waiting. She had known somewhere inside her to bring this particular music, even if consciously such knowledge was impossible.

'What a stroke of genius,' the minister beamed. 'Just how did you find out what my sermon was going to be?'

'Ah – I doubt whether you would believe me if I told you,' she admitted.

Ellen had grown up with this musical talent. Born just before the war into a small community she excelled herself by gaining an arts degree and teaching music. She loved her creativity, either painting or writing compositions. Often these would simply flow into her mind in such an easy manner that it was a joy and no effort at all to proceed. At the conclusion of this frenzied spell she would feel very tired but greatly elated.

The channelling of creative juices came in the same way as her intuitions, where she often knew who was on the other end of the phone whenever it jangled. Sometimes she would think for days on end about a person she had neither seen nor heard from in years. Suddenly they would be in touch or there would be news about them.

It began to seem like a psychic memo pad that constantly jogged her memory about the past.

As a child she had grown up with a family who owned the village store. They had a huge family among which were three young daughters for Ellen to play with. Eventually the youngsters moved away and the parents became too old to manage the store, so they retired out of the district.

Ellen now had her own problems. Her grandmother was a handful to look after and her father, who had suffered a stroke and was sometimes hardly able to speak, was an extra worry on top of her two young children who had not long commenced school. Then, when her husband suffered an accident at work, he too became an added burden to slot into her hard-pressed schedule.

There was no time to think about creative pursuits, intuitions or long-gone friends and neighbours. Far more important tasks had to be performed.

But then a vivid dream struck Ellen out of nowhere. In it she saw her old friend the store owner lying supine in a hospital bed. She saw the form of his elderly wife hovering above him in much despair. Ellen was soaking up the fear and turmoil of her friend and the pain and suffering of the woman's husband.

It was far too real to be a dream. And yet it *was* a dream.

Ellen Taylor plunged out of the nightmare into the cold reality of the bedroom. 'He's dying,' she blurted out aloud. 'Or maybe he is dead already.'

Nobody understood what she was saying.

Such was the conviction of this experience that it haunted her throughout the morning. Normal household duties were impossible. She knew that she must call and check on her old friends. But how did you phone someone and say that you had seen them die in a dream?

Instead, Ellen called a mutual friend, asking if she had heard anything about the old couple.

'How odd. What made you ask that this morning, of all mornings?'

'I ... just wondered. It's been a long time since I heard of them. Years in fact.'

Her friend was sombre. 'Yes, well, one of their sons is close to my husband, you know.'

Ellen said she knew.

'He was here only minutes ago. He had a call to go to the town where his parents had moved. It seems that his father had a severe stroke during the night and they've rushed him to the local hospital.'

Ellen was shocked. 'Um, I see,' she acknowledged. 'How is he?'

'Bad, I'm afraid. They don't think he'll make it. In fact they are talking about hours or days at the most.'

'How awful,' Ellen said, the words being hopelessly inadequate.

A few days later Ellen Taylor received a phone call. Would she play the music in church at the man's funeral. He had survived only forty-eight hours.

Now she knew the truth. Something about her was able to reach out and touch the minds of others – to empathize with their moods and their feelings.

Call it telepathy, or call it something else. But Ellen knew that the human mind – or spirit – had no boundaries and could reach you wherever and whenever you were needed.

The St Patrick's Day Demon

———————— ◆ ————————

Three miles to the east of the Cheshire market town of Warrington lies the Birchwood housing estate. The development, with its modern shopping and leisure centre, is now an established feature of the area, nudging close to the Risley Moss nature reserve. But little over a decade ago there was nothing there. At least no *houses*, no *people*. On this vast tract of land, currently providing the habitat for a population of 20,000, clung the broken and derelict remains of another time.

During the last World War, the entire area was a huge munitions dump. Up until the advent of the housing development, its concrete bunkers and rusted wrought iron buildings were still visible, weed-choked and long since abandoned. Signs proclaiming: MINISTRY OF DEFENCE – KEEP OUT, were visible from the nearby main Culcheth to Warrington road.

In February 1947, the Ministry of Supply took over a small part of the area and developed the UK Atomic Energy Authority complex, comprising offices and laboratories. Back in March 1978, the area had changed little in thirty years. The UKAEA installation was bordered by Daten Avenue – a service road which connected with the nearby M62 motorway. Also close by Daten Avenue, on the opposite side, was an AA Relay Station, and a university research building. It was a quiet, lonely road, but one Ken Edwards knew very well . . .

Ken, tall and gangly, was a very affable man in his late thirties. He was a service engineer who lived with his wife, Barbara, in a bungalow in Risley. On 17 March 1978 – St Patrick's Day – Ken had been to work as usual, arrived home, washed and changed, then rushed out again to attend a trade union meeting in Sale, south of Manchester.

The meeting was routine. He had had little to drink, having to face the forty-minute drive home afterwards.

The motorway shone blackly in the headlights of Ken's van as the wide petrified river of tarmac flowed alongside the unspoilt wastes of Chat Moss. 'The Moss', as local people called it, is ten miles of desolate peat bog lying between Manchester and Warrington.

Ken was tired. It had been a long day. Driving through busy streets, stop-starting at traffic lights, changing up, changing down, it all took a lot out of him. Now it was late, and it was dark, and he was thinking only of the warm bed awaiting him.

About a mile and a half from home, he slowed down, indicated, and left the motorway at Risley via an unsign-posted slip road. This was used mainly by maintenance vehicles, but provided a handy short cut for local people too. He had left the meeting at 11 p.m. He glanced at his watch and saw it was now approaching 11.30 p.m. Good, soon be home.

The van rattled along the road, the proposed new housing estate still just a sheaf of blueprints on the planners' board. There were no other vehicles. The total darkness was eerie, his headlights pushing it aside as if it had substance, like thick black treacle. Ken knew that beyond the glare of the headlights huddled the twisted skeletons of long-abandoned World War Two ordnance factories. A generation before, hundreds of people had toiled there with the machineries of death.

As he approached the AA Relay Station, Ken changed down to negotiate a small island, before continuing slowly up Daten Avenue. He was just moments away from an event that was to change his life for ever.

Up ahead, to his right, was a grassy embankment skirted with bushes and small trees, beyond which lay the university building. On the left, just coming up, was a ten-foot-high chain-linked security fence surrounding land belonging to the UKAEA. On the embankment, the van headlights illuminated an unbelievable sight – an incongruous figure.

Ken stared goggle-eyed as his brain tried desperately to

find a nice comfortable niche for the incongruity which was now only a small distance away. At the same time he slowed down the van until it was stationery at the side of the road. Ken tried to place the figure within the cosy framework of his day-to-day life. Could it be someone, anyone, a prankster perhaps – even at this late hour, climbing in such a peculiar fashion down the embankment?

The tall, likable man in the car was like a rabbit hypnotized by a snake – helpless. He realized that if the strange figure was not a joker, he was trapped out there on the lonely road. He watched, entranced, as the bizarre event unfolded.

As the 'thing' walked down the steep embankment it held its arms out straight from the body like someone sleep-walking. Furthermore it was walking at *right-angles* to the ground – an impossible stance. Anyone walking down the slope would have to tilt their whole body *backwards* in order not to topple *forwards*. At last the figure reached the foot of the embankment and stood on the wide verge staring across the road. Now Ken had a much better view of it, and for the moment at least it seemed oblivious of him, the van and its lights.

The 'thing' was over seven foot tall and was covered almost entirely in silver. Its black head was shaped like a goldfish bowl and sat on a broad body. But the most alarming feature was its arms. Like something from a nightmare they grew out of the *top* of its shoulders! Ken felt panic rising from the pit of his stomach as he realized that the thing was real, and furthermore *it was not human.*

Ken Edwards sat crouched in the seat, gripping the steering wheel, wishing fervently he could disappear. But there was no chance of that, no possibility of reversing and driving away, or of opening the car door and making a run for it: he was unable to move.

Several days later, the bewildered man described the way he had felt:

'My head was swimming with strange thoughts.

There were hundreds of them, all racing through my mind at once ... I also felt very odd. It was a sensation like two enormous hands pressing down on me from above. The pressure was tremendous. It seemed to paralyse me. I could only move my eyes. The rest of me was rigid.'

Suddenly the figure was on the move again. It took a few steps to cross the road, but it seemed ill equipped for this most simple of manoeuvres. The entire body moved very stiffly, the legs articulating from the hips – no evidence of knee joints at all. Then it stopped. Right in the middle of the highway. And Ken knew he was not going to escape so lightly. *The thing knew he was there.* Slowly its head began to swivel, and for the first time he noticed it had eyes – or something which resembled eyes – set at the top of its head. From these 'eyes' projected two pencil-slim beams of light. They pierced the windscreen for about a minute, it seemed, pinning the man like a butterfly in a case. Then the head turned again, and the thing continued its laborious walk across the road and onto the verge opposite.

What would it do now? The high chain-linked fence blocked its path. Would it turn right, or ... The alternative started the panic again in his stomach. *What would he do if it turned towards the van?* It did neither. The 'thing' walked up to the fence, raised its arms again, *and walked right through it.* It was as if the fence did not exist, as if at the moment of contact the atoms of the fence had become benign, changed their orientation, and allowed the entity to pass through unharmed. The entity shambled up the slope on the other side to become swallowed by the darkness.

A range of emotions flooded Ken's thoughts. He had just met and been greatly affected by an unfathomable 'thing', something his own mind would normally have rejected as having no basis in reality. But he had *seen* this 'thing' with his own eyes, watched it walk – impossibly – down the slope, stop at the road and then turn those penetrating eyes on him ... Then there was the fence. The fence! *My God*, he thought, *MY GOD*! With difficulty, he managed to get the van into gear.

Ken retained only a vague memory of the short drive home. And there was further confusion. The experience had seemed to last just a few minutes, but he discovered from the clock in the kitchen that it was 12.30 a.m. when he arrived home, a discrepancy of roughly three-quarters of an hour!

He pushed his way into the house and uncharacteristically went straight to the drinks cabinet. Barbara followed him into the lounge and watched as he gulped down a large whisky. She was already worried because of his late arrival, and now she was convinced something awful had occurred – a road accident perhaps.

'What's wrong, Ken, what on earth's happened?'

He looked at her blankly. She noticed the blood-drained hand gripping the whisky glass, as he struggled to reply. The words tripped out, making no sense, words that slammed into one another. Words laced with *fear*.

'*I've seen a silver man.*'

When he had calmed a little, he told her the whole story. Barbara was flabberghasted. How could she believe such a tale? The whole thing was insane. Yet, she knew her husband well. He was a straightforward, stable person, not one to tell lies, *or* tall stories. But above all it was obvious that *something* very disturbing had happened to him. It was written on his face, the way he kept nervously combing his hands through his hair. *And what was that curious burn mark, on the inside of the fingers of his right hand?*

Ken Edwards started undressing for bed hoping that routine would anchor him back into the world of normalcy. It was useless. He had to tell someone, had to report his bizarre experience. Barbara looked aghast as he began dressing again.

'I think I'd better go to the police,' he mumbled. 'Will you take me?'

He huddled into the passenger seat for the short journey to Padgate police station. The officers on duty were not amused. At first they thought it was a prank – March 17th was St Patrick's Day. But they, too, quickly became convinced of his sincerity. Besides, the man was clearly in a state of shock. Crazy though the story was, they decided to mount an investigation immediately.

A call was put through to the UKAEA plant. A police car with two officers then escorted the couple home. They dropped Barbara home, but Ken went with the officers to the plant. There waited a surprise. It was still the early hours of the morning and the darkness remained complete, giving the lonely road an eerie, expectant feel. And there, straddling the width of the avenue stood a large group of uniformed men.

They numbered about twenty-five altogether, all armed with batons and electric torches. They were security officers from the UKAEA, alerted by a call from the police.

Ken climbed out of the car, and at the invitation of one of the policemen, nervously recounted what had happened at that spot just a short time earlier. Perhaps it was the atmosphere of the place, but there was no smirking nor derision from any of the men. Several of them fingered their batons and looked about warily. They examined the chain-linked fence but found it completely undamaged. Then a general search of the area on the other side of the road, where the entity had emerged, was made. When Ken pointed out he had last seen it heading towards some trees, none of the officers would volunteer to venture there in the dark. Finally, the officers drove Ken home where he tried to get some sleep.

But this was not the end of the story. In fact it was only the beginning. The end was to be much more devastating.

Within hours, the police had leaked the story to the press, and during most of Saturday, and much of the following week, Barbara and Ken Edwards were besieged by newsmen and weird religious cultists. They were not prepared for any of this – in fact they could have done without it. But Ken, having that kind of nature, patiently spoke to all of them. Naively, perhaps, he trusted that they would faithfully report his story, and inject it with the sincerity he projected towards them. Because of some spurious UFO sightings in the area, and the release of the Spielberg film *Close Encounters of the Third Kind*, the experience was linked with UFOs, and this produced a lot of silly headlines in the Sunday Newspapers. Members of a religious group known as the Aetherius Society, reportedly called on Ken offering him long discussions about their beliefs that Earth is being visited by benevolent aliens from Venus. He was not impressed. Ken had never put any interpretation into his story – he always told it just as it happened.

As all the fuss died down, he had time to think more deeply about what had happened. Several things worried him. Something was wrong with the *time*. He had left the union meeting at 11 p.m. and had come off the motorway about half an hour later. Normally he would have been home by 11.45 at the latest. The experience had *seemed* to last only a few minutes, so why did he arrive home at 12.30 a.m. – three-quarters of an hour after coming off the M62?

Did he just sit there for all that time, suffering from shock? As far as he knew, he had left the van engine idling, yet it failed to show a large consumption of petrol. Could there be another answer, something with more sinister connotations?

Although Ken Edwards did not know it, 'time-lapses' occur in many cases where people have witnessed strange phenomena. Many of these victims, from all parts of the world, from different cultures, have been hypnotized by qualified psychiatrists and clinical psychologists, in attempts to 'fill in' the missing time. The scenario which emerges is nearly always the same.

The witness is abducted and taken into a featureless white room. There he is made to lie down on a table where movement is impossible. The table is then surrounded by several grotesque-looking beings who carry out physical and mental testing on their captive. Finally the witness finds himself back behind the wheel of his car, with no conscious memory of what occurred during the missing minutes or hours . . .

Would a similar 'memory' have emerged if Ken Edwards had been hypnotized? His watch had stopped at 11.45 – several minutes after the onset of the experience. Because of subsequent events, we shall never know . . .

However, there were other, more tangible indications of the reality of the experience. On the Monday morning when Ken drove to work, he tried to use his radio transceiver but it failed to operate. Company electricians took the machine apart and were mystified. An enormous power surge – possibly through the aerial – had burned out the entire transmitting diode circuit. Most of the capacitors in the circuit were also destroyed. Because of the enormous cost of repair, it was decided to scrap the unit and fit a new one.

Then there were the burns – similar to sunburn – which marked several fingers of his right hand; the hand which gripped the steering wheel when the entity aimed the beams of light into the vehicle. If there was a connection, then what kind of energy could burn out a radio transceiver and affect human skin in this way?

In the aftermath of the experience, several odd things occurred. There were a number of strange phone calls from strangers. One came from a man with a Geordie accent who claimed to represent NASA! Four of these callers wanted to put Ken under hypnosis, but at that time he refused. Another call came from a man who said he was a private detective, hired by someone else, to prove that Ken was a liar. Then one caller, who said he was a radio presenter in Birmingham, asked if he could do an interview. By this time, the Edwardses were heartily fed up and Ken refused.

A few weeks later, Ken went to Birmingham on business and called in at Radio BRMB, thinking, perhaps, he had been a little hard on the telephone caller. But when he asked for the presenter, it was found that no one of that name worked there. The caller had given his name as 'George King'. Coincidentally, George King, now living in California, is the London taxi driver who founded the Aetherius Society. This was not the same man.

So what had this amiable service engineer experienced on St Patrick's Day, 1978?

There were two theories which would explain the incident, partly at least, in mundane terms. Rumours of a stunt by a nearby local college were investigated by the police, as PC Roy Kirkpatrick explained.

'The college did get up to stunts back then, you know, stealing wheels from cars and so on. But we looked into the idea. There was no rag on at the time and nobody ever admitted it. We never could find evidence for such a link.'

Ken Edwards was unimpressed by the rumours too.

'I wish he or she would come forward and tell me how they did it ... How they blew up my radio and walked through the fence! It was some stunt!'

Could it have been a fireman in a silver-foil radiation suit attached to the UKAEA complex?

The police, in conjunction with staff at the UKAEA, arranged a little subterfuge. Officers called at Ken's house, and asked him to accompany them to the nuclear research plant for further questioning. At a pre-arranged signal, one of the staff wearing a fireman's suit, strode out in front of the car. The officers carefully watched Ken's reaction.

'That was what you saw – wasn't it?'

Ken never batted an eyelid.

'Nope! Nothing like it,' he told them.

If there is a paranormal explanation, then are there any clues regarding the source of the apparition?

The village of Risley was founded by Thomas Risley, and the church he built was one of the oldest Presbyterian buildings in England. But when the M62 scythed through the area, the church was swept out of its way. The graveyard remains, just a short distance from Daten Avenue. There is a strong belief in 'leys' – invisible lines of energy which reputedly cross the Earth in straight lines through old burial mounds and church sites – many of which have been built on for hundreds of years. Could a violent disruption of a ley by the advent of a motorway,

71

with all its attendant noise and pollution, cause 'things' to happen?

In 1987, investigators of the paranormal uncovered some other very interesting factors. The university building on that side of Daten Avenue where the entity appeared, is jointly owned by Liverpool University and the University of Manchester. There is a small nuclear reactor in this building – hence the presence of the radiation suits across the road at the UKAEA. But more interesting are the experiments carried out in the sensory deprivation unit here.

The purpose of these units is to totally isolate a human being from all exterior stimuli for long periods of time. During these experiments, participants have reported very vivid mystical and hallucinatory experiences. Occasionally angelic or demonic beings are conjured up. Are these from the inner space of the mind, or from some exterior source? Was there an experiment underway on the night of 17 March 1978?

Could Ken Edwards have been witnessing someone else's nightmare?

Certainly there is a strong belief in the East that certain priests can create 'thought forms' or 'tulpas' – entities that once conjured by the mind of the priest, might sometimes take on a life of their own for a short period. The act of meditation in isolated mountain caves and temples is not dissimilar to modern experiments in isolation units.

Ken Edwards was to see his entity one more time.

On 23 March a UFO investigator from Leeds came down to see him, and Ken agreed to visit the site of his encounter. Once there, Ken began to feel dizzy. From the corner of his eye he momentarily saw the entity, visible for just a few moments.

From that time, things did not go well with Ken Edwards. Less than a year after the encounter he began to feel lethargic and suffered stomach cramps. A specialist diagnosed cancer of the kidneys. In early 1980 Ken underwent emergency surgery, and it seemed to be successful. But a few months later he developed cancer of the throat, and in 1982, aged just forty-two, Ken Edwards died.

It would be circumstantial to link his premature death with the strange experience. Although, as Barbara pointed out, here was a phenomenon which could stop a watch, cause burns and destroy a radio transceiver. *What might such energy do to the long-term health of a human being?*

APRIL

2nd In 1973, a huge block of ice fell from the sky into a Manchester Street, just missing scientist Dr Richard Griffiths who studied the mystery.

14th Formulator of the 'ancient astronauts' theory – that the Earth has been visited in the past by extraterrestrials – Erich von Daniken, was born on this day in Switzerland, in 1935. Daniken rose to fame with his first book *Chariots of The Gods*, and quickly followed it up with several more, including *Return to the Stars* and *In Search of Ancient Gods*. The books have sold millions of copies around the world. However, when he was taken to task over his book *The Gold of the Gods*, he admitted that although it was written in the first person, he had no first-hand experience of some of the events in it. Some of his 'evidence' of extraterrestrial visits has been debunked, even by those who are sympathetic to his views.

On the same date in 1933, there occurred the first widely publicized sighting of the Loch Ness Monster.

17th Famous American contactee George Adamski was born on this day in Poland in 1891. Adamski claimed to have met a 'man from Venus' in the Arizona Desert. There were six witnesses. He went on to describe meetings with other aliens and also trips into space. Although most ufologists are satisfied the case is a hoax, some wonder who exactly was doing the hoaxing, and why. The famous photographs have not so far been proven fraudulent, and there are claims that in some way the CIA were implicated.

23rd This day in 1960 was when an unemployed engineer, Tim Dinsdale, took a controversial film of an alleged monster which appeared off the shore at Lower Foyers, Loch Ness.

24th In 1964, police patrolman Lonnie Zamora was chasing a speeding black car in New Mexico, when he saw something come down from the sky into a gully. There, he observed an egg-shaped object on the ground, with two four-foot humanoids standing nearby. The strange beings then entered the craft and it took off, leaving three holes in the ground where its landing pads had been.

On the same date in 1965, a UFO landed at Scoriton in Devon and its occupants allegedly reported that George Adamski – now dead – was with them!

My Guardian Angel

◆

It was April 1981. Mona Juarez was many miles from her native Texas amidst the stark landscape of Oregon, on the north-west coast where the USA blends unobtrusively into Canada.

Mona had work to do. She was part of a research team studying the eating patterns of local population groups. It was a fascinating, if exhausting activity, necessitating much travel.

Returning to the motel after one gruelling session, Mona was puzzled to find the room in a disordered state. Images of theft and burglary briefly filled her head, but then she realized that such a worry was premature. This was a strange sort of disorder. Not the kind of mess a criminal might leave behind.

The bedclothes were all askew, as if the maid had not been in to make the beds that day. And on top of these was a huge pile of coat hangers, simply cast there.

As she looked at this odd scene Mona was suddenly overcome by a terrible premonition. This is a sign. It meant something. It was telling her that something was wrong with Daddy.

Without waiting for any explanation or a chance to allow second thoughts to take over, Mona sat by the bed and dialled the number of her Texas home. The phone gave the endless tone which signified that nobody was answering.

Something was wrong. She knew it. Why wasn't her father at home?

She replaced the receiver and keyed in the number of her aunt. If there was any reason why Daddy was not at home, then she would know about it. Her aunt spoke into the phone: 'Mona – thank God you called.'

It turned out that Mona's father had suffered a ruptured gall bladder and he had been rushed into hospital. They had operated right away to remove the diseased organ, and he was fighting to recover.

'Pray for him,' was the advice proffered. Not something Mona needed to be told. As a good Catholic she knew that there was a God and, if it be His will, that her father would pull through.

Later that night, after lengthy sessions of prayer, she got through to the hospital. Her father was well enough to be able to speak to her.

'Daddy – something really strange happened in the motel.' She explained what had taken place.

'Don't you worry about me,' he grinned, 'I'm a real tough egg.'

Three days later he was up and about, on his way home and heading for a complete recovery.

Not long afterwards Mona enlisted in the Navy. Being extremely keen on fitness and health this offered scope to develop her talents and to improve her own physical and spiritual being.

'Boot' camp was in Orlando, Florida, a sprawling city in the centre of a state which is surrounded on three sides by water. It sticks out southwards like a pointing finger, known as a tourist centre the world over, with Walt Disney World and many other attractions, it is blessed with a year round sub-tropical climate and offered a pleasant environment in which to face the rigours of training that would lead the new recruits towards an overseas posting.

After eight weeks of tough initiation, a necessary precursor to embarkation was 'having the shots'. A sailor can be sent anywhere in the world at a moment's notice and inoculations are essential to protect against the most common forms of virus.

The armful of jabs all went in at once – painfully – but a recruit was supposed to be tough and take what came.

'You'll feel minimal pain and perhaps just a touch of fever,' Mona was forewarned, almost casually. That was certainly not an underestimate of the situation.

As an officer in charge of part of the group, new recruit Juarez had some privileges, including a top bunk. This afforded some air and a little bit of peace for the night. She swallowed two aspirin, said her nightly rosary and settled down in the hope that she could sleep off the results of the injected medications.

An unknown time later Mona awoke, burning with fever, sweat beading across her brow, mumbling and calling out for 'Daddy'.

During this time the 'Roving Rat' passed by. This nickname is given to the unfortunate on night patrol, whose task is to stalk the area surrounding the bunks and make sure that everything is all right with those lucky enough to be able to sleep in them.

The woman on duty that night heard Mona muttering and groaning. She saw her toss and turn, but put it down to a combination of the heat, the jabs and a bad night. She was, after all, by no means the only fresh graduate who was suffering such after-effects on that particular night.

Hearing the call 'Daddy! Daddy!' several times the 'Roving Rat' did smile faintly. Somebody was homesick already, but everything else was normal and Mona had seemed to settled down soon enough.

However, Mona was experiencing things in a quite different manner. Burning up with the pain, she felt her entire body about ready to explode. Then a hand touched her own and she felt the rosary back within her grasp. She knew that it had fallen to the floor during her feverish turmoil and the only way to reach it back for herself was to get out of the bunk. Now here it was again – magically in her hands.

Then she felt gentle hands comforting her and easing her posture, and then a palm was mopping her sweating brow. The pain and fever were quietly to be soothed away.

In moments she was back in a peaceful sleep and did not wake up again until the morning, which seemed to arrive in the blink of an eye.

Feeling fine, Mona wrote to Daddy to tell him what had happened. He answered, telling her that there was nothing to be disturbed about.

'It was just your guardian angel.'

For four years Mona enjoyed her life in the Navy, in which her duties eventually took her to Spain. In April 1985 she was at one of the US commands there, serving as fitness coordinator. Not only did this entail devising and teaching exercise routines for the other recruits but she also had to take part in several competitive events herself.

Right now she was training for a forthcoming athletics meet.

Running at some pace alongside a colleague, they passed a marker and Mona suddenly lost sight of her fellow runner. She turned to see what had happened, and that proved a fateful mistake. There was a terrible crunching sound and at the same time she felt a sharp pain in her foot; she knew instinctively that her left ankle had been badly damaged.

Hobbling back to the base gymnasium the stricken runner got dressed and drove over to the hospital, fearing the worst. Nothing was apparently broken, although the ankle was severely sprained and all the attendant ligaments had torn. A plaster cast was fitted immediately and she was given a pair of crutches.

'What about the race?' Mona enquired.

'When's that?'

'Two weeks.'

The doctor negated all hope of that possibility: 'You must not run, or even walk, without the crutches. Indeed you had better not put any pressure on that ankle or do anything strenuous at all.'

For a fitness coordinator that was not far short of a death sentence.

Being such an active person, Mona was furious – both with herself and the turn of events. She entered a highly depressive state and hated having to rely on her fiancé to do everything for her. She wrote home, expressing all her anger and anguish to her sympathetic father.

At church and at home in her modest apartment she would constantly pray to God to heal her quickly, but the weeks went by and her recovery seemed to be taking an age. Her foot kept swelling up like a balloon and was a mass of ugly purple bruises. Mona began to get seriously worried that she might be in danger of major complications, that she might even need to have the foot amputated! She again wrote back to Daddy, expressing her self-doubts and grave discomfort. But the doctors simply told her it was going to be fine, and would just take time.

One of her church friends advised her to look upon the injury as a learning experience. She was reminded how saints had used such tribulations long ago in an effort to help them evolve as a person. Meditation and prayers focusing on the pain and suffering could be a most enriching life experience.

It sounded very strange, but she tried it and it did seem to help.

Yet the pain was still awful. It felt like a blade shaving away the bone one thin slice at a time, as if she were on one of those cutting machines in the supermarket. Although she was sleeping with her damaged foot placed on top of

79

two pillows, it was not allowing her any rest and her work was suffering.

But then, during one of these painful nights, Mona awoke with a very strange feeling. It was so strange that she sat up straight and looked around her little room.

Directly in front of her were her day clothes, casually left on a chair as she had struggled into the semi-comfort of the bed. But by the chair was something else – a figure standing in the shadows. Not just any figure – it was Daddy!

There was absolutely no fear in her mind. The silent figure was looking at her, smiling and radiating love and peace. Throughout every pore of her being Mona felt the joy and the comfort that her father was bringing.

She knew that this experience could not *really* be happening to her. Daddy was thousands of miles away in El Paso. Yet *somehow* he was also here in this little Spanish apartment. He had come to rescue her.

But Mona did not question the strange manifestation. She just accepted that her father was communicating with her, directly into her mind, telling her not to be frightened and not to worry.

'You're going to be all right. You will be okay,' he whispered now, as he moved in her direction and touched her injured foot. He stroked it and she knew that it was getting better.

Daddy smiled and spoke once more into her mind: 'You must rest now.'

The next thing Mona knew it was morning and she was opening her eyes to greet the new day. Her pain was subsiding. Her foot was getting better. It even looked better.

She told her fiancé of the experience, but he laughed. He rationalised: 'It was just a dream.'

What about the recovery of her foot? she enquired.

'It would have got better anyway.'

Perhaps so, but Mona needed nothing to convince her of the miraculous events which had taken place. She knew that Daddy had been there in her room – sent to her by God.

Was the visitation a powerful dream that she conjured up to rescue herself? She thought about the possibility, but dismissed it.

Was it her guardian angel again? No – it was definitely Daddy.

She later talked to him about it. He said that he had been praying for her and sending out waves of love to heal her foot. In reply she told him that miracles were possible and that God allowed them to happen – if you believed enough and if you were worthy.

Mona said to her father, 'You *were* there in my apartment.'

He was unperturbed by her statement, to him it was quite natural that she should have felt his presence there.

'Daddy, I *saw* you,' she emphasized.

He shrugged and simply agreed . . . 'Yep.'

The Easter Monday Poltergeist

◆

Easter is a time of both sorrow and joy – the sadness of Christ's crucifixion and the joy of His miraculous resurrection. But the thing which wreaked havoc in the cellar of the Bull's Head public house in the early hours of Easter Monday morning, had no respect for the celebrations of the holy feast. In fact the unknown power which was resurrected in that cold ancient place generated only feelings of pain and fear.

The pub squats on the corner of Chorley Road and Station Road, in Swinton, near Manchester. Its heavy-leaded arched windows and weather-scarred walls give the impression of a huge dormant prehistoric *something* waiting to stir. Not quite that archaic; the building is, however, steeped in history.

It was established during the sixteenth century but rebuilt in 1826. Opposite, stood a small chapel which was replaced in 1869 by the much grander St Peter's Church. In fact Station Road was originally called 'Burying Lane' – aptly named, as horse-drawn hearses passed directly by the Bull's Head travelling to the graveyard in front of the church. Apart from providing food and ale, the pub has played a leading role in Swinton society over the centuries.

At the rear was a field where cock fighting and bull and bear baiting took place. In the nineteenth century, members of the 'watchers club' kept vigil from the upstairs rooms watching over the graveyard for body snatchers and resurrectionists. At this time it was also a coaching house, serving as the first stage on the Manchester to Lancaster route. The Bull's Head was also a dropping-off place for mail during the embryonic years of the postal service.

But what of the frightening events about to unfold during that Easter weekend in 1985? Was there a precedent for them? Did the pub have a history of hauntings?

Although some of the contemporary staff had experienced strange events, no history of hauntings could be found. Even local historian, Neil Richardson, found this odd.

'Funnily enough, I didn't come across any mention of ghosts in the course of my research, which is unusual for pubs the age of the Bull's Head!' he told an investigator. Another branch of enquiry also met with negative success.

Rumour had it that there was a bricked-up underground tunnel which linked the pub with St Peter's. As one of the events might indicate a link with the church, or chapel, this could prove very interesting. And in fact there *is* a bricked-up archway on the south-westerly wall of the cellar. But time spent examining old history books in Swinton Public Library uncovered no mention of a 'secret' tunnel. Another mystery would remain.

So what happened? Why should a place be 'normal' for

hundreds of years, then become suddenly haunted, and in quite a vicious way? A possible answer to this question emerged only much later ...

Easter Sunday, 8 April 1985 – a time of celebration. Susan and Donald Flint, newly installed managers of the Bull's Head only months before, decided to throw a party. Susan invited her mother and stepfather, James Kilroy, for the weekend. Also present was family friend, Andrew Cameron, an electronics technician in the RAF.

It was a successful day. Everything had gone well, and that night the party was in full swing. Finally, towards midnight, things cooled down somewhat, and Susan Flint's guests and staff gathered around the bar for a nightcap. As with any other gathering of people on a social occasion such as this, the conversation switched back and forth from cheerful banter one minute to a reflection on more serious issues the next. But eventually someone brought up the subject of the pub's ghost ...

Apparently some of the staff claimed to have experienced strange phenomena in the building. There was much talk about 'cold spots' and the sighting of an apparition in the cellar. To those who had not been involved these stories were received in a light-hearted vein, and two men in particular, James Kilroy and Andrew Cameron, were highly sceptical.

The discussion became a little more heated when someone challenged them to spend the remainder of the night in the cellar. Both men laughed and agreed to do just that. It seemed a bit of a lark. Back at work they would be able to tell their colleagues how they had bedded down in a haunted pub!

At long last, the staff drifted off home, those remaining preparing for retirement. The two men were given sleeping bags and then led down into the ancient cellar by the Flints. Access was by stone steps hemmed in on either side by thick four-hundred-year-old stone walls and above which was a low whitewashed ceiling. Evidently, landlords in the sixteenth century were much shorter, stouter men than their twentieth-century cousins. Partway down, a single room led off to one side, then it was down, down into the bowels of the old tavern.

There, pipes criss-crossed the low roof, coupled up to barrels and leading to the pumps above. At the foot of the stairs and around a corner was a small room with an alcove opposite. Adjacent to this was a narrow archway through which there was a much larger room, used to store twenty to thirty kegs of beer.

The men decided to 'kip down' on the floor of the smaller room. When they were comfortable, and Susan and Donald were satisfied that everything was in order, the landlord and his wife switched off all the lights and retired upstairs. It was late, and they were asleep in no time. The Flints would need to be up early as usual, in preparation for morning opening.

James and Andrew did not immediately fall asleep. They talked for some time, finishing off the drinks they had brought down with them. The whole exercise seemed like a joke, despite the pitch blackness, the chill atmosphere and the isolation, the mocking sound their voices made echoing back off the stone walls, buried in this pit of antiquity . . .

The two men eventually dozed off. How much time passed? It is hard to say. But James Kilroy, Susan's stepfather, was rudely awoken, disturbed by the younger man. Cameron was babbling incoherently.

There in the alcove opposite, just yards away, were several orange and red lights! They hung like a row of vertical three-foot fluorescent tubes, the light flickering, dancing almost. One of the men said afterwards that they resembled prison bars except for the crazy colours running up and down, up and down, like molten coiled snakes spitting and fighting.

Suddenly there was a flash as of lightning, and the lights had gone, swept away by this new manifestation. This was too much for the RAF technician. Even though it was pitch black again, he jumped to his feet, screaming. He had to get out of there. He had to ...

But it was not over, not by a long chalk. In the adjacent room something terrifying was starting up. Beer barrels could be heard rolling about, knocking into one another. Andrew knew that if one of them should fall through the archway and strike him he could be maimed or even killed. But he could not run. He was completely disorientated, and it was black, so utterly black. He just stood there, petrified, rooted to the spot. Then a new sound began, a loud 'swishing' which seemed all around him, like someone going ten to the dozen with a broom.

James Kilroy hoisted himself up onto his elbow and decided to make for the cellar steps. He squirmed out of the sleeping bag, and was prepared to move when a heavy hand suddenly clamped firmly onto his left shoulder. A voice whispered harshly in his ear: *James* ... The voice sounded male. Panic took control and he moved quickly, but never made it to the cellar steps ...

Meanwhile, the 'swishing' sound stopped, and in the darkness Andrew felt something thrust into his hands. The lights went on, and the sleepy faces of the Flints peered around the corner. Alerted by the sounds of bedlam they had rushed downstairs and now stood in shock and dumb horror.

Andrew Cameron was crouched in a defensive position, his hair awry, hands gripping the handle of a broom, terror written across his face. James Kilroy lay at the foot of the steps, blood from his head staining the cold stone floor ...

James was rushed to nearby Hope Hospital, treated for shock and received eight stitches to a nasty gash over his right eye. Once he had calmed down sufficiently, Kilroy added his voice to that of Andrew Cameron's in an attempt to explain exactly what had occurred. The wound had been caused when Kilroy's head collided with a stationery beer barrel, but did he fall *or was he pushed?*

Understandably, the middle-aged man was in much confusion at the time and he may have tripped in the dark. But what was clear enough, was the alteration in Mr Kilroy after the events of that night. According to his wife, Joan, he had undergone a dramatic personality change.

This sceptical, jovial man became introverted and would not venture anywhere near the cellar of the Bull's Head – even in daylight. He *knew* something horrible had gripped his shoulder and whispered in his ear. No longer was it a bar-room joke.

'He was full of life, always telling jokes, but this experience has changed him,' Joan said. 'Now all he wants to do is put it behind him. Forget about it.'

But did paranormal events really occur, or was it just a practical joke which went tragically wrong? There had been a party, plenty of drinks, they had gone down the cellar for a joke anyway – had one of them decided to frighten the other then it had gone out of control?

Oddly enough, the idea of a prank had been voiced by Andrew Cameron. He wondered if the pub manager, Donald Flint, was the culprit, but his wife confirmed that he had been upstairs until the time they heard the screams from the cellar.

But if it was a prank which had been perpetrated by Cameron, then one would expect the man to shoulder a certain amount of guilt for something which could have ended even worse than it did. James Kilroy might have lost his life. Cameron, however, does not mind talking about the incident, but he, too, will not go near the cellar.

There were two other things which also did not support the hoax theory. Why 'invent' the atypical manifestation of the 'bars of light'? It would have been more logical and believable to have made up the sighting of an apparition.

The second point? Oh yes, there were other frightening incidents which occurred both *before* and *after* that Easter Monday.

Susan and Donald Flint, and their two boys aged five and six, moved into the Bull's Head during January 1985. Just one month later, the first inexplicable phenomenon occurred.

For security reasons the accounting is done in the small

room just off the cellar stairs. The walls are of thick stone, no windows, just one entrance – more like a cave really. It is deathly quiet down there, just the sort of atmosphere conducive to concentration when figures have to be balanced, money counted.

Saturday night. *Late* Saturday night. All the pubs have been emptied, people gone home to their beds, or on to a club or all-night restaurant. Susan Flint was down in the cellar, in *that* room, checking the night's takings, quite, quite alone. She was sitting facing the doorway, when her concentration was rudely interrupted by a loud scraping noise from behind.

Startled, she twisted around, and was astounded to see a small wooden stool moving across the stone-flagged floor *of its own volition*. Several times it moved a foot to the left, then back again, a foot to the right, *as if someone invisible was pushing it.*

She ran upstairs to her husband and blurted out what had happened. Donald went back down with her but everything had returned to normal. Could traffic on the road outside have set up a vibration which caused the stool to move? Susan tried to convince herself that this was the case, even though there was no traffic at that hour, or if there was, it was so light as to have no such effect. Later, tests were carried out at peak rush hour. Even then, no vibration at all could be felt through the solid stone of the cellar, never mind enough to move furniture.

Nothing else happened until after the near-fatal events of Easter Monday. Then, in August and September, several things occurred.

It was in August that the Flints decided to organize a fancy dress competition for charity. It was a very successful evening. At 12.30 a.m. the staff were still clearing up. On the wall behind the bar hung a large white clock. It had been there for years. Some money raised during the evening was piled beneath it. As one of the staff reached out for the money, the clock suddenly seemed to jump off the wall and then shatter on the floor. There were several witnesses to this, including Susan Flint. They were all adamant that the clock did not just 'fall', but actually 'jumped' off the wall. The nail which had been holding it there, was still firmly embedded in the plaster.

Not long after this, the Flints' two boys became involved in an incident. After school, between 4 and 5.30 p.m., the youngsters were allowed to play in the pub, as the bar was closed. On this particular day Susan was upstairs preparing tea when the youngest boy suddenly appeared, breathless and looking scared.

'The little one came running upstairs, saying "There's a man in the pub, Mum,"' Susan said. 'I told him not to be silly as the pub was closed, but he was insistent, so I followed him down to where his brother was waiting. There was no one there now, but the boys were certain that a man wearing a blue jumper had been sitting in a corner.'

But what happened afterwards, one evening when Donald and Susan were preparing for bed, was more frightening.

After making sure the pub was secure and all the alarms were set, the couple started upstairs. The landing lights were always left on in case either of the boys woke up during the night and wanted to visit the bathroom. But, as Susan and Donald made their way along the connecting corridor, inexplicably, *one by one the bulbs went out* ...

In the darkness they found their way into the bedroom, and Donald fumbled for the light switch. Nothing happened. There was no rational explanation. If a fuse had blown, then all the lights would have gone out instantaneously – not individually, one at a time. Too afraid to investigate, the couple locked the bedroom door but lay awake in bed.

Now they could hear footsteps, coming closer and closer, obvious indications that someone – or some *thing* – was abroad in the pub. Yet although the floors were fitted with wooden boards, the footsteps were clearly being made on solid *stone*. The pair shrank beneath the sheets as the footsteps seemed to pass and fade out of hearing. This was no ordinary intruder. They would not investigate. Just wait, until the morning.

At daybreak they decided to take a look around. The two boys were still fast asleep and oblivious to the night's happenings. *Yet every light in the building was on, including those downstairs in the bar.*

The family experienced a final incident just a few weeks before they were due to move out to another public house, in December 1985.

'Flannel', their bull terrier guard dog, had remained silent during the night of the ghostly footsteps. He now became agitated and destructive. The final straw came when he ripped out all the telephone wires on the flat roof outside the kitchen. Poor old Flannel had to be destroyed. A British Telecom engineer arrived the following afternoon, when the pub was closed, to repair the damage.

There was only Donald and Susan Flint and the engineer in the building. When the latter had replaced all the faulty wiring he asked if it was okay to use the phone in the living room to call his office. The couple thought he had a crossed line, when they heard him say:

'Can you put the phone down please, I want to ring out.'

He replaced the receiver then tried again.

'Will you put the phone down please!'

Donald asked who he was talking to.

'There's someone downstairs talking on your extension.'

The pub manager told him that was not possible. They were the only people in the building. Susan later told an investigator:

'Donald and I ran downstairs and found the phone off the hook. Of course there was no one there. The phone worked perfectly after that.'

The Flints left the Bull's Head just before Christmas, but the manifestations continued ...

The current manageress is a Mrs Hattersly – a no-nonsense woman with a sceptical attitude to the whole subject of ghosts and poltergeist activity. Yet she does not deny that members of her staff have experienced something inexplicable on occasions.

In 1986, a cellarman claimed he saw a hooded figure, like a monk, while he was changing a barrel down in the cellar. And Mrs Hattersly's fierce fifteen-stone German Rottweiler, 'Hassa', will not go through the door leading into the cellar on any account.

Then in 1987, a barmaid was about to climb the stairs from the pub to the living quarters above when she saw something standing at the top. It was 2 a.m. As she watched, the figure – a vague outline of a monk – glided silently down the stairs. She has no clear memory of what occurred next ...

Why does the Bull's Head have no long history of hauntings? Did the Flints stir up something which had lain dormant in the building?

One theory to explain poltergeist phenomena is that they are the result of repressed emotional energy externalizing itself.

Not long after the Flints left the Bull's Head, the couple separated. Was there hidden emotional tension during their stay at the old inn? Did this externalize in the form of phantom footsteps, mysterious voices and the inexplicable movement of furniture? Or did this energy merely feed a malevolent force?

Could this be the reason why it was at its most virulent in the early hours of Easter Monday – a most holy of holy days? *Was this why a man received head wounds, and needed hospital treatment?*

MAY

1st Birth date of Professor J. Allen Hynek in 1910. The Chicago astronomer is widely regarded as the father of the UFO movement. He worked as civilian consultant to the US Air Force in the forties, fifties and sixties. His 1972 book *The UFO Experience* formed the basis for Steven Spielberg's epic UFO movie *Close Encounters of the Third Kind* (and Hynek invented the classification scheme from which this title emerges). He had often said that he was born when Halley's comet appeared and expected to die on its return. Shortly after viewing its next close encounter with Earth in 1986 he did indeed pass over.

11th In 1950 farming couple Paul Trent and his wife took what are widely considered the most evidential UFO photographs, depicting a disc over their land at McMinnville, Oregon. All analyses have found the pictures to be genuine.

13th At Barnsley, South Yorkshire, in 1983 a dog using amazing ESP abilities saved the life of another dog. Being wrongly presumed dead, this had been buried in its owner's garden. The psychic dog was able to help pull the injured animal from its grave and it made a full recovery.

16th A crocodile was reported by motorists crossing the M55 motorway in central Lancashire on this day in 1980!

18th In 1909 a man named Lethbridge observed an airship over the Caerphilly Mountains of South Wales and also saw two 'pilots'. This was the first recorded close encounter of the third kind in Britain.

20th Canadian Stephen Michalak received severe chest burns in 1967 from what he said was a strange craft that landed in a swamp. He later suffered vomiting and nausea and visited seventeen doctors – at his own expense – in an effort to resolve the alleged long-lasting physical effects.

21st In 1977 travelling magician and showman Anthony 'Doc' Shiels became the first person to film *two* different water monsters, by capturing remarkable close-up colour shots of Nessie in Loch Ness, to add to his pictures of a sea monster off Cornwall. His Loch Ness photographs were taken near Urquhart Castle on the very day when Britain was at the height of its greatest ever wave of UFO sightings.

30th A couple travelling by car between Zimbabwe and South Africa claim that it was lifted off the road and 'flew'. It reputedly crossed hundreds of miles without consuming any petrol.

The Ones That Got Away

◆

'I wonder what we'll catch tonight?'

The question was a familiar one. Dave McCrimmon would talk the matter over with his two sons as they made their way towards Seaforth Rocks at the mouth of the River Mersey.

Waddling down there with all the fishing tackle was a great family outing. It was like an adventure trek.

Dave sounded a bit like John Lennon, drawling his words in that delightful Liverpudlian manner, he had other traits of the Merseysider too. He was a painter and decorator, but like many thousands of men in this job-starved city, work was something he could usually only dream about. It was a dim memory from the past and a fond hope for the future.

There were other problems in his life at this time also. He had two sons, Carl, who was ten, and David, three years older, the latter better known to friends and family as 'the 2½ million dollar man'.

David suffered from a serious illness that was proving to be a serious drain on the family's mental and physical resources. He had been flown to the USA several times where the delicate and lengthy bone surgery could be carried out.

The 'spare parts', as they called them, which were being liberally sprinkled around the teenager were the source of much amusement to some people – hence the jovial name that had been applied. But, of course, there was a much more serious side to what was happening, and they all knew that only too well. Yet the family faced this adversity with stoicism and they saw things through with remarkable composure and courage. These regular fishing expeditions were an excellent way to forget their cares and worries for a brief time and pit their wits against the sea and its marine life. Out there you did not need money in order to be the victor.

On a Saturday night such as this one in early May 1988, the two boys would go with Dave. There was no school the following morning, and they loved it out there in the estuary, where one of Britain's major rivers flowed into the Irish Sea between the sand banks.

Behind and around them lay the old docks, now being refurbished in parts and creating homes for yuppies or tourist museums and art galleries. But the terraced streets of Seaforth were still pretty much unchanged. Once, thousands of dockers had inhabited them. Now the seafaring life of the city was cut back to its bare bones. No longer did clippers or dozens of container ships sail with every tide to the Americas. There was little traffic now in the wake of economic cutbacks and the rise in swift air transport, although the port had survived better than some.

Still, the Seaforth streets were the same as always. Only the people who lived in them were different. Now there were fewer who could make ends meet. That was all.

Dave, Carl and David met up with some regular fishing friends in the shadow of the rocks. This was a popular spot for catching the night tide, even if you couldn't see the fish until you hauled them in.

Out in the middle of the river you just had the lighthouse three miles away for company. Otherwise you were swallowed up by the night. The beacon's steady blink was some reassurance, but, as if it was yet another local thumbing its nose at the past, this was run by computer rather than by a human being.

The time was around midnight. The fishermen lost track of time out there and often stayed until near dawn. It was a warmish night – there hadn't been much of a winter. The stars dotted the sky, wavering in a slight breeze, and the moon sat low near the horizon. Yes, it was very pleasant indeed. Here one could forget about the real world.

Suddenly, someone started chattering about a strange light in the sky. The tension in the air began to crackle. A second ago, all had been peaceful. Now they were in a scene out of *War of the Worlds*.

The words 'flying saucer' sprang to someone's lips and the calm night took on a terrifying new dimension.

'What is it?' Dave asked.

But he had no need to ask the question, for he saw what was happening himself. Emerging from some spot to the north, just behind them, came an object that had no right being up in the sky.

'A banana – a flying banana!'

That was a fair description. The 'thing' looked to be several feet long and was crescent shaped, curving up at each end. However, it was a dazzling orange and much bigger – as big as a small car – than a banana.

The incredible 'thing' was descending all the time until

it disappeared silently into the water not very far from the nearby shore.

'How deep is it there?'

'Deep enough.'

'Where's it gone?'

'Dunno.'

But these meaningless questions were swiftly replaced by new ones, as a second object appeared from the same direction and made an identical diving plunge towards the water – disappearing underneath.

'What the devil are those things?'

'I don't have a clue – and I'm not sure I want to find out.'

As if to reaffirm their mounting panic a third, then a fourth and a fifth object completed the formation – each falling into the water like ill-fated dive-bombers crashing at more or less the same place.

They were all talking at once now, desperately trying to figure out what these things could be.

'Can you see them?'

'No – they've gone right under.'

'Perhaps they were birds.'

'Birds that glow orange and look like bananas?'

The question easily demolished such a rational suggestion.

'I reckon it's a government project,' one chap offered.

'A project to do what?'

The answer was a shrug.

'Do you reckon we should get closer?'

That brave suggestion was not pursued. At least they were fairly comfortable at a safe distance of several hundred feet.

'We don't know what they are or what they can do.'

'They're flying saucers – UFOs' – the letters drew themselves out.

They eyed the water as if on a wartime cruiser and every moment they were anticipating the torpedo wakes that might streak from some deadly and invisible submarine.

The nightmare continued. Their breathing was heavy. The minutes passed by.

Then there was a commotion in that same part of the sea, and out popped one of the 'flying bananas', reversing its course and heading straight out to sea.

'There's nothing out there – just Ireland.'

'And the Isle of Man.'

'Yeh, but that's nearly a hundred miles.'

'What on earth are they?'

Dave could hear something as well. 'Listen – there's a sort of noise.'

Sure enough it was a faint buzzing or humming – something like a small rotor might make, or the motor attached to a model aeroplane. Bees, too, that was another comparison. It was decidedly odd.

'The sound is coming from those things,' Dave said with conviction.

But as they stood there, staring into the darkness, watching the glowing forms rise one by one out of the sea and climb away, they knew even then that there was not going to be an answer.

At least not an answer that any of them would care to choose.

'I tell you – I am damned scared.'

'Me too.'

The others were too frightened even to *say* that they were scared. They just stared, wide-eyed, at this impossible scene that was unfolding into stark reality right before them.

'So much for a quiet night's fishing.'

'You don't expect to catch something like this.'

'I doubt we *could* catch one of those if we tried!'

Dave looked to see how his two sons were coping. Carl, particularly, was terrified. Like several of the men he was visibly shaking. But it was not cold weather that was bringing these shivers. It was pure, unshamed fear. The sort of fear which anyone facing up to that kind of shock would be bound to feel.

'They're gone. Wonder if they'll come back?'

'I don't care. I just want to go home,' Carl insisted. His father and David were in no fit state to argue.

Back at the house they had to justify why they had left the rocks. There was nothing else to do but tell the truth.

'Well, if it's true, and I'm not saying I believe you mind, then shouldn't you call the police?' What Dave's wife said seemed to make sense.

'I guess we should – but if *you* find it hard to believe, what do you think the police are going to make out of it. 'Scuse me, officer, but I was fishing and nearly hooked these spaceships that landed in the river.'

His wife saw the point.

'No – I think the police are the last people we ought to tell.'

Several Saturdays later the idea of going back out to Seaforth rocks was tentatively mooted in front of Carl.

'You know I never believed in flying saucers. Well not really. You read about them and think that those who see them have got to be nuts. But then, when it happens to you, it's completely different. It was scary, real scary . . .'

'Dad?' Carl said.

'Yes.'

'I don't want to go out there again.'

'Not tonight?'

'Not on *any* night.'

The Whit Monday Mystery

◆

The mysterious disappearance of people will always create newspaper headlines and arouse varied speculations. But what of the other side of the coin? What if a person, without identity, without memory, *should appear out of nowhere*? This is precisely what happened in the city of Nuremberg, on Whit Monday, 26 May 1828, to a man who became known as 'Kaspar Hauser'.

At the beginning of the nineteenth century, Nuremberg, Bavaria's second largest city, was in decline. The old order of things had passed, taking the romantic splendour of the old place with it. The new wealth of the Industrial Revolution was still around the corner. Nuremberg had lost much of its social sparkle by the late 1820s, and it was ripe for mystery and intrigue.

The citizens from the surrounding country, shops and offices were celebrating the annual public holiday, when a number of people became aware of a strange youth walking through Unschlitt Square. His legs were unsteady and he looked totally bewildered, dressed as he was in ill-fitting labourers' clothes. A cobbler approached him and asked if he was all right. But he seemed oblivious to his surroundings and muttered incoherently. In his hand was clutched a letter, which the cobbler saw was addressed to 'The Captain of the 4th Squadron, 6th Cavalry Regiment.' Supporting the boy, the cobbler led him to the Captain's house.

When they arrived, a servant let them in, but informed the cobbler that the Captain was out. However, he agreed they could wait, and offered them refreshments in the meantime. Both men watched with bemusement as the strange boy wolfed down copious amounts of bread and water, but drew back, as if revolted, by an offer of meat. When a foaming pot of beer was put in front of him, he just stared at it in bewilderment. It was the same with other things too – everyday items that the people of Nuremberg took for granted. To this strange youth who could neither talk nor walk properly, he was mystified by all around him. It was as if *he had never seen these things before in his life.*

When the Captain returned, the boy, catching sight of the officer's uniform and sabre, became very excited and repeated over and over: 'Want to be a soldier like father.' 'Horse horse.' 'Don't know.'

The youth, judged to be about seventeen, handed over the envelope and it was found to contain two letters, one of them in Latin, allegedly written sixteen years apart. The first purported to be from his mother. It stated her son had been born on 30 April 1812, and that she was turning him out. She begged the finder to 'Take care of my child. He has been baptized. His father was a soldier in the 6th Cavalry.'

The second letter, allegedly written by the labourer who had taken on the boy, contained the bizarre admission that he had kept him in a locked room totally shut off from the outside world. He had now decided he could no longer support the lad along with his own ten children, and was sending him to Nuremberg.

When the Captain attempted to question the boy, all he received in reply was gibberish. Convinced he 'was either a primitive savage or an imbecile', the Captain handed him over to the police as a 'foundling'. Already, news of the strange affair was spreading across the city, and a small crowd of people followed them to the police station, where they waited outside for news of the boy who had 'appeared out of nowhere.'

The police were unsure how to treat the situation. In the meantime they put the youth in a cell and carefully observed him. While his behaviour backed up the assertion that he had been kept in solitary confinement, his appearance did not. One officer commented on his robustness and healthy-looking complexion, and noted the softness of his palms. Yet another officer made the following observations:

'He can sit for hours without moving a limb. He does not pace the floor, nor does he try to sleep. He sits rigidly without growing in the least uncomfortable. Also, he prefers darkness to light, and can move about in it like a cat.'

A doctor was called and he had no doubts about the prior predicament of the youth.

'This man is neither insane nor dull-witted, but he has

apparently been forcibly prevented in the most disastrous way from attaining any personal or social development.'

When he was given pen and paper, only three words could be discerned from the childish scrawl. 'Reiter', meaning 'cavalryman', and 'Kaspar Hauser'. Everyone presumed this was the boy's name, although initially he never reacted to it.

But despite its inconsistencies, the story seemed clear. The infant had been cast out by his mother, for unknown reasons, bearing a letter. Kaspar was then taken in by a labourer, who after this initial display of kindness, proceeded, again for unknown reasons, to keep him locked up in a dark room for sixteen years! Then, suddenly deciding he could no longer afford to feed the boy, the man abandoned him on the outskirts of Nuremberg with a new letter, indicating that the holder should be introduced into the army, 'like his father'.

However, the initial acceptance of this bizarre story began to crumble when the two letters, supposedly written by two different people sixteen years apart, were expertly examined.

It was ascertained that *both* letters were written on the *same* paper and – although one was written in Latin – with the same ink. What further confused (or clarified) the matter, the second letter stated: 'I have taught him to read and write, and he writes my handwriting exactly as I do.'

An examination of the words the boy had written at the police station, compared with the writing in the letters, showed some similarity. Was the entire affair then a hoax perpetrated by the youth? Was he only pretending to be illiterate, and had he in fact written all three letters? If so, for what reason?

Another mystery arose during the police investigations. Although plenty of witnesses testified that they had first set eyes on Kaspar Hauser at the New Gate area of the city, no one could be found who had seen the boy prior to this. The odd way he walked, his apparent drunkenness or idiocy, were certain to draw attention, yet no one had seen him on the road leading to the New Gate.

Kaspar Hauser had literally appeared out of nowhere.

All these facts caused Anselm von Feuerbach, a citizen of Ansbach, to comment much later:

> Kaspar Hauser showed such an utter deficiency of words and ideas, such perfect ignorance of the commonest things and appearances of Nature, and such a horror of all customs, conveniences and necessities of civilized life, and withal such extraordinary peculiarities in his social, mental and physical disposition, that one might feel one's self driven to the alternative of believing him to be a citizen of another planet, transferred by some miracle to our own.

Charles Fort, an early twentieth-century collector of 'odd' stories, commented that Kaspar Hauser's case was similar to other, less publicized stories of people who had 'appeared out of nowhere', as if they had been teleported from 'elsewhere', and in the process suffered amnesia. Perhaps the labourer, conjectured Fort, had found the youth in this distressed state, and kept him for only a few *weeks* in confinement, before getting rid of him after forging the letters to give him a new start. In support of this, Fort cites Hauser's later assertion that although the boy had been treated kindly, on one occasion he was struck for being noisy. Fort believed this meant that there must have been people living nearby who might hear the strange boy, and give his presence away. Therefore he could not possibly have been kept locked away with no one else finding out, for a period of sixteen years, as one of the letters claimed.

Kaspar admitted he had no real concept of 'time' during his confinement, and stated that 'the man' who looked after him had repeated over and over again, just two sentences for him to learn. One of them was that he wished to join a cavalry regiment, and the other was simply: 'I don't know'. This latter was perhaps meant to hide the fact that he was almost illiterate.

Kaspar Hauser became an overnight sensation. One policeman gave him a small wooden horse, and his enjoyment of this toy captured the hearts of the crowds who regularly turned up to watch him eat, sleep and go about his toilet. Well-wishers sent him gifts of similar horses.

Eventually, Kaspar was brought before the town council where he was asked to explain his predicament. With the extra German words he had picked up, he gave a fuller account of his vague and sketchy memories. The council published a statement shortly afterwards.

He neither knows who he is nor where he came from, for it was only at Nuremberg that he came into the world. He always lived in a hole, where he sat on straw on the ground; he never heard a sound nor saw a vivid light. He awoke and slept and awoke again; when he awoke he found a loaf of bread and a pitcher of water beside him. Sometimes the water tasted nasty. When he fell asleep again, he woke up to find he had a clean shirt on; he never saw the face of the man who came to him. He had two wooden horses and some ribbons to play with; he was never ill, never unhappy in his hole ... One day the man came into his room and put a table over his feet; something white lay on the table, and on this the man made black marks with a pencil which he put in his fingers. This the man did several times and when he was gone Kaspar imitated what he had done. At last he taught him to stand and to walk and finally carried him out of his hole. Of what happened next Kaspar has no very clear idea, until he found himself in Nuremberg with a letter in his hand.

The authorities went to great lengths to solve the mystery. A reward was offered for information, and throughout Germany posters appeared everywhere. The investigation even spilled over into Hungary, and writers in France and Britain took up the story. People travelled from all over Europe to see him, and theories about Kaspar Hauser's origins were a constant source of discussion.

This 'Child of Europe', as he was known, became Nuremberg's adopted son. A Professor George Friedrich Daumer saw the youth as a great challenge, and took him into his home. Daumer was a leading educationalist, and saw Kaspar as a prime example of a 'feral' child – someone who has been cut off from normal human contact during his formative upbringing. The scientist kept careful notes, and recorded examples of the boy's sharp 'animal senses', in particular his sense of smell. Kaspar was able to track different kinds of animals, 'smell' different types of trees, and even recognize people in the dark through their own peculiar odours. Yet he seemed quite ignorant of mirrors, flames and the difference between living things and inanimate objects. He attempted to find the 'person' in a mirror by looking behind it, attempted to pluck a flame from a candle and thought a grandfather clock was a living creature because it ticked and had moving parts.

But in every other respect he was quick to learn from his very able tutor – unnaturally quick. The semi-paralysis of his legs wore off, and he soon learned to speak German fluently, but with an indefinable accent. He also possessed a photographic memory, and his mental development was incredible to say the least. On top of all this, the 'boy from nowhere' displayed an enviable artistic talent for finely executed drawings.

All this caused the critics to announce that Kaspar Hauser was not a fast learner at all, but was merely *re*-learning things driven into the back reaches of his subconscious mind by some sort of shock. Others went a stage further, and declared the entire affair was a hoax, and that Kaspar was just a skilled actor out to achieve notoriety.

But most people accepted the story at its face value – that the youth had been held captive for sixteen years, by an unknown jailor for unknown reasons. But if the facts were unknown, there were plenty of people ready to supplant them with gossip and speculation.

The rumour soon gathered strength that he was really the illegitimate son of an aristocratic family who had locked him up to avoid a scandal. This caused a great stir in Nuremberg society, especially when Stephanie de Beauharnais – the Grand Duchess of Baden – was linked as the guilty party. In the end, the Grand Duchess had to threaten legal action in a futile attempt to silence the gossips.

Kaspar revelled in all the attention. A thorough police investigation turned up no clue which might lead to an end to the mystery. Even though posters showing his face were circulated all over Germany, no one came forth to say they recognized the teenager, which is surprising if he was merely a hoaxer. Neither did enquiries with the 6th Cavalry lead anywhere.

A year after Kaspar Hauser's mysterious appearance in the streets of Nuremberg, he sat down with Dr Daumer and wrote his autobiography, in an attempt to set the record straight.

If anything, this was an anti-climax, as little which was new was revealed. On the other hand, it was a very important document, as it showed that Kaspar was not prepared to embellish his story for the sake of sensationalism. But just two months after the publication of his book, events took a dramatic turn.

Kaspar was discovered lying prostrate in Professor Daumer's cellar, with a bloody head wound. The youth was carried upstairs and laid down on a bed. He claimed that a man with a 'black face' had appeared out of nowhere and attacked him with a knife. Although no one had been seen running away from the scene of the crime, the Nuremberg citizens were convinced someone was out to assassinate their adopted son. He was moved to another address and for the next few years was constantly watched over by two police officers.

Nothing untoward occurred until two years later, in the May of 1831. One of the officers assigned to watch over him was alarmed to hear a shot issue from a room in the house. He rushed in to find Kaspar once more wounded in the forehead, but this time, he explained, it was of his own doing. He was standing on a chair, reaching for a book, he explained, when he over-balanced. His hands struck out wildly and one of them grasped a gun mounted on the wall. The pistol had discharged itself.

People began to murmur the word 'suicide' and some of Nuremberg's more prominent citizens started grumbling about the cost of keeping the boy under police protection. The authorities were in an awkward situation. What if they withdrew the police protection, and someone successfully murdered the young man? Fortunately a solution presented itself in the form of a wealthy English eccentric.

The Nuremberg councillors allowed Lord Stanhope temporary custody of Kaspar. Stanhope had taken a close interest in the case from the start, but unfortunately he seemed to view Kaspar as some sort of amusement to entertain his rich friends.

He took Kaspar on a tour of Europe, but eventually the pair quarrelled. In 1833, this influential Englishman persuaded the Nuremberg Council – against their better judgement – to allow him to lodge the young man with a friend, a Dr Meyer, who lived some twenty-five miles away in the town of Ansbach. This proved another, and ultimately, fatal mistake.

Dr Meyer had very firm plans. First of all he had Kaspar confirmed as a Protestant, then he attempted to teach him Latin and History. Kaspar perhaps resented the way he was being forced into all this. After all, he was no longer a child. Consequently, Dr Meyer found him to be a very poor pupil. It is possible too that Kaspar was missing the glamour conferred on him by his friends back in Nuremberg.

The doctor completely lost interest, bitterly declaring that, in his opinion, Kaspar Hauser's supposed superior mental abilities were a complete sham. If anything, he was retarded!

Kaspar was planning to return to his friends in Nuremberg when he was savagely murdered.

It happened on 14 December 1833. The young man had gone out for a walk around town, and Dr Meyer was surprised by his sudden and premature return. Clutching his side, Kaspar gasped: 'Man stabbed! Knife! Park! Gave wallet! Go quick!' Then he collapsed in a pool of blood. As Kaspar lay in bed seriously ill, he revealed more details of the attack.

A stranger, 'tall, with dark whiskers and a black coat' had approached him as he walked through the town. 'Are you Kaspar Hauser?' the man had asked. Kaspar nodded, and the stranger said he had some information regarding his origins, then led him into the nearby park. There he handed Kaspar a wallet, and as he opened it, the stranger stabbed him in the side.

The police found the wallet where it was dropped, and inside, on a piece of paper, was written a nonsensical message in 'mirror' writing. It said: 'Hauser will be able to tell you how I look, whence I came from and who I am. To spare him the task, I will tell you myself. I am . . . from . . . on the Bavarian border . . . on the river . . . My name is MLO).'

The peoples of Ansbach and Nuremberg were outraged by the attack, and once again posters were distributed far and wide in an attempt to throw light on this final mystery connected with the life of the man known as 'Kaspar Hauser'. But even as he lay dying, some cast doubts on whether an attack had occurred at all. No one in the town remembered seeing the stranger, nor anyone suspicious leaving the park. And earlier it had been snowing heavily, yet at the place of the alleged attack, there was only one set of footprints, leading into and out of Ansbach park . . .

Had the young man stabbed himself to obtain public sympathy at a time when he was obviously unhappy? But what was the point of the wallet with its nonsensical message?

Yet that was what Dr Meyer believed. But if that was the truth, Hauser had gone too far, penetrating the left side of his chest, damaging his lungs and liver irreparably. Was this possible?

Two physicians who attended Kaspar Hauser gave the opinion that he could *not* have injured himself in this way. But a third indirectly commented that he could have executed a bizarre suicide bid.

But the 'Son of Europe' denied it to the end. He died, after complications set in, on 17 December 1833.

Just who was the man known as 'Kaspar Hauser'? The debate never waned from the time of his almost supernatural appearance near Unschlitt Square, to his bizarre death five years later. Yet much of the story seems nonsensical. Letters allegedly written sixteen years apart, on the same paper, and in the same handwriting ... a healthy outdoor complexion ... an ability to sit perfectly still for hours on end ... never seeing the face of his jailor ... no memory of how he arrived at Nuremberg ... two attacks on his life when no evidence of an attack could be proven ... and another strange message on a piece of paper ...

If Kaspar Hauser was merely a hoaxer, then his hoaxes were full of holes, dangerous and finally fatal. If he was telling the truth, then perhaps we should consider the theories of Charles Fort and those proponents of the illegitimacy theory. Perhaps Kaspar Hauser was murdered before his full memory returned. Also, after his death, some very prominent Nurembergers died under mysterious circumstances, including Burgermeister Binder. Did they know something Hauser had secretly told them?

We will probably never learn the true identity of Kaspar Hauser, whom, the Nuremberg councillors claimed '... it was only at Nuremberg he came into the world.'

Large crowds followed the body to its final resting place. A monument was erected to mark the place of the fatal stabbing in Ansbach park, and on his headstone is written:

Here lies Kaspar Hauser
The riddle of his time
His birth was unknown
His death mysterious

MARRIAGE

After the Wedding

———————◆———————

He could see his body in a tangle of sheets, next to Mary, his wife. His slumbering, soulless body – down on the bed, while *he* was up there, near the ceiling, wondering what to do.

Larry had been trying for some time to bring about what parapsychologists call 'an out of body experience', or 'OBE' for short. Now he had achieved it through concentration and trance. Or had he? For a moment he doubted it. 'What an imagination I have,' he thought, and chuckled inwardly.

But it *felt* real, everything *looked* real; *vividly* real. The bedside table with the long scratch down its door, the alarm clock – a present from his brother last Christmas – exactly where he had placed it after winding it up earlier, the worn patch on the carpet . . . If it was all a dream, then it was a remarkably detailed dream.

But what happens now? he thought. He looked through the bedroom window, and wondered if it was possible to reach the railway line a hundred yards away. No sooner had the thought formed, than he found himself drifting through the closed window as if it was not there. Out through the bricks and mortar into the night air.

He reached the line easily, stopped, looked back at the bedroom window and was troubled at how small it appeared. But he *could* go on . . . he knew it, he could go on and on . . . well, for a short way, at least. Larry followed the line like a balloon on the end of a piece of string, the wooden sleepers lost in the dark, the steel rails reflecting wanly the vague tatters of starlight. It was exhilarating, it was *weird*. What really impressed him was how *un*familiar this familiar landscape looked from his vantage point over the railway track. This was his neighbourhood which he knew intimately, but it was like a foreign land viewed from this new perspective.

Then something happened which broke his reverie. There, up ahead, was a tunnel-like patch of mist about twenty feet long, hanging in the sky at a slight cant. It was as if some celestial god had collected all the steam ever issued from all the old steam engines which used to run up and down the track, then woven it into a strange cotton-wool-like cocoon. Larry was drawn towards its swirling white mouth, the entrance to this misty tunnel. He had to get in there and see what there was to see. This same curiosity which had made him experiment in the first place, now drove him even further . . .

Larry was inside. And trapped. Hundreds of hands shot out from the floor of the tunnel and gripped frantically at his ethereal legs. One hand caught an ankle and held it tightly. Then Larry panicked and fought frantically to escape, yet all the time in the forefront of his mind remained the desire to find out what lay at the end of the tunnel.

Suddenly the mist cleared and he could see ahead. There was the most beautiful mountain range he had ever seen in his life. A golden sun shone in a sky almost washed out of blue. The mountains themselves dominated the scene with their beauty. Light brown in colour, they rose and fell in petrified splendour.

The scene hung tantalizingly ahead of him. It would be so easy, he felt, to give up the struggle and carry on into the paradise ahead. But something told him *no, not yet, not yet* . . .

He fought back with renewed vigour as the disembodied

109

hands grasped frantically to hold him. Then it was all over. One moment he was struggling for his life, the next he was back in his body, sitting up in bed, gasping for air, feeling his sweat-soaked pyjamas sticking coldly to his body.

The bedside light flashed on and for a moment stung his eyes. The worried face of Mary clouded with sleep hung before him.

'What's a matter, Larry? What's wrong with you?'

His head flopped back on the pillow and he stared up at the ceiling for a moment. Then he told her what had happened. She made him promise never to try anything like that again.

The year was 1973. Larry Mayer kept that promise to his wife. But fourteen years later events were to take place beyond his control.

Larry had not always lived in Manchester. He was born near Sheffield, and had spent some time living in the small town of Stocksbridge, surrounded by rough moorland and pine forests, at the southernmost tip of Yorkshire. Most of his relatives still lived there, and he visited them regularly. But now there was a problem. His brother's daughter, Pamela, was getting married in a few weeks' time, and of course, he and Mary had been invited to the wedding. Since Larry's retirement, money had been in very short supply. It took every penny they had spare to maintain the old Volvo they used to get around in and to ferry the local old folk to the community centre. The last thing they needed was the expense of a wedding present. In fact they just could not afford it, and to buy something absurdly cheap would only cause more embarrassment. As the date drew nearer, they decided that Larry would attend the wedding, to 'show his face' as it were, but Mary would remain at home.

It was Saturday, 19 September 1987, Larry set off especially early that morning because he had offered to drive some of the guests to the church. He arrived at his brother's house in plenty of time amid the hustle and bustle and near-panic of the final wedding preparations. There was perhaps an extra nervousness in the air because this was Pamela's second try at marriage, and everyone wanted the day to go without a hitch. Larry congratulated his niece on how nice she looked, then melted into the background.

The ceremony was to be held in the methodist church in Stocksbridge. The weather was a bit showery, but not too bad considering it was the tail-end of a not too brilliant British summer. Larry helped transport some of the guests, then took his place in the church, waiting for the ceremony to start.

There was organ music playing gently in the background, intended to relax everyone and prepare them for the entrance of the bride. But Larry Meyer was troubled, and he did not know why. Was it the church? Did he feel uncomfortable because he was about to take part in something he had no particular belief in? Not the marriage itself, but the hymns and prayers he was expected to sing and parrot, even though their words meant nothing to him. No ... not the church ... something else which was going to happen or had already happened a long long time ago ...

The organ music penetrated his thoughts for a moment, and he almost expected to hear a heavenly choir ...

How old had he been? Yes, three, just three years old. He was a bit of a scamp, he remembered, always running off and playing quietly on his own. Of course, in the 1930s, a child could do that with no fear of ending up in the clutches of a sadistic killer. The only danger was that such a small child might come to some harm in a brook swollen by winter rains, or become lost on the moors and die of exposure ...

At this time, the young Larry Mayer lived with his parents on a small estate near Sheffield. Close by was a park.

This particular evening, Larry wandered off as soon as his parents' backs were turned and found himself drawn

111

towards the park. As he neared the trees, he heard the most beautiful singing he had ever heard in his young life. To him it sounded like the voices of angels.

Like a child of Hamlyn, he followed the sound further into the park, and finally sat down on a bench. The heavenly voices were above him. His gaze turned upwards. It was a clear starlit night. At the spot from where the singing seemed to emanate was – nothing. It was as if a hole was punched through the sky; a black circle of nothingness where no stars shone.

The little boy's attention was drawn back down to the bench, and he gasped. Beside him was a large glossy book, its cover composed of the most magnificent colours. He carefully picked it up and stared at the illustration on the front. In the bottom left-hand corner was depicted a Stone Age man. The figure was staring upwards, his face full of wonder. The object of his attentions was the full moon.

Larry placed the book down again and sighed. I'll take this home with me, he thought, but when he looked again, the book had gone.

As he sat in the church, he pondered on the meaning of this and several other strange experiences which had plagued him during his sixty years. Suddenly the note of the organ changed, and everyone stood up. The bride was coming down the aisle.

As far as weddings go, it went well. After the ceremony, the guests were transported back to the home of the bride's parents for a buffet lunch and drinks. Larry stayed until after tea, making conversation, laughing and joking with his brother, yet all the time that uneasy feeling which had begun in church was with him.

An evening reception had been planned at a club in the town. But Larry was teetotal so he declined the invitation, and instead, at six o'clock, went to visit his sister and brother-in-law who also lived in Stocksbridge.

Brian and Sarah Brooks were pleased to see him. Larry

felt so relaxed he failed to keep track of the time, until he suddenly looked at his watch and saw it was 9.25 p.m. Good grief, he thought, Mary will be wondering what has happened to me! He bade his relatives goodnight and left at once.

It was dark and still now. The showers which had blotted the day were gone. Larry started his car and waved goodbye to Brian and Sarah. He set off through the Garden City area of the town then turned left onto the Manchester to Sheffield road. That strange feeling returned; the sensation of unease he had first experienced sitting in the pew of the methodist church just hours earlier. Why had it come back?

At the top of Langsett Hill something made him slow down. Inside his head, a voice seemed to say, take your time. Stocksbridge was now a mile or so behind him. All that lay ahead was the dark moors, a few scattered farms and, running parallel with the black ribbon of road, a pine forest.

Larry was doing thirty miles an hour or less by the time he reached the edge of the forest. A few hundred yards further on he exclaimed to himself. As the car had passed a clearing he had seen something which had confused and astounded him. It was only a fragmentary glimpse, but it was as firmly etched in his mind as the other strange things that had happened down the years.

A bright red light had drawn his gaze. But there was much more. There were several strips of lights, about three feet long and eight inches deep, coloured red, then white, alternately. The arrangement gave the strong impression that the strips were attached to something circular, hovering about fifty feet off the ground near the tops of the trees. More than this, these powerful lights were *pulsating*, having an almost hypnotic quality to them.

A hundred yards down the road, Larry pulled into a layby. Just what exactly *had* he seen back there? He climbed out of the car and stood staring back at the forest. It struck him that his whole surroundings were unusually quiet. More than that, since he had left Stockbridge there had been no other cars on the road. Larry knew the route well, and on a Saturday night one could expect to see two or three cars every minute. There were none.

Just the silence, the *complete* silence.

He lit a cigarette and wondered what to do. He could easily walk back to the entrance to the clearing and take another look. Had he really seen a UFO? Then another thought struck him. Supposing it was some sort of vehicle connected with drug smuggling or maybe gun running? He could stumble into something he might regret. But those bright lights, those pulsating hypnotic lights – they seemed to be attached to something which was *hovering*. He could take no chances. Larry put out the cigarette, climbed back into the car and drove away.

About four miles further on, near the top of Woodhead Hill, he came across an accident. Near a small bridge over a stream, a car had completely turned over onto its roof. A few people stood around and the situation seemed to be under control, so he did not stop. A few minutes later an ambulance and a fire engine passed him travelling from Manchester in the direction of the accident. But Larry's mind was still too full of the scene he had witnessed in the forest to take much notice, and he continued his journey home.

He walked into the house, head buzzing, and looked quizzically at his wife as he greeted her. She was wearing her night clothes and drinking a mug of coffee.

'Hello, Mary,' he said, 'you're ready for bed early?'

Now it was her turn to look askance at him.

'Well, it *is* ten past eleven!'

He glanced at the wall clock as if suspecting a trick.

'Ten past eleven? But I set off before half past nine . . . It should only be about ten o'clock!'

Larry collapsed into an armchair. How could he have possibly lost an hour of time? None of it made sense.

The experience became something of an obsession. For months afterwards, Larry, accompanied by two of his nephews, visited the location at Stocksbridge and drove around the area looking for clues, often until the early hours of the morning.

Investigators from the Direct Investigation Group into Aerial Phenomena and the Manchester UFO Research Association (MUFORA) made enquiries about the case.

Larry Meyer was not alone in his belief that he had experienced unusual phenomena in the Stocksbridge area that month. Less than a fortnight before his curious encounter, things had been going bump in the night on the side of a hill overlooking the town where a bypass was under construction. Pearoyd Lane, descending from high up on the moors, crosses over the new road before plummeting towards the British Steel works below. Two security men, patrolling at this spot, started off the scare.

It was just after midnight when Steven Brookes and David Goldthorpe arrived at the location to check out the site. They could not believe their eyes. Just a short distance away, beneath an electricity pylon, a group of 'children' were holding hands and dancing in a circle. The men drove past and parked their vehicle, but by this time the small figures had vanished. The location was particularly difficult to get to, and there seemed no way the children could have disappeared so quickly. The men searched the ground beneath the pylon and found another mystery. Although there was fresh mud beneath the steel struts, *there was no sign of footprints.*

Steven Brookes and David Goldthorpe made some enquiries. They discovered that workmen living nearby in caravans had heard children's voices in the dead of night. A local farmer, too, had reportedly sighted a circle of dancing children at the same spot.

Not long after the initial incident, the scene was set for a much more frightening experience. At midnight on Monday evening, 7 September, Steven and David were driving slowly along the partially built road towards the new bridge which would allow Pearoyd Lane to continue its ancient passage over the bypass. At this stage the bridge

115

was uncompleted, and not linked either side with the lane. Without ladders it was impossible for anyone to get onto it. Imagine their bemusement then, at seeing a hooded figure clinging to the parapet along the top of the bridge.

They stopped the Landrover a few yards from the base of the construction; the figure, apparently that of a man, stayed where it was. They decided to reverse and drive up a slip road onto Pearoyd Lane, where they would be able to get around to the back of the 'man'. As they neared the gap between road and bridge, Brookes put the headlights on main beam. *The light shone straight through the hooded man who then disappeared.*

Now they were terrified. This was too much. What exactly was going on? The men had heard rumours that the new road cut through an old graveyard, and speculated that this had disturbed *something*. They were so upset that just a few hours later at 7 a.m., they woke the Reverend Simons, a local clergyman, and told him the story. Would he carry out an exorcism? The vicar did some checking and confirmed that a graveyard had *not* existed at the construction site. Because of this fact, he decided an exorcism was out of the question and advised the men to refer the matter to the police.

Police Constable Andrew Bentley was initially sceptical. But Steven and David's boss, Mike Lee, himself a former Rotherham police officer, phoned the constable to say his men were genuinely distressed. He was convinced they had experienced something truly bizarre. Both Brookes and Goldthorpe were trembling like jelly, he explained, and refusing to work at the site again unless the matter was sorted out. All this started PC Bentley thinking.

That Saturday night, the twelfth, Bentley and Special Constable Michael Keen went up to the location around midnight. None of their colleagues knew what they had planned. According to PC Bentley, this is what happened.

We went up from Deepcar and drove up to the bridge, parking roughly halfway between the pylon

116

and the bridge where the two sightings have supposedly been. We turned all the lights and radios off. It was a clear sky, virtual full moon, and after a while we could see very well. If anyone came near us we could see them.

We'd been sat there a couple of minutes. Up by the bridge I'd already noticed a large container which was like a white painted box. I'd been looking at this for quite some time, and I asked Mike if he could see anything amiss. We both decided there was something moving across and around this box. We could see a shadow, so I put the full beam on the car and saw nothing at all. After our eyes had adjusted, we drove up and got out – not a damned thing! We drove back to where we were before, and lo and behold, there was something moving around the box ...

We went up again – nothing at all! We decided that the lights from the steelworks in the valley below were reflecting off the box and causing shadows. Back at our original spot I put my window down. It was a nice night. I was sat in the driver's seat, Mike was in the passenger seat. Suddenly I had a feeling, unlike any I'd had before, just as if someone had walked over my grave, because I froze. And what was so odd, I went cold without knowing why. A few seconds after I had another feeling that someone was stood at the side of me. I turned my head slowly, and saw something by the side of the car.

It definitely gave me the impression of it being a person, a man. He wore light clothing and a 'V' on his chest. I could see it in the moonlight.

Suddenly it was gone and then *instantaneously* reappeared at the passenger side of the vehicle. Special Constable Michael Keen let out a scream and hit his colleague on the arm. Keen got a more detailed look at the figure.

To me, what I saw of him, it sort of connected to the

1820s – that kind of era. But I just looked at its face, which I presumed was a man, and it was just literally staring, and to me it looked like he had some kind of cravat on, and a waistcoat. It looked like something out of Dickens' day. But I looked again and tried to focus, and it was gone . . .

Not long after, when they tried to alert other officers, something thumped loudly on the back of the car.

Had all this any connection with Larry Mayer's post-wedding experience, exactly a week later? At about the same time, it transpired, two officers in a panda car on Lodge Moor, observed a group of brilliant lights moving at low level in the area of Redmires Reservoir.

On the night of 8 December, a team of MUFORA investigators accompanied Mr Mayer and his nephews to the location of his experience and reconstructed the event. They took the same route as Larry and drove past the clearing at thirty miles an hour. It was determined that, even at this slow speed, it was not really possible to have taken in as much detail as Larry claimed to remember. There was only time enough for a glance. Did this mean that his imagination had played a trick on him, exaggerating what was really just a few distant lights? Or was there some connection with the missing period of time? Had something happened during that unaccounted-for hour which was wiped from his conscious mind?

The police were contacted regarding the accident, to see if the timing of that would resolve the anomaly of the missing hour. This move proved to be of no help, but the Chief Superintendent of the South Yorkshire police commented that from the position of the alleged UFO sighting, car headlights can be seen coming over Bord Hill, some two miles away. He suggested these might be the lights Larry had seen.

But the investigators already knew about this effect – and so did Larry Mayer. They had observed them on the night of the reconstruction. They looked like what they were: distant pinpricks of light – car headlights.

Larry had been adamant from the first. He had observed *long strips* of red and white lights which *pulsated*. And they had not been anywhere but in the forest. The pine trees behind the phenomenon had been clearly lit up.

Was there really an hour of missing time? If there was, then what could have happened during that period?

Brian and Sarah Brooks were of no help. They could not remember clearly at what time Larry decided to leave, except it was 'late'. However, Larry was genuinely puzzled by the apparent discrepancy. There are many other cases on record where people – sometimes whole families – cannot account for an hour or so, after seeing a UFO. Under hypnosis, they describe being in a white room undergoing examination by strange alien beings ...

Larry Mayer was offered the services of a clinical psychologist to probe his subconscious mind for any possible 'hidden' memories. This man is a skilled scientist who has worked on several other similar cases with amazing results. Larry Mayer refused.

Perhaps he would rather remain ignorant. Perhaps the details of that missing hour are too fearful for him to face. In his heart he might already know what happened. Perhaps ...

Recently, strange images have been creeping into his mind. In one, he is standing in the forest, looking up at a brightly lit object no higher than the trees. In another, there is a face staring at him. The head is pear-shaped; there is a slitted mouth, large round eyes and a long pointed nose.

Is there any link between these experiences and the other incidents of contact with the unknown in this man's life, or did he just happen to be in the wrong place at a time when strange paranormal phenomena seemed to have invaded the Stocksbridge area?

What really happened to Larry Meyer, after that wedding?

JUNE

2nd On this date in 1964, a group of children near Gateshead in Tyne and Wear reported strange little 'elves' playing on haystacks.

5th Europe's most impressive set of UFO photographs was taken on this day in 1955 when a disc was filmed flying in and out of a curious vapour trail left behind above Namur, Belgium.

On the same date in 1983 there were extensive falls of strange objects from the sky above southern England, ranging from a crab in Sussex to small pieces of coke in Dorset. Freak weather conditions were blamed for this common phenomenon known to paranormal researchers as 'fafrotskies' – falls from the skies.

19th Five witnesses claimed to be abducted by a UFO from a road near Farringdon in Oxfordshire on the return trip from a family funeral. The 1978 encounter was extensively documented by university lecturer, Frank Johnson, in his book – *The Janos People* – although most researchers are not persuaded by his literal interpretations, or his proposal that the New Zealand government empty one of its two islands to allow the Janos aliens to land en masse and populate the vacant space!

20th Major Donald Keyhoe, who became an important figure in the UFO controversy, was born this day in 1897, in Iowa. He died in 1988.

23rd On this day in 1744, Daniel Strickett, his boss William Lancaster and family observed troops on horseback on the slopes of Souter-Fell, Cumberland. Altogether, 26 witnesses in cottages round the mountainside saw wave after wave of phantom troops, for a duration of $2^1/_2$ hours, walk up impossibly steep slopes and over precipices.

26th Mr Smellie, author of *The Philosophy of Natural History,* made a pact with the Rev. William Greenlaw, that the first to die would return and visit the other. If a year elapsed and nothing happened, it was to be concluded the visit was not possible. The vicar died first on this day in 1774. The year was almost up, when Greenlaw appeared to the writer while he was relaxing in an armchair, and told him he had experienced great difficulty in getting through.

30th In 1908 a huge 'fireball' exploded in the sky over Tunguska, Siberia. It sent a shock wave twice around the world, and the effects were felt up to 600 miles away. Twenty square miles of forest were blown down and set on fire. Theories range from the disintegration of a comet to the explosion of a nuclear-powered space craft.

A Haunted Family

◆

The light pierced through the window, spearing Barbara's very youthful eyes. From outside a fearful racket bombarded all her senses. It was like a thousand machine guns rat-tat-tatting at once. It was a terrible experience.

Barbara *knew* that she was tiny – very tiny – and trapped in a bigger world. Indeed, she knew an awful lot of things that later would seem hard to comprehend. Right now they were just a matter of course.

The girl surveyed the scene from her cot. Yes, her *cot,* she thought. I am just a baby, less than a year old. Still unable to walk. But here I am alone in this bedroom with the chest of drawers to my right and the big window ahead.

Even with the heavy drapes the glow of the searchlights was obvious and the piercing wail of the siren that had preceded the guns had warned of these forlorn efforts to shoot the German bombers from the sky.

Barbara was alone and dreadfully scared. It was 1942 and a fierce air raid was pounding South London. The docks were under heavy attack and her Balham home was in the way, as Hitler tried once more to thrash Britain into submission. He knew that the tide of the war had turned against him.

Is this how adults behave? Barbara tossed the question around like a salad. What an awful time to be born into.

Using her babyish voice, which was all that her vocal chords could muster, she screamed and yelled. Somebody had to come for her. It was not safe up here. Outside in the garden there was a shelter. Why wasn't her aunt or grandmother coming to take her to that haven?

Still the noise and the light continued and Barbara, thinking in a strangely adult way despite her youth, also knew why all this was happening.

She had been *sent* to this place.

Barbara had been born during another air raid the summer before. But she was now well aware that such an entry into the world was somehow preordained. There was a memory of a time even further back – beyond conception – of events *before* she was born.

Young and innocent – and yet so wise – Barbara could see herself suspended in the blackness of space looking down upon a blue and white ball of earth. The home to which she was about to be sent. It felt like an exile. There was a terribleness about it, yet also an inevitability.

Beside her in this limbo were two men – at least she sensed that they were male. They seemed to hesitate, as if they had come too far already and could not go past the barrier at which they all stood.

'You do not have to go, you know,' one of them thought (in a speechlike manner but direct into her mind).

'I know that, I want to,' she replied. They seemed to be

laughing at her curious determination.

The other man was quite firm. He insisted. 'It is important that you go there.'

'I know,' she told him.

'There will be difficulties. Your life will have obstacles.' The voice explained what some of these might be, and the other man confirmed the facts.

Barbara needed no persuading. She told them: 'I can do that easily.' They laughed again.

The memory of all this faded with time. Only a peculiar sensation – like a feeling tickling inside – remained as she grew. It was a knowledge that some great secret was understood by a hidden part of her mind, but it was always out of reach. Always tantalizingly close, but just beyond her comprehension.

Barbara's family treated her well, and she grew to love them. But there was constantly this forbidden truth lurking inside. They did not own her. She owed allegiance to something greater. And she was her own person.

Whilst still a small child, inside Barbara was more than that. Far more.

At last the war was over and something like a normal childhood became possible. Recollections of these fantastic experiences were now dim. But they were there. Barbara always knew there was more to life than simply evolving as a form of animal. She began to respect other species. To care about conservation and recognize that life was sacred.

She became a rebellious spirit, challenging convention, and found that her family understood this extra dimension to existence.

Her father was deeply religious. He would consume the Bible avidly. Yet at the same time he revelled in the occult.

When she was still at primary school Barbara heard her parents talking feverishly about some American chap called George Adamski, who had met spiritual masters from another planet. They seemed to believe what he said.

She was meanwhile developing her own talents, learning how to handle something her father had called astral projection.

Soon the feelings began to come naturally. At night Barbara would drift into a strange state of consciousness. It was almost as if she had disassociated her mind from her body and was hovering on the edge of a huge chasm. Dare she leap off and fly into the air, or would she crash to the ground?

It was frightening at first, but became less so as she got used to it. Yet never would she bring it on at will. It brought back too many echoes of that distant memory ... floating above the Earth in a place that she could not remember, but which she knew that she had reluctantly departed.

Her very own garden of Eden.

The family was living in Brixton now. This was an area full of old houses crammed close together. The streets that had survived the Nazi bombs were intermixed with those that were scarred and ravaged. By 1949 there was a new air of optimism about the country, but still a great deal of postwar austerity. The money to fix all the damage simply wasn't there. Bomb sites of rubble were fun to play in, but they were also a terrible memento of what the human race had done in a frenzy of masochistic hatred.

In their grand new house the eight-year-old Barbara had a room to herself way up on the top storey. Apart from the bedroom this floor held only the toilet and a ladder leading through a skylight onto the flat roof.

This isolation did not worry the adventurous youngster. In some respects she actually enjoyed it. The room was directly above the lounge and she had been given a stick with instructions to bang this on the floor if she ever needed anything after going to bed. She used it very sparingly; knowing only too well the consequences of overuse.

On this particular summer night Barbara was in bed early. Her father worked as a technician at one of

London's still thriving theatres. He left at about 7 p.m. and she had to be in bed and settled before he departed. But outside it was light and sleep was often elusive.

Rolling over to face the bookshelves and dressing table, Barbara suddenly jerked upright. She was confronted by a strange figure, a man sitting quietly in the little chair by the side of her bed.

She stared at him, her heart thumping. Who was it?

It was certainly not her father, nor anyone she knew. Yet he did not seem to be evil. In fact he radiated a kindness into her mind.

My God, it's Robin Hood, was the girl's first thought. For the man was dressed in a skin-tight one-piece suit with what looked like a short cape at the back. But then she realised the silliness of this idea. This was no ordinary man. He was quite different in every respect.

For one thing he was so small and delicate: almost effeminate. The chair had been designed for a child, yet he fitted into it snugly. He was completely in proportion, not like a circus midget might be. Yet in height he could have been only about three feet tall.

In other words – *he wasn't human*!

His features were weird. He had an oval face with a very pointed chin and his knee joints seemed angular as well. She had never seen anyone remotely like this and her head became filled with strange impressions. Perhaps it was one of her comic-book characters; 'Jack Flash' maybe. He did not look right for that, but the green cloak was similar.

Barbara hardly dared to breathe. The intruder was still sitting there quietly, as if he had a right to be in her room. Then 'Jack' was talking to her, but not with words. The thoughts were entering her head and then disappearing, as if they were raindrops being absorbed into the sea. Nothing was sticking in her memory. She seemed under a magic spell.

Then the figure vanished. Free of the grip that was holding her, she hit the floor with her stick and yelled out.

'I've seen Jack Flash. He was here in the bedroom,' she

told her father when he scurried upstairs.

He smiled and tried to reassure her that she had only been dreaming; it was nothing to be afraid of. But he was anxious to get off to work and these dismissals were not in the least convincing. Barbara knew that the encounter had been real and had meant something.

In fact, it had forced open a door inside her mind, awakening many other mysterious images. The bedroom visit from 'Jack' was to be the start of a lifetime of impossibilities.

Almost immediately the bad headaches struck Barbara. Every few days they hit her out of nowhere. Her head would pound and burn up as if something was alive inside and trying to kick its way out. The pain was awful. When she complained about them she was told that it was all part of growing up, and that they would fade in time. They did not do so.

Much later she was led to believe they were attacks of migraine – a persistent, if unexplained, head pain. Barbara even contemplated that she might be suffering from epilepsy – and that there was some form of disorder in her brain. Doctors were consulted but still the headaches continued until she was adult, with a daughter, and ceased only when *she* took on the legacy.

Soon after the little man materialized in her bedroom, Barbara began to suffer from sudden floating sensations. She felt her body going further and further away and a dreamy timelessness and space disorientation took over. It was frightening. But there was nothing she could do to stop it happening.

Often Barbara delayed bedtime as long as possible, using any pretext she could find.

'I want a glass of water,' she would tell her mother. Half an hour later she would demand another. Barbara knew that to submit to sleep would be to give in to this horrible drifting sensation. It would creep up on her in the dark hours, stalking her out, waiting to pounce. The moment she dared to let go of consciousness, it would grab her and try to tear her free of her body.

In that terrible instant she would jump up, yelling 'No! No!'. Then it would go away – until tomorrow.

Eventually all that Barbara could do was learn to cope. By living with and accepting it, so that it disappeared.

Oddly, the bedroom did not become a place to be avoided after such traumas. It seemed a happy corner in which to spend time. Indeed she took her friends there without ever telling them what happened there at night.

It seemed that all would soon be well.

And then the voices came.

They called out to her at night. Reverberating inside her head and filling the room. She did not know who they were – but they appeared to be female.

'We will not hurt you,' they whispered.

Barbara looked around the room, expecting to see something – anything. There was nobody there.

'You are safe – Dee-Dee.'

The use of the name shook her rigid, it was a family term of endearment. Only those very close ever used it. Yet these strange, invisible phantoms were talking to her as if they were entitled to treat her as a relative. Who were they?

Barbara turned over, bringing the sheet up to mask her face. She faced the wall, her mind begging the voices to go away.

Yet still they continued. Sometimes they went on all night.

At first she thought she was losing her sanity. Then she assumed that the room was haunted by unseen apparitions. She contemplated the possibility that the creatures were fairies. Was the little man their king? Yet there was no sense of the ghostly about the place. Only the voices.

Paralysed with fear, she now never used the stick to bring her parents running. Somehow she knew that this was not the answer. That the ones behind the whispers in the night would never understand. Her parents probably would not hear the voices anyway. These were *her* ghosts.

They would go only when they were good and ready.

And – not long afterwards – they did.

Barbara grew up and married young but she still had strange and vivid dreams, some of which seemed to foretell the future.

Once, in 1963, around the time she became pregnant, she experienced a terrible dream in which a huge tidal wave swept over her. She awoke in a sweat and fought to shake off the images. Minutes later, switching the radio on, the newsreader reported a disaster in the Far East. A tidal wave had struck and many coastal inhabitants had been killed.

But the allegorical nature of the dream might be more significant. Soon afterwards Barbara was struck by her own tidal wave – a terrible illness, the dreaded disease, tuberculosis.

In hospital they struggled to save her life. Barbara was pumped full of drugs and kept drifting in and out of consciousness. One night she awoke and felt strange. A sense of foreboding dulled her senses. Looking round, she saw why. She was no longer *on* the bed, but floating several feet above it!

Desperately Barbara tried to scream, but her voice would not function. Then, there was an awful churning sensation like a lift plunging out of control towards disaster, and she was back in her body in the bed.

As soon as she could drag herself from bed, Barbara discharged herself from the hospital. The doctors protested furiously. There was damage to her lung. If she did not carry on with the treatment she could very well die. But it was all to no avail – there was nothing that would make her stay.

Her father told her not to worry. Wise in the ways of the occult, he led the sick young woman to a nearby wood and they sat and soaked in the calm surroundings. He explained about healing and the way that the body needed balance. All you had to do was restore the current imbalance in energy fields. Barbara gazed into his warm, loving face and took hold of his hands. They felt very hot as if some power were pouring from them and entering her.

Shortly afterwards when the doctors examined Barbara, they expressed amazement. The lesion in her lung was gone. Spontaneous healing had taken place.

Of course, she did not tell them *how* it had happened.

Barbara's daughter, Connie, was born soon after the tuberculosis episode. Thankfully she was normal and full of health, despite all the problems that surrounded her birth.

Everything seemed to be going well with the family for a change. But this was only to be a lull in the proceedings. Very soon the disturbing pattern was set to renew itself. The supernatural was ready to take over their lives.

Connie was about as old as her mother had been when the experiences first began. One day while she was in the room with Barbara, and her mother was just about to sit down in a chair, Connie yelled: 'Don't sit there, Mum!'

'Why ever not?' Barbara cried, pausing in mid air.

'There's a lady there already. She's got a little baby with her.'

Barbara was confused. What on earth was the youngster talking about? There was nobody else in the room. She looked at her daughter with a puzzled expression: 'There's nobody there. The chair is empty.'

'I saw someone,' Connie insisted.

Later they did some checking on previous occupants of the house. It was then learnt that a young woman had committed suicide there and, being unable to part with her babies, she had taken their lives as well.

Was this who Connie had seen?

In *1973*, Barbara's father spoke to her in serious tones, announcing that he was about to die. He had seen it in his mind. It was inevitable. There was nothing to be concerned about.

Barbara was frightened, for he did not seem at all perturbed, but in fact, was totally calm.

A week later he was dead.

A couple of years after her father's death, Barbara had a second child – a son called Philip. His sister was now a teenager and Barbara's marriage was breaking up. It was a very trying time. Then her favourite aunt passed away also.

Days later, as Philip slept in bed with his mother, Barbara awoke with a vivid picture in her mind. It was a country scene with green trees and a narrow lane. Her aunt was there, saying, 'Dee-Dee. It wasn't as bad this time. Not like when all the children took me.'

Barbara was bemused by this. What did it mean? She forced open her eyes. There, just above the bed and floating inches over Philip's head, was a cloud of white mist.

She stared at it, unable to move for some minutes. Despite all that had taken place, nothing like this had ever happened. But at least it was somehow not so frightening any more.

She drifted back to sleep, content in the knowledge that her aunt had said goodbye.

During this period – 1977 and 1978 – everything changed. It seemed to centre on Connie, who was at first a happy-go-lucky teenager, enjoying partying and clothes. Suddenly she became a highly strung and very nervous person.

One night the girl ran screaming into Barbara's room at about three in the morning.

'My bed is floating!' she kept repeating.

Barbara tried to persuade her daughter that it had been a dream, recalling similar explanations once offered so unconvincingly by her parents. But Connie insisted and dragged her mother into the room. There was nothing amiss. The bed had not *really* moved.

Then, later on, electrical equipment started to malfunction. Connie only needed to stand near a kettle and the socket would explode. Once a table-top shattered into a thousand slivers of deadly glass while the girl was beside it.

The family became convinced that the teenager had been taken over by a poltergeist; and there were some useful side-effects of the disruption.

Their neighbours at the time were constantly upsetting the family. Connie and her mother persuaded themselves that by combining wills they could wreak a form of psychic revenge.

'We'll screw up their electrics!' they decreed, after one turbulent incident.

Soon after this, the neighbours went to use their car, but the battery was drained of all power and the vehicle would not budge. Barbara and Connie felt sure this was their doing.

By 1979 the strange phenomena in Connie's life began to subside. By now almost an adult, she eventually moved into a flat of her own with some friends.

But Philip was already beginning to take over the mantle of family psychic. It became impossible to play board games with him at one point as he seemed able to control the dice and make it throw a six almost every time!

One of the few comforts in this period was the family's lovely cat. But one night disaster struck the faithful pet. He dragged himself into the house with a gaping injury in his side. Blood oozed out and the bone could be seen deep in the wound. He looked to be in a desperate condition.

They were not on the telephone, so Connie jumped onto her bicycle and raced to her grandmother's and summoned the vet.

He took one look at the terrible wound and shook his head, giving little in the way of hope for the poor creature.

'There's not much I can do, I'm afraid. I'll give him an injection, and the tissue will either heal or it won't. If it doesn't then you must think about having him put to sleep. It would be kinder.'

Barbara and the children looked at the injury, which measured several inches across. It was hopeless. The cat was doomed. And they loved him so desperately.

That night in bed, Barbara felt a presence. It gently teased her into wakefulness. She gazed across the room – certain it could only be her father. She knew that as a healer he would have saved the cat, had he been alive to do so.

Suddenly the room was filled with swirling patterns. It was like being sucked into a multi-coloured tunnel of light. Then, as quickly as it began it was over. But Barbara was left with an absolute and overwhelming certainty that the cat was going to make it through.

Next day the wound was seen to be already closing up. When the vet visited again he pronounced the good news. 'It looks as if he's going to be all right.'

And so the magic went on. Hardly a day passed without something taking place in the lives of this haunted family. It seemed as if their strange ability to commune with things that are lost to the rest of us was handed down across the generations as if it was there within the genes.

One Christmas Eve, just before Connie moved out, Barbara collapsed into bed exhausted after completing all the necessary tasks. A normal two-parent family usually finds these jobs taxing. Having to do them all alone left Barbara shattered.

Lying in bed, mulling over whether she had successfully finished everything, Barbara realized that her five-year-old son was quite likely to be up and about at 4.30 a.m., desperate to get Christmas Day underway as fast as possible.

Suddenly a patch of light appeared in the bedroom. Barbara stared at it and blinked. It began to solidify into a clear and firm image, with nothing ghostly about its nature. This was her father, complete from the waist up. He had now been dead for six years.

He spoke softly into her mind, using the familiar pet name: Dee-Dee.

132

'Do remember that it's Christmas,' he told her. 'Don't be nasty to your mother.'

Barbara felt instant guilt. Her one surviving parent was staying over the holidays and Barbara knew she had been complaining to herself about the extra work this inevitably brought. It was not a serious gripe, but an understandable one. But it was wrong.

She smiled at her father's request, somehow conveyed to her across time and space.

Barbara drifted back to sleep. Now she knew: this was going to be a very happy holiday.

In Broad Daylight

◆

24 June 1947 was clear and sunny over Washington State on the west coast of America. This purity of the atmosphere served to enhance the natural beauty of the Cascade Mountains visible from the cockpit of the light aircraft.

Pilot Kenneth Arnold, with over four thousand hours flying experience, was not the sort of man his peers might accuse of hallucinating, or making up tall stories. He was a businessman who sold and installed The Great Western Fire Control System – an apparatus he had designed and patented himself. He was also flying deputy for the Ada County Aerial Posse, acting deputy federal United States marshal, and a member of the Idaho Search and Rescue Mercy Flyers. A responsible man with a responsible position in society. Yet something was set to happen that day which would turn his life upside down and give the world a new term – as well as much food for thought.

The day started just like any other, as Arnold was later to explain.

I had just finished installing some fire-fighting apparatus at Chehalis, Washington. The job finished, I began a chat with Herb Critzen, chief pilot for Central Air Service. We talked about the possible location of a lost Marine transport which had gone down in the mountains. I decided to look for it. It meant a $5000 reward and I hoped that via my proposed route to Yakima, Washington, I might be lucky enough to find it. I decided to spend enough time in the air in the vicinity of Mount Rainier to make a good attempt at locating the wreckage.

His own aircraft, a single-engined Callier, was specially designed for mountain work, capable of landing in rough fields and pastures. At 2 p.m., the thirty-two-year-old businessman took off to start his search for the Marine Curtess C-46 Commando transport plane which had disappeared somewhere in the mountains, and had so far eluded discovery. Arnold figured his journey to Yakima would be delayed about an hour while he searched the 14,400-foot-high plateau of Mount Rainier.

The charisma of the snow-covered mountains and deep rugged valleys below was not lessened by familiarity. As Arnold concentrated his search for the wreckage, he looked beyond tragedy and saw the real magical beauty of Nature. The sky was so clear he could see for miles – an added advantage when searching ravines and mountain slopes for the relative insignificance of chunks of burned-out twisted metal and broken human debris.

Kenneth Arnold never did find that aircraft. But he found something else instead, or *it* found him.

It was during this search and while making a turn of 180 degrees over Mineral, Washington, at approximately 9,200 feet altitude, that a tremendously bright flash lit up the surfaces of my aircraft. I was startled. I thought I was very close to collision with some other aircraft whose approach I had not noted.

He spent the next thirty seconds or so searching urgently for that other aircraft before a collision might take place. Where had the flash of light possibly come from? Then he *did* see another aircraft which he identified as a DC-4 probably on its regular flight from San Francisco to Seattle. But this was to the port side and rear of him, and surely much too far away to have caused the light phenomenon. He conjectured that possibly a P-51 had buzzed across his nose to give him a fright, the sun reflecting off its wings.

As he continued his search for this speculative other aircraft, a second flash occurred, only this time he was able to pinpoint the direction it had come from. He followed his line of sight, and his brow furrowed in puzzlement. From the north, near Mount Baker, flying close to the mountain peaks at incredible speed, was a formation of very bright objects.

Arnold judged they were about a hundred miles away and therefore too distant to make out any features. However, they were approaching him at an angle and steadily nearing the snow border of Mount Rainier.

All the time I was thinking that I was observing a whole formation of jets. In group count, such as I have used in counting cattle and game from the air, they numbered nine. They were flying diagonally in an echelon formation with a larger gap in their echelon between the first four and the last five.

But Arnold noticed something disturbing. None of the aircraft had tails! Once more his rational mind sought out an explanation. He knew the Air Force were very good at camouflage. Had they perfected it to a degree that appendages, such as tailplanes on an aircraft, could be rendered as good as invisible?

They were now about twenty miles distant. If they carried on their present course they would pass between Mount Rainier and Mount Adams. Using the mountains as

135

markers, Arnold timed their passage between them using his wrist watch, hoping to work out their speed later.

I was fascinated by this formation of aircraft. They didn't fly like any aircraft I had seen before. In the first place, their echelon formation was backwards from that practised by our Air Force. The elevation of the first craft was greater than that of the last. They flew in a definite formation, but erratically. As I described them at the time, their flight was like speedboats on rough water or similar to the tail of a Chinese kite that I once saw blowing in the wind. Or maybe it would be best to describe their flight characteristics as very similar to a formation of geese, in a rather diagonal chain-like line, as if they were linked together.

Another characteristic of these craft that made a tremendous impression on me was how they fluttered and sailed, tipping their wings alternately and emitting those very bright blue-white flashes from their surfaces. At the time I did not get the impression these flashes were emitted by them, but rather that it was the sun's reflection from the extremely polished surface of their wings.

The direction of the flight never varied, although the individual objects did swerve in and out of the mountain peaks – flying in front of some, disappearing momentarily behind others. Between the two mountains there is a very high plateau. The pilot observed that as the first unit of craft cleared the far southernmost edge of the plateau, the second part of the echelon was just entering the opposite, northern edge. That meant the formation was five miles long!

As the nine objects flew out of sight, Arnold unsuccessfully tried to explain them away in his own mind as some sort of technological wonder belonging to the Air Force.

I definitely did have an eerie feeling about the whole experience. I tried to focus my mind on a continued search for the downed C-46 which had crashed some months earlier with thirty-two Marines aboard, but somehow the $5000 didn't seem important. I wanted to get to Yakima and tell some of the boys what I had seen.

At around four o'clock, Kenneth Arnold landed at Yakima and went straight to see Al Baxter, general manager of Central Aircraft. Arnold told Baxter he had to see him alone. The men went into the general manager's private office and Arnold related his story and drew some pictures. Baxter was bemused. He knew Arnold was neither crazy nor the type to pull a stunt. Arnold was level-headed, and an experienced pilot. Besides, he had nothing to gain from making up such a story, and everything to lose ...

Yet Baxter could not disguise his feelings of incredulity. It was written all across his face, and Arnold saw it. *Was* there a rational explanation for the experience?

Al Baxter called in several of his helicopter instructors and flight pilots for their opinions. After listening carefully to the story, they discussed it amongst themselves. Arnold relates what happened next.

'The high point of my enthusiasm got its top knocked off when one of the helicopter pilots said, "Ah, it's just a flight of those guided missiles from Moses Lake."'

Arnold had to think about that one. He gathered his wits together, returned to his aircraft and took off for Pendleton, Oregon. Was that the explanation? He was not even aware of a base at Moses Lake. And besides, he had not mentioned the incredible speed of the objects, nor the fact that one of the craft looked different from the rest. This had been darker, crescent-shaped, with a small dome on top. If they *had* been missiles they were of a completely new and previously unknown design. The other eight objects had resembled pie pans – so shiny they reflected the sun as efficiently as a mirror.

News travels faster than a light aircraft. As a matter of routine, the officials at Yakima had to notify those at Pendleton of Arnold's imminent arrival. With this information, human nature being what it is, went news of the businessman's strange sighting. When he landed at Pendleton, a group of people were waiting for him. There was an atmosphere of uncertainty between the two parties. Arnold knew that they knew about his experience, and they in turn, knew he knew they knew ... No one, it seemed, wanted to mention it first. But eventually the subject was broached and the ice was broken. It seemed that everyone at Pendleton wanted to hear the story. Using the figures Arnold had recorded at the time of the incident, it was calculated that the objects had been travelling at around thirteen hundred miles per hour! The thirty-two-year-old pilot was now certain of one thing. If they were terrestrial they were remotely controlled. The human body could not survive the terrific 'G' forces generated at such speeds.

Armed with his maps and calculations, Arnold decided he should report the incident to the FBI.

'I thought it was my duty to report these things. I kind of felt I ought to tell the FBI because I knew that during the war we were flying aircraft over the pole to Russia, and I thought these things could possibly be from Russia.'

Ironically, when he arrived at the FBI office, he found it shut!

Instead he went and saw Nolan Skiff, editor of the 'End of the Week' column in the *East Oregonian*. Initially, Skiff was sceptical, but became convinced by the pilot's credentials and sincerity. Another journalist, Bill Becquette, was also present, and he realized the story would have national interest. He sent off an Associated Press despatch. It was while Arnold was trying to explain the strange movement of the aircraft that he unwittingly gave the media a phrase they grew to love, but one which later ufologists loved to hate.

'*They flew like a saucer would if you skipped it across water.*'

138

With those few words, the term 'flying saucer' was born. The despatch, which was to ensure Kenneth Arnold's place in history, had this to say:

PENDLETON, ORE, June 25 (AP) – Nine bright saucer-like objects flying at 'incredible speed' at 10,000 feet altitude were reported here today by Kenneth Arnold, Boise, Idaho, pilot who said he could not hazard a guess as to what they were.

Arnold, a United States Forest Service employee engaged in searching for a missing plane, said he sighted the mysterious objects yesterday at 3 p.m. They were flying between Mount Rainier and Mount Adams, in Washington State, he said, and appeared to weave in and out of formation. Arnold said that he clocked and estimated their speed at 1200 miles an hour.

Enquiries at Yakima last night brought only blank stares, he said, but he added he talked today with an unidentified man from Utah, south of here, who said he had seen similar objects over the mountains near Ukiah yesterday.

'It seems impossible,' Arnold said, 'but there it is.'

There it was. It said a lot for Kenneth Arnold's credibility that the story was reported seriously and matter of factly. But even Bill Becquette could not have realized the *inter*national ramifications of the incident, which captured the imaginations of the news media across the world. Arnold, like so many unprepared victims of anomalous phenomena, had unwittingly opened up his life to the media circus.

I could have gone to sleep that night if the reporters, newsmen, and press agencies of every conceivable description had left me alone. I didn't share the general excitement. I can't begin to estimate the number of people, letters, telegrams and phone calls I tried to answer. After three days of this hubbub I came to the conclusion that I was the only sane one in the bunch. In order to stop what I thought was a lot of foolishness and since I couldn't get any work done, I went out to the airport, cranked up my airplane, and flew home to Boise.

But Arnold was naive if he thought the interest would remain behind at Pendleton. And up until speaking to Dave Johnson, aviation editor of *The Idaho Statesman*, he was still convinced the objects were of advanced terrestrial origin.

When I caught the look in his eye and the tone of his words, flying saucers suddenly took a different and serious significance. The doubt he displayed of the authenticity of my story told me, and I am sure he was in a position to know, that it was not a new military guided missile, and that if what I had seen was true it did not belong to the good old USA. It was then I really began to wonder.

Dave Johnson told him that the Wright Field Base wanted a report so they could check it out. They were not the only ones. Journalists and TV crews besieged the home of Doris and Kenneth Arnold.

Around that time there were other sightings too. United Airlines pilot Captain E.J. Smith and co-pilot Ralph Stevens observed something unexplained during flight. On 26 June, the *Chicago Tribune* reported a sighting made by a Pendleton couple. On the same day as Arnold's sighting, a prospector from Portland called Johnson claimed to have witnessed five or six discs around the region of the Cascade Mountains. There were 850 sightings reported between June and July.

All of this left Arnold confused. It seemed that everyone was jumping on the bandwagon. It was true that prior to his sighting the phenomenon of 'flying saucers' was not generally known. But why were all these reports coming in *now*? Perhaps there were two simple explanations. Arnold's sighting had acted as a catalyst. No doubt some people caught up in the excitement were going out *looking* for saucers and then mistaking aircraft landing lights, bright stars and weather balloons for something more exotic. Others, however, were perhaps experiencing something truly mysterious ... All Kenneth Arnold had done was give people the confidence to speak out instead of skulking away afraid of ridicule.

Not that Arnold escaped ridicule himself. Once people started interpreting his experience as proof of an *extra*-terrestrial invasion the de-bunkers were not slow in coming forward. As he told ufologist Greg Long in 1981: 'These nameless, faceless people ridiculed me. I was considered an Orson Welles, a fraud. I loved my country. I was very naive about the whole thing. I was the unfortunate goat who first reported them.'

He sent a detailed report to the Air Force who carried out an investigation. At that time, astronomer Dr J. Allen Hynek was their UFO consultant. Many years later, after realizing the Government were hoodwinking the American people into believing that every sighting had a rational, normal, explanation, he founded CUFOS – the Centre for UFO Studies.

Dr Hynek found several discrepancies in the story. Arnold's estimate of a hundred-foot 'wing span' did not bear out for the alleged distances involved. At twenty-five miles away – never mind a hundred – something only a hundred feet wide would be invisible to the human eye. This meant the distances must have been much less, which also reduced the calculated speed of the formation to subsonic figures. Therefore the objects *could* have been terrestrial aircraft. There was only one problem with that. Everyone denied there was any aircraft in the area at that time.

However, if it was the estimate of *size* which was wrong, and the distance was about right, but the objects were much larger than Arnold had thought, then the speed of around 1300 miles per hour was about right.

The case was never solved, although there have been plenty of theories, including that of mirages. More recently it has been suggested that Arnold observed 'earth lights' – luminous balls of electro-magnetic energy allegedly released into the atmosphere along fault lines in the Earth's crust at times of underground stress.

As far as Kenneth Arnold was concerned, the formation of nine objects he saw moving across the crystal-clear Washington skies 'like a saucer would if you skipped it across water', was only the first of several similar experiences.

Although not generally known, Arnold had many more sightings. His eighth, in 1952, was of two objects – one of which was transparent.

'They looked like something alive,' he said. 'I've had the feeling with these things that they are aware of me, but they made no effort to come close.'

Then in 1966 he took some 16-mm cine-film of a glowing 'cylinder' over Idaho Falls, Ohio. Although the object looked similar to an atmospheric balloon, it was travelling at speed into a northerly wind.

Whatever he experienced on 24 June 1947, Arnold retained his passion for the subject right up until his death in 1984. Such longevity would seem to have stemmed from something much more tangible than just imagination.

An FBI agent who saw Kenneth Arnold at the time of the original incident, thought so, too.

It is the personal opinion of the interviewer that [Arnold] actually saw what he states he saw in the attached report. It is also the opinion of the interviewer that [Arnold] would have much more to lose than gain and would have to be very strongly convinced that he actually saw something before he would report such an incident and open himself up for ridicule that would accompany such a report.

JULY

1st The charred remains of Mary Reeser were discovered in her apartment in St Petersburg, Florida, on this date in 1951. No explanation was forthcoming for her grisly death, and some experts believe she was a victim of spontaneous human combustion.

4th In 1966, a police officer taking part in the hunt for the 'Surrey puma' saw a huge cat in Worplesdon and photographed the creature.

5th In 1977, an impressive colour picture was taken of 'Champ' – a creature who allegedly inhabits Lake Champion, USA – by Anthony and Sandra Mansi.

7th In 1553, Sawston Hall, Cambridgeshire was torched, and Mary Queen of Scots driven out. Since her death, Mary's ghostly presence is said to haunt the building.

18th In 1963, 126 policemen, 21 dogs, 30 soldiers, ambulancemen and RSPCA officials searched south-east London in vain for a mystery 'cheetah'.

25th 1977. Ten-year-old Marlon Lowe of Illinois was playing hide and seek when a giant black bird with white rings around its neck, picked him up in its claws and tried to carry him away. Hearing his screams, his mother ran out and scared the bird into dropping him.

26th Swiss psychologist Carl Jung was born on this day in

Kesswil in 1875. He sought answers to occult and UFO questions through applied psychology, and formulated the theory of 'synchronicity' – a study of 'meaningful coincidences'.

29th During a solar eclipse on this date in 1878, astronomers observed a planet-like object close to the sun, and concluded this was a hitherto undiscovered world. Later observers could find no new planet and refuted the earlier observations.

Just a Phone Call Away

———— ◆ ————

It was a wicked summer's night. Dark, ominous clouds hung heavy over the docks. The endless cobbled streets of Birkenhead were already slick beneath the incessant rain. And the rumble of thunder merged with the chugging of the steam engines, shunting cargo and ferrying commuters home across the Wirral.

Lucia Saddler was always sensitive to storms. It was something she had grown up with. Whenever they were coming, she *knew* it. Whenever they were around, she *felt* it. There was a kind of prickling and tickling that affected her skin and seemed to fill it with painful static electricity.

It was probably just the way she had been made – somehow she was a human lightning conductor.

Ignoring another peal of thunder and not watching the window for the coursing streaks of light, Lucia decided to concentrate on her ironing.

This was still a new life for her. The war had been over four years now, but as a German citizen living in England there were those who could not forgive and forget very easily. This she quite understood. So many had suffered, that much time would have to pass before all the scars were healed.

At least she had been lucky. Her English soldier husband had rescued her from the nightmare, sweeping her into his arms and back here to his home town. After being demobbed he had found a good job at an office in the centre and they were building a future for themselves.

There were regrets, of course. But most of those were back in a fractured and shattered Germany. A land she would never see again, could never bring herself to face with pride – ever.

The phone rang. Pulling herself from her memories, Lucia picked up the receiver.

Her right hand continued with the ironing, maintaining the smooth rhythm that she had built up over the last hour or so. Outside the crashing storm was further away, at least it seemed so in her mind.

Without looking at the receiver she spoke softly in her barely Anglicized accent: 'Hello.'

The voice that came in reply was faint and distant. But it was unmistakably that of her husband.

'I love you,' he said, almost in a whisper.

This was a welcome, but vaguely strange, greeting.

'Speak up,' Lucia requested.

'I love you,' he repeated, still very faint.

She was confused. The telephone was not something she was unfamiliar with. In Germany the system had been excellent. Her father used one frequently. Perhaps it was the storm that was causing this loss of signal.

'Where are you?' she asked. He ought to be on his way home by now, she thought. The idea dismissed itself.

'I am so very far away,' came the answer as if being carried off on a gentle breeze, not the buffeting winds coming in from the sea.

This disturbed her. 'Hello? Hello?' she called again.

What was he talking about? The answer was ridiculous. He was only a couple of miles away. How could he be *very far away*?

There was silence in her ears. Her husband was not answering this time.

Lucia suspected now that this was some kind of prank; perhaps someone who thought it amusing to play a joke on a foreigner – especially an exile from Germany. But it seemed a bit too subtle for that.

She switched her attention away from the ironing now, laying the hot implement on its end with her right hand and turning her head ever so slightly to face the phone in her left hand.

Only there *was* no phone in her left hand.

Lucia's fingers clutched at empty space. Now she remembered. *They did not have a telephone!*

The puzzled housewife sat down and pondered this unnerving experience, as outside the storm began to disappear into the distance.

It was utterly weird. But it was one of those things to add to her life story that was already more dramatic than a movie script.

She took her thoughts back over four years, to a very different kind of storm in a very different world. A time when her life was unrecognizable from what it was now.

Her father had been a businessman and the family were fairly well-to-do. But by the winter of early 1945 nobody in Germany was rich. The country was being crushed between the grip of the invading Russians and the advancing Allies, led by American and British troops who were determined to end six years of suffering.

But the Nazis clung stubbornly to the final twitches of their existence, knowing that the game was lost, but yet unable to concede defeat. Meanwhile, as the generals sat in their concrete bunkers beneath Berlin, the ordinary citizens lived through ceaseless bombardment from tanks, guns and waves of enemy aircraft.

That particular February night her father was due on Home Guard duty. He was too old to fight, but protecting the city was important work. They all knew that the punishment for desertion would be as severe as in the front line.

Yet he astounded Lucia and her mother by announcing: 'Tonight I am not going. There are more important things to do.'

They looked at him in confusion as he gathered up all the household valuables and put them in the cellar. 'Tonight we go to the shelters,' he announced proudly.

His wife pleaded with him: 'This is madness. The British will not come here tonight. They will never come. Dresden is a city of art and museums. We are not makers of war. They would not punish us.'

He looked at them both sympathetically, but made clear that it was not a suggestion. He was giving an order. So they went to the shelter and readied themselves for a long night of refuge.

As darkness fell, wave after wave of bombers flew over the city, discharging thousands of tons of explosive in a never-ending rain of death. It was the biggest single attack of destructive bombing ever launched against any city anywhere. Within hours, Dresden was flattened.

Driven from their shelters by the heat, the citizens of Dresden had wandered round the Armageddon landscape in an uncomprehending stupor. A firestorm was sucking up the oxygen and funnelling walls of flame into the sky. Those who had survived the incomparable destruction now faced death from suffocation and lung devastation from burning gases.

In panic, Lucia fled with her parents on to the only raft of life that remained, along with thousands of other fortunate citizens. They commandeered rowing boats or simply waded the few hundred yards to the island in the centre of the lake that had once sat very proudly within the city zoo.

Here the flames could not reach them directly; although the acrid smoke descended all about them like curling tongues of death. The air was thin and choking as the fire consumed everything.

But there was now a new and awesome terror. The bombing had released the animals from the zoo. Those that had survived were already half crazed with fear and hunger – and a hundred tasty meals were ready and waiting just a short swim away.

Trapped between the inferno of the city and the preying animals that stalked the night with poisonous and carnivorous teeth was more than some could face. They jumped into the lake and were never seen again.

Fortunately, the lions and tigers were too scared and dazed to be a real threat, but the snakes and crocodiles made the watery trek and were constantly a danger.

It was several days before the heat and flames subsided and those lucky few who had made it through an experience few human spirits could survive, were able to return to the city.

Scenes of horror awaited them. Every member of the Home Guard who had shown up for duty on that fateful night had died beneath the onslaught. Only instinct had kept Lucia's father away.

As they wandered around the smoking rubble, with bricks too hot to touch even days after the bombs fell, Lucia and her family could not find their house. They could not even find the *district* in which they had lived. Everything was gone. Just an endless sea of human debris lay before them.

Having lost everything, the shock left Lucia and her parents standing in bewilderment along with many others. But she was well into her twenties and she saw her responsibility. Lucia insisted that she would walk to Munich and seek help and restitution. For all that these beleaguered citizens knew, the world really had come to an end on that terrible night. They had to do something, go somewhere.

Lucia waved goodbye to her parents, knowing it might be a very long time before she saw them again. But her father, smiling, was too old to make the trip so he and his wife decided to stay behind. Someone must try to rebuild the city that had disappeared overnight.

Lucia made her way painfully towards the southerly roads, setting her feet between the bodies and the desolation, knowing only one thing: she must find some hope for the future.

At home in Birkenhead, these memories from such a short time ago seemed as if they came from another lifetime. Lucia's husband-to-be had rescued her from the practical reality when he found her in Munich months later, but the image in Lucia's mind would never go away. Not so long as she lived.

How had her father known what was going to happen? What strange sort of sense had driven him to insist on rebellion and in the process certainly save the life of his daughter and his wife? And was it in any way connected with the odd hallucination that Lucia had just now experienced as she busied herself with the ironing?

That phone call from her husband – on a phone that wasn't there. What did it mean?

She looked at the door and then at the clock. He ought to be home by now. Was this phenomenon meant to be a warning, trying to tell her he would be late? Had he suddenly been called away somewhere and been unable to tell her by any conventional method, finding this psychic bridge instead.

Or was this all stuff and nonsense, just as it seemed? Maybe she had been overdoing things and it was just a silly dream.

It had seemed like a dream then, Lucia remembered, as she set off to march towards Munich. The German countryside was in despair and, although the war had but a few weeks left to run, danger still lurked around every corner.

It took seventeen days to struggle the two hundred miles from Dresden in the far east of the country towards the less affected streets of Munich in the south. But before reaching the city of hope she encountered hordes of Russian troops sweeping in arcs across her path. As a bedraggled young woman picking her way down the cratered roads she often had no way of knowing which side of the invisible dividing line she occupied. Was she still in what remained of free Germany or in already captured territory?

One morning the awful truth hit home with a vengeance. As she struggled along in the company of some other local women, a rustle in the trees ahead announced the arrival of foot soldiers. The women glanced around quickly, searching for a place to hide. There was no escape.

The platoon marched towards them. They wore the red stars that marked them as Russian; mostly very young, battle-scarred and overtired and hungry. After what the Nazis had done to their Soviet homeland during the initial invasion, these men had little respect for any German.

The women were rounded up and bundled roughly into a captured cottage. One by one the soldiers came at them, raping and beating whoever they chose. Drinking stolen wine they embarked upon a constant drunken binge which only fuelled their violent depravities.

Lucia took the only chance that came her way. After many hours during which the confusion increased, she ducked to the floor and rolled swiftly underneath the bed. The men around her were so wrapped up in their drinking and the other women crushed beneath their arms that her move went unnoticed.

For twenty-four hours she remained there, cramp biting at her legs and body. She dare not move or hardly breathe, lest the slightest noise be detected. All around her the terrible scene continued, with constant screaming and brutality. Lucia was only inches away from becoming the next Russian victim. Any second she could be spotted and would be thrashed into submission; possibly left to die when they had had their fill.

Suddenly there was a thud and one of the Russians fell

like a toppled tree onto the floor. He rolled around and groaned, his eyes briefly staring straight into her face. Less than a yard from her his rancid breath assailed her nostrils. This was it. Finally the end. There was no way forward now.

But then the soldier's eyelids fluttered again. He groaned one last time and collapsed into unconsciousness; deeply asleep.

A long time later, with the room quiet except for snoring and heavy breathing, Lucia knew this was her only hope. She plunged from underneath the bed and out into the night. If just one soldier awakened she was doomed. But they were all so satiated that they were sleeping the sleep of the dead.

Lucia made it to freedom, and shortly afterwards arrived in Munich. But home was in Dresden and after the war Dresden was in Soviet hands. It was now part of the new satellite of Communist Germany – sacrificed by the democratic Allies to appease the ravenous USSR. A hunk of the German nation hacked off and given away by Churchill and his peace-making friends.

Lucia's parents were 200 miles away under the rule of the Red Army. To the victor the spoils and those spoils had included her family.

Lucia knew that she could never face a Russian man again. Not after what she had lived through. Her father had saved them from the British, but he could not stop the British giving Dresden away.

Just as surely as if they had died, her parents were lost.

About an hour after the phantom phone call, with the ironing still not done, Lucia was shaken from her reverie by a knock at the door.

Her husband did not need to knock. He had a key.

She gathered her thoughts and opened the door without caution, especially when she was confronted by a policeman.

The officer led her inside, sat her down and suggested a cup of tea.

'I'm afraid I have some very bad news . . .'

Lucia sat there, barely taking in what had happened. On his way from the office a couple of hours earlier, her husband had surprised a car thief. Bravely he had squared up to the man, who panicked and pulled out a hand gun. He shot Lucia's husband at very close range before fleeing.

Passers-by had called an ambulance, but her husband had died before reaching hospital.

'When was this? When did he die?' she asked, with sudden understanding.

'About an hour ago, I believe,' the policeman told her.

The *same* time that her husband had contacted Lucia – just a phone call away.

When the Lights Go Out

———————◆———————

Something woke her up. She did not know what it was, but Diane Jordan could *feel* it inside.

She sat up, propping her arms against the pillow. There was no sound. Outside, the New Jersey night was proceeding as normal, even though this was Independence Day, when many celebrations would doubtless soon begin.

She turned to her husband, William, and nudged him. But he did not stir. He seemed lost in his sleep. She tried again. It was no use.

The time was 3 a.m., Diane noted. She had been in bed only about an hour, after a heavy night out – although not one spent drinking alcohol.

From the bedroom of their nineteenth-century cottage there was a fine view out across the marsh and meadows that littered the coast around Port Monmouth. In the distance was a highway and a railroad track. Further away was an airfield, a US Air Force Station and a massive naval ammunition dump.

Things were always going on around here. It was probably just something connected with one of these establishments that had disturbed her. A noise, now ceased, that had woken her up.

Yet out by the irrigation ditches, a few hundred yards in front of their home, there was definitely an odd sort of light. It glowed a strange white colour, and seemed to be bouncing about all over the wild mass of rough grass that thrived in the watery conditions.

But stranger still was that Diane's eyes were focused on the light, which was not drowned out by the streetlamp outside the house. In fact, the streetlamp was switched off, which was most peculiar. She had not known that to happen before.

Diane watched the bouncing 'ball' for some quarter of an hour. Its size seemed to be bigger than a garage and it had a ring of lights around its circumference that were flashing red. They reminded her of the back of a car.

Something or nothing? How did you tell? But then, suddenly, the streetlamp was back on again. The 'ball' was swallowed up. And Diane drifted off into a deep sleep.

Being only in her early thirties and yet the mother of a large family of eight children, including twins, life could get to be a tiring business. She had little time for this sort of UFO stuff. It was all silly nonsense, anyway, she had assumed.

True enough there had been a few puzzling events during Diane's life. Those dreams which seemed to predict the future, like that time they won all that money. Or the sadder, more personal, images that were connected with the death of her lovely little baby.

And then there were those stories about the haunting in Grandma's house, which did seem to have something in them. Odd happenings had gone on around there when she was young.

But not this. She had certainly never expected to meet up with a goddamned flying saucer.

Around five o'clock she woke again. It was light now, and the fog was rolling in from the bay as it did every so often. Even if the light were still out there she wouldn't be able to see it now.

At breakfast she told her husband and the children what she had seen. The kids were furious. Why hadn't she woken them up so 'they could go across the meadow and chase the thing? Some of them scuttled out to see the place where their very own 'spaceship' had been engaged in a cosmic dance.

William was less convinced. He just assumed there would be some sort of explanation. At least he did – until her eldest son, Billy, aged fifteen, came scurrying back indoors yelling that the UFO had landed out by the ditches.

You could tell, because it had left great big marks!

'They're in a triangle,' Billy announced. 'I don't know, maybe 20 to 25 feet across and 30 to 40 feet apart. All the grass is just squeezed down flat like something has sat on it.'

Further explorations were inevitable as the day progressed. They found tracks leading to or from one of the straight ditches that cut through the meadow. It looked as if something had been dragged along there. They started or ended near the flattened area where the thing had come down.

'Never seen anything like them before,' they all agreed.

After these experiences all sorts of weird things started to happen around the house. It was as if a curse had been placed on the electrical equipment.

The TV broke down, so they had a repairman in and he fixed a new tube. It just flickered, but never worked again. The car too was giving them endless trouble. It kept breaking down on the road outside the house. They had a new ignition fitted, but it did no good. Later, when it was working again, they were told that there must have been something amiss with the spark plug.

Then the phone started giving trouble. Although their number was unlisted, call after call kept flooding in all through the day. When someone picked it up, there would be nobody at the other end of the line. It was suggested that it might be a crank caller, but it went on for a long time.

Connecting the escalating incidents together, Diane took it upon herself to call the intelligence officer at the army base. He listened to her story, asked quite a lot of questions but basically told her it was probably nothing and the best thing they could all do was go away and forget about it.

A couple of days later several military helicopters appeared, flying low over the meadows. This in itself was not especially unusual, but it did seem that on this occasion the choppers were *studying* the area where the UFOs had been reported.

It was a very odd coincidence that such unexpected interest followed on so rapidly from Mrs Jordan's report.

The official advice to forget about the incidents was easier said than done, because one night Diane went into the bedroom and was overcome by a terrible odour – a foul noxious smell. It was suddenly all around her and it was not coming from the meadows. There had never been anything like it before. She shut all the windows and went back to bed, but the smell remained.

Like a powerful narcotic it drugged her into sleep. She fell into a state of almost coma-like proportions. And while in that 'coma' she had a dream.

The dream was horrible. She 'saw' a strange light descend into the meadows. Water was surrounding them. Everything was in great confusion and panic. She took the children up to the bedrooms and locked shut all the doors and windows. The nightmare increased its intensity and Diane found herself rushing around and crazy images beginning to take over. She thought that she saw vague, shadowy figures by the bathroom window. They were not human ... and they were trying to get in!

In the morning Diane woke with nasty shooting pains around one knee. It was just like a needle being stuck into the joint. She went to see her doctor, but did not tell him about the dream or the UFO. Eventually the pain went away of its own accord. The medic had found no obvious cause.

Berthold Schwarz, a kindly psychiatrist who lived locally at the time and worked at the Brain Wave laboratory in Cedar Grove, became fascinated by the case. He had studied previous similar UFO encounters and was well aware that the witnesses were generally sincere.

He arranged for samples to be taken from the meadows and studied. But no unusual radiation effects were found there.

It was a week after the 4 July encounter. Because the weather often got quite muggy out here in midsummer, Billy was sleeping on the front porch, which afforded a fine view across the meadows.

Around 4 a.m. Diane suddenly woke up. This time she was overwhelmed by a feeling that something was about to happen. It scared her, particularly as it was an extremely real sensation.

Tonight Diane was taking no chances. She pounded on her husband's chest until the pain forced William awake.

Diane told him: 'Something is going to happen. I sense it.'

He looked at her quizzically. Then the streetlamp went out.

From the bed, they gazed out of the window and a few minutes later saw a ball of yellowish/white light appear. It came from the far distance, descending towards the meadows.

Diane went to the phone and called the police.

Out on the porch Billy was wide awake. He saw the grey oval shape that poured out light. It was heading towards them emitting a noise like a faint engine in the distance. It seemed to be rotating, because three blobs of red light on the side kept circling the disc, taking a couple of seconds to make one revolution.

By now the police had arrived and were obviously taking no chances. They had their guns drawn ready for action. Barking orders, despite the hour, they rattled up the stairs towards the main bedroom, from where Diane and William had seen the thing come down. It was hoped they might get a better view from this elevation.

Suddenly, Billy saw the UFO rising out of the grass only 60 feet in front of him. Here the grass was twice the height of a man. More than enough to hide this object.

'Look! Look!' he yelled, after overcoming the shock.

But the police were inside and there was a great deal of toing and froing. Nobody appeared to hear him.

'Mom, look!' he tried again. But it was no use.

The grey oval was at first climbing vertically and very slowly. Now it seemed to be gathering speed. As it did so the humming engine-noise increased.

Very quickly it raced away into the distance, disappearing towards the coming dawn. The encounters were finally over ... For now.

AUGUST

2nd In 1973, Swedish Fisheries Officer Ragnar Bjorks fought off a 12-foot 'fish' on Lake Storsjo. At one point it threw his boat some 9 to 12 feet in the air!

4th In 1951, two English women on holiday in Dieppe, France, heard gunfire, divebombing and screams. Were they experiencing the sounds of battle from nine years before? Also, during Sunday service in 1577, a large black dog suddenly appeared in Bungay Church, Suffolk. As it passed two people knelt in prayer, it deftly broke their necks and then injured a third person. Afterwards it appeared at nearby Blythburgh Church and caused more deaths, leaving burn marks on the church door.

6th Charles Fort was born in 1874 in Albany, New York. He became an avid collector of accounts of anomalous phenomena, from falls of fish to reports of blood-draining sheep killers. Such phenomena are now termed 'Fortean', and the magazine *Fortean Times* carries on in Fort's tradition.

10th In 1901, Charlotte Moberley and Eleanor Jourdain were on holiday in France where they visited the Petit Trianon, Versailles. Apparently, they then slipped back in time to the eighteenth century, and observed people of this period including Marie Antoinette.

13th In 1956, a UFO was sighted both visually and on radar by RAF and USAF personnel at a NATO base in

Lakenheath, Suffolk. The incident was investigated by a US government commission and considered very significant. A British Ministry of Defence under-secretary, now retired, has recently stated that this encounter seriously disturbed the government. RAF jets were sent in pursuit.

19th In 1978 a teenage girl, Genette Tate, disappeared from Aylesbeare in Devon having just been seen by two friends before she rounded a corner on her bicycle and vanished. The police utilized psychics extensively in an effort to find the missing girl, but no clues to her whereabouts ever emerged.

25th In and around Fobbing in Essex a major spate of sightings of a mysterious big cat were reported and followed up by researcher Michael Goss. As is often the case, no trace of the animal was ever found and the creature behaves more like a ghost than a real feline.

31st A house in Enfield, Middlesex, was invaded by a poltergeist from this day in 1977 onward. It became subjected to one of the most intense investigations ever mounted by researchers Maurice Grosse and Guy Lyon Playfair. Their book – *This House is Haunted* – recorded some of the main events, which included a tape recording reputed to be the spook using a terrible guttural voice and describing its own grave.

Terror in the House of Dolls

———————— ◆ ————————

It was a warm summer's evening on 12 August 1979. Not sticky, but comfortable, torpid. The sort of night when a disturbance; a noise in the house, the banging of the garden gate, might cause you to start drifting out of sleep.

But halfway you realize how good it feels in this protective womb, and sink back again into sweet restful bliss. Only in the morning does concern arise about those anonymous sounds in the night.

That is how it was, that night, in their Gateshead semi, for Carol and Steve Fellon. They were a married couple in their early twenties, with a three-year-old daughter called Nicola. The little girl had a room of her own. Her special friend was their Yorkshire Terrier, 'Wolfie'.

Carol lay with the quilt tossed back from her bare shoulders and one arm wrapped around Steve. Deep in the abyss of sleep, something reached down and lightly prodded her. She stirred slightly, but her own internal clock told her to stay put – it was not time to get up. But the prodding became more insistent, and a part of her wondered if Nicola was crying.

She dragged herself out of sleep and prepared to climb out of bed in her usual sleep-walking fashion. But there was no need. It was nothing to do with the little girl. Something entirely different had disturbed her. Was she going crazy? She picked up the clock on the bedside table. Its fluorescent face smiled back sarcastically. Half past one. *What on earth was someone doing mowing their lawn in the middle of the night?*

At least that was what it sounded like. Steve was awake now, and rubbing his eyes. They both sat up in bed, listening intently. Steve commented afterwards: 'It was like a lawn mower going at full blast, with a bleeping sound mixed in.'

Suddenly the noise stopped – just like that.

The following day, Carol learned from some of her neighbours that they too had heard the 'lawn mower' and several had seen something odd in the sky.

A few nights later, Carol and Nicola were alone in the house. Steve was now working night shift. Carol went to bed as normal, but could not sleep. One of her teeth, which had been mildly irritating her earlier in the day, was now hurting badly. She tossed and turned until 2 a.m., then slipped on her wrap and went downstairs to make a hot drink. The house was quiet, sleeping, Carol decided, as she could not.

The kettle seemed to take for ever to boil. At last the coffee was made, and she carried the steaming mug upstairs. After propping up the pillows, she settled down with the drink, hoping it would take away some of the pain. The curtains were closed, the bedside lamp lit, yet she could see a bright red light shining through the curtain material and into the room. She climbed out of bed and put the mug down, drawing the curtains aside. What on earth was *that*?

The window looked out onto a field about a hundred yards wide. It separated the row of houses where she lived from others on the far side. Unusually for August, the atmosphere appeared damp and misty. Above the roofs of the houses opposite, hovered a mysterious object. It consisted mainly of a group of orange, red and white lights, set beneath a dome of some sort. Suddenly, all but the red light went off. Now she could see the thing more clearly. The remaining light was attached to the object's underside, which seemed to be about the same size as one of the houses. After a few minutes, Carol was shocked as the 'thing' spiralled upwards and silently disappeared from view.

The young woman climbed back into bed. After draining the mug of coffee she settled down again and tried to sleep. But it was no use. Apart from the toothache, she kept thinking about what she had observed. Had it any connection with that awful noise both of them heard several nights before? A low rumbling sound came from just outside the bedroom window. Her head snapped round. *There, hovering at the top of the curtains, was a perfect miniature of the object she had just witnessed outside.*

It was a flattened bell-shaped craft, about eighteen inches in diameter, lit from within by a pale grey light. But there was more. Behind the disc hung a cloud of tiny glittering objects, like a swarm of insects.

Carol was terrified. Was she hallucinating, going mad? The affair was so *insane*. Now the disc was moving with the swarm on its tail. It stopped close to the lamp shade. *What was going to happen next?* She soon found out.

The swarm left the object and descended on her. She had no time to scream or bury her head beneath the quilt. There was no escape. It covered her face like a caul, flooded her open mouth, and exerted a terrible pressure that seemed to drag her down ... down ... There was a tingling sensation dulling her senses, subduing her terror, while in the background was a loud buzzing noise.

After a while the swarm lifted and returned to the curious object still hovering by the lamp shade. Carol felt like someone coming out of anaesthetic, only her recovery was much quicker. As she returned to normality, the disc, with its attendant swarm, moved off across the room towards the open door. There it paused, passed through, returned for a final 'look', then left altogether.

Carol's sigh of relief was short lived as she realized that the 'thing', having finished with her, might now be on its way to deal similarly with her tiny daughter ...

'My God! My God!' she muttered as she threw the quilt back and stumbled out into the dark passageway and into Nicola's room. The light clicked on, and thankfully the phenomenon was nowhere to be seen. But Carol was taking no chances. She picked up the sleeping child and carried her to her own room. As Carol lay, clutching the little one tightly, she barely controlled the inner hysteria striving to escape. When Steve had taken the job which included night shift, they had both discussed their fears concerning break-ins. But this was something worse, something so *awful*. And it was not over – entirely. Outside, the mower sound droned away. At around five thirty, the exhausted woman began to nod off when the tingling sensation took hold again. She gave a start and it was gone.

Steve came home from work around seven. He called out but there was no reply. Strange, little Nicola normally

162

made sure her mummy was up by the time he arrived home. He went upstairs and found his wife still in bed. Carol was crying and obviously in a state of shock. She pulled him to her and sobbed out her unbelievable story.

Steve did not know what to make of it. Certainly he had heard that noise himself a few days before, but *this*? He did not *dis*believe his wife, but . . .

After the incident, Carol felt hot and flushed. During the next few days, there was a pain in her left cheek and jaw, although this was probably connected with the toothache. But there was also a rash on her neck. Over the next thirteen days nothing untoward happened, except a frightened and apprehensive Nicola invaded her parents' room a number of times – something she had not done before.

On 30 August, Carol was woken up by the sound of Nicola crying. She climbed out of bed quickly before Steve was disturbed. Having settled the child, she turned to leave when she was suddenly overcome with the terrible tingling sensation. Her gaze dropped, and there on the floor, beside Nicola's bed, was the bell-shaped object. Curiously, it was on its side and much more brightly lit than before.

Abruptly it disappeared. It was as if the spell was lifted. She was free to move, free to . . . Before she could call out, the tingling returned and so did the object, this time near the ceiling and the right way up. Slowly, as she watched in her paralysed state, the disc moved towards the window and *passed right through the glass*. Now she *did* scream. Steve rushed in and was in time to see a flash of light outside.

In the morning, the family seated themselves as usual for breakfast. Neither of the adults were saying much, their thoughts being filled with the events of a few hours earlier. Carol in particular was depressed. She noticed Nicola squirming in her seat.

'Do you want to go to the toilet, love?'

Nicola nodded her head.

'Up you go then, to the bathroom.'

163

'Don't want to,' she said defiantly. Carol was about to reply sharply when Steve cut in.

'Why not, Nicola?'

'Won't go upstairs.'

'But *why*?'

'Hulk. *He's* up there. He pushed me down!'

Steve knew that Nicola was an avid viewer of *The Incredible Hulk*, and referred to anything out of the ordinary, or frightening, as the 'Hulk'.

Carol had had enough. If she was going mad, maybe she could live with it, but not when it was infecting her child. She decided to seek professional advice. Bravely, she went to her doctor and told him the whole story. Dr Bevis promptly told her she was hallucinating, and prescribed tranquillizers.

But if it was an hallucination, then Steve was affected by it too. Two days later, he lay awake for much of the night listening to the mower noise. It sounded like something was circling the house.

Steve was soon on night shift again. Carol made up her mind not to sleep in the house alone – at least not for the time being. Instead she made arrangements for herself and the child to stay at her mother's house, a short distance away. Apart from her mother, Mary, there was also her father, Richard, and brother, Walter. That night, Carol settled down with Nicola in the spare bedroom.

At around midnight, Walter was awakened by a 'mowing' sound which seemed to be in the room. Before he could put on the light, a tingling sensation overtook him, and he drifted back into unconsciousness. It was 4 a.m. before he awoke again. Something drew him out of bed towards the open bedroom door. Outside in the passage was a curious light, heading towards his sister's room . . .

Walter could not explain why, but instead of alerting his sister to the phenomenon, he walked back into his own room and quietly went back to bed. Yet at that precise moment, Carol was awake and fighting the crippling tingling sensation. But it was much too strong for her; an almost complete paralysis took over. Her legs, trunk and arms were beyond her control. She was unable to call for help. With difficulty Carol turned her head.

The miniature disc was in the room, hovering about five feet off the floor, in a corner. There was no interior light this time, but she could plainly see, even in the darkness, its dull grey body. And there was something different about it. Projecting from its upper surface was a narrow tube-like appendage.

The paralysis wore off and was replaced by a feeling of incredible relaxation, as if she was floating. In this new state she looked away for a moment, and in this short time the object had gone. Something even more bizarre was in its place. *The room was filled with a group of small beings!*

Some were standing, others kneeling, and a few hung back near the door. As one, they drew closer to the bed, about twelve entities in all. Carol's glasses were on the floor so she was not able to make out as much detail as she did on a later occasion.

The figures were about thirty inches tall with proportionally larger heads than bodies. They had broad foreheads, large pale eyes and full lips. It was not possible to decide what gender they were, but their faces were feminine and strangely beautiful. Their skin was pale and the hair close-cropped – unreal, like doll's hair.

They wore white clothing, and one had a white cloak. This individual stood right beside the bed and touched Carol's eyes, although she could not *feel* the touch. It seemed particularly interested in her eyes, and the spectacles, which it seemed to be examining, although she could not be sure, as the entity had bent down out of sight. Then it spoke. She heard the words although its lips never moved.

'She's just like any other earthling!' it said, and the others made a series of unintelligible clicking sounds.

The 'earthling' turned her head away, and the floating sensation left her. Her heart thudded as she slowly, very slowly, looked across the room. It was empty, normal, but outside the mower noise had started up. She glanced at Nicola. The child seemed to have slept through it all. Through the window, the street lights were flickering.

All that day, Carol was withdrawn. Walter knew something had occurred, and managed to persuade her to speak. Then he told her what had happened to him ... Now Carol was sure Dr Bevis was wrong – it could not be an hallucination!

Steve was still on night shift, so Carol and Nicola stayed again in her mother's house. Mrs Conway knew something very strange was happening to her daughter and other members of the family. She suggested that Carol and Nicola sleep with her while Mr Conway and Walter shared a room.

Richard Conway did not mind the temporary arrangements. The things his children had talked about were crazy, but hadn't his son-in-law also heard this 'lawn mower' noise? Whatever was going on, Mary seemed worried by it.

At 2 a.m. Mr Conway woke up. Was it the strange bed? No, there was a tingling sensation all over his body. He momentarily panicked. Wasn't pins and needles in the arms a prelude to a heart attack? But then it quickly subsided. Just after four o'clock it returned, but he succeeded again in fighting it off and drifted back into sleep. Just half an hour later, it was Walter's turn. The sensation was very strong. As he strained and tensed every muscle in his struggle against it, his ears were assaulted by the deafening noise of the manic lawn mower. Just as his strength was giving out the fight was over, and he shouted out in terror and relief. The noise woke the entire household. His mother ran into the room. Richard was just stirring, while her son was sweating profusely and shaking uncontrollably. He was murmuring over and over: 'I'm burning up ... please ... I'm burning up ...'

By morning a rash had developed on his neck.

The family felt isolated. Isolated from the community and from an understanding of the reality they had all been

166

taught to believe in. Embroiled in a madness they could neither understand nor attempt to explain to outsiders.

The sleeping arrangements were the same for the following night. Everyone went to bed with a degree of apprehension. Around eleven, Carol woke her mother.

'Can you hear it, Mum?'

The older woman stirred.

'Yes ... yes ... I can ... that noise ...'

Although Mary Conway could hear the noise, it sounded far away. This bemused Carol. To her, it was very loud, very near. An hour later, Carol began to shake. Mrs Conway hugged her daughter to her.

'It's trying to get me!' Carol said between clenched teeth. Through her determination she fought it off. It struck twice more in the next hour, and on both occasions she again triumphed over it.

Over the next three weeks there were no more incidents concerning Carol, although her brother twice experienced the tingling sensation. The second of these occurred in the first half hour of 30 September.

Later that morning, at 7 a.m., Steve left the house for work. Now he was on day shift, Carol and Nicola were back home. Carol was still in bed, and her daughter was asleep in her own room. It was Sunday. Ten minutes after Steve's departure, Carol felt the tingling sensation briefly, then it passed away. But the mowing noise had started up outside. She put on her glasses and climbed out of bed and looked through the window. Seeing nothing, she turned away, and stopped in her tracks ...

There, beside the door, stood one of the tiny doll-like entities.

It was the being with the cloak, the one who had come right up to her and examined her eyes like a senior doctor in front of a group of students.

'She's just like any other earthling,' it had said – at least that was how her mind had interpreted the communication. Now it had returned, alone, and stood with its back pressed up against the door, cutting off her escape. Wolfie lay on the bed, totally unconcerned, or unknowing of the intruder.

The creature lifted up one arm and seemed to be offering her something. It held a white object in the palm of its hand. Carol went cold, her stomach tangled up in knots as she realized this time – *this time* – she was not under 'their' control. There was nothing to subdue her natural emotional reactions to this living nightmare.

This time Carol was able to scream.

All the fear, frustration and tension which had built up during the last six weeks was released in that scream. It was not just a cry of pure horror for the indignities she and her family had endured, but a cry for the futility of trying to understand such an alien phenomenon. A phenomenon which Society did not acknowledge, something which could make them outcasts with their friends and neighbours. No victim of robbery ever had those fears. To be *controlled* and *used* in this cold callous way ...

The being, perhaps not surprisingly, vanished.

Over the next few weeks, various members of the family, in both houses, experienced the immobilizing sensation, and heard, quite distinctly, the noise like a lawn mower going at full power.

There was a distressing episode where Nicola woke during the night screaming and thrashing wildly. Was this the result of a nightmare, or was it directly connected with the other events? The dog, too, was finally drawn into the arena, when it began racing around the living room, barking and yelping madly at something unseen. Something it patently did not like and feared.

Carol saw the disc on just one more occasion. During the night of 1 December, she was in Nicola's room comforting the child who had been disturbed. While she was there, a noise sounded in her own room. Heart thumping wildly, she peered cautiously around the door. The object was moving across the width of her bed, as if searching for her ...

Just what was it that first invaded the lives of the family

on that warm August night? Is there an 'easy' psychological explanation? Did mass hysteria play its part, or is there a deeper, more terrifying explanation? *Were the five adults and one child part of an experiment contrived by visitors from Elsewhere?* If that is the case, then what they have told us may only be the tip of the iceberg. *The real horror of what they experienced may be buried deep in their subconscious minds – for their protection and ours.*

Friday the Thirteenth

———— ◆ ————

The small suburb of Abram lies near the Lancashire border with Merseyside, just six miles from Wigan. Abram is a legacy of the Industrial Revolution, with its old mine workings and run-down mills nudging uncomfortably with a scattering of farms set in acres of flat rugged countryside. When George Orwell wrote *The Road to Wigan Pier*, he could not have guessed at the strange drama which was to unfold in the area many decades later.

Dominating the skyline for miles around are the steep slopes of Winter Hill, its only mark of civilization a television mast servicing the towns and villages in the vast sweep of land below. Our story begins at about 9.45 p.m. on Friday, 13 August 1982 – a warm summer's evening, when the unexpected arrived.

Linda and Mike Meadows live on the edge of a council estate overlooking fields which converge abruptly with the winding gear of Bickershaw colliery, about a mile away. The couple have a son – then ten years old – who was out playing with friends. Dusk was changing into night proper, but there was still enough light for Mike to carry out some chores at the front of the house. Inside, Linda sat watching television with the lounge curtains still open.

Suddenly she let out a cry. The front door was wide

open, and Mike, hearing her, ran inside to see what was wrong. She was staring through the window at something hanging in the sky. Mike followed her gaze and gasped. The couple moved out into the garden for a better view.

There, they observed a cigar-shaped *something*, moving hardly at all in a west-to-east direction. It was light grey, with a row of square 'windows' along its length, and was fin shaped at the back. The rear glowed red, leaving a slight trail of sparks in the sky.

Mike and Linda heard voices in the field next to the house. They belonged to Mr Walker, a neighbour, and his nephew who was a police forensics expert. The couple joined them, and they too were bemused by the strange aerial display.

As they discussed the matter, their attention was drawn away from the cigar-like object towards some distant colliery lights. There, two small lights were circling like moths around a flame. If this was not enough, a *fourth* object streaked silently across from the vicinity of Winter Hill, joining the two around the colliery lights.

This was also light grey in colour, shaped like an ice-cream cone, with two orange lights at the rear. There were also two white lights, one on the nose and the other on the underside, casting a fan of illumination. In the meantime *something* was happening to the primary object. It seemed to be moving *sideways* towards them. The emission from the rear had ceased, and the 'windows' grew dim then bright again, as if they were pulsating.

At this juncture, the three objects circling the colliery lights began travelling towards the strange cigar-shaped craft. The 'cone' accelerated away from the two lights and disappeared. The lights continued until they had reached the 'cigar', whereupon they either went *into* it, or *behind* it. The group were flabbergasted. What could they do? Mike suggested to Linda they drive down nearby Park Lane. There they would be much closer to the object and would obtain a clearer view. Hesitantly, she agreed.

The journey to Park Lane took about five minutes.

During that time, because of streetlamps and tall buildings, the couple lost sight of the nocturnal aerial show. Before long, they turned off the main Wigan road, and darkness closed around them. Park Lane is little more than a track that leads to two small farms, but partway down is the premises of a company called Abram Alloys. Mike was beginning to get an attack of the creeps, as if the ride was not such a good idea after all, but he said nothing to Linda in case she became frightened too. There was a security light outside the plant, so he parked opposite it because, as he said later, 'it made me feel safer.' But what Mike failed to realize, was that the light also made the vehicle's presence obvious . . .

It was now just after 10 p.m. The 'cigar' was still there, positioned close to a dense area of trees known as Crankwood. The two lights were hovering nearby, as if undecided what to do.

'It was as if they were waiting for orders,' he told investigators.

After a minute or so, one of the lights dropped almost to ground level beside the wood. Slowly, it began following the shallow valley towards Park Lane. Linda did not see this as she was still watching the 'cigar'. It was moving off, and carrying out a very strange manoeuvre just before disappearing from sight behind some trees. *It moved from the horizontal plane to the vertical – then back again, several times.* It was like someone slowly twiddling a biro back and forth between forefinger and thumb.

Mike was ignorant of all this. He was becoming increasingly nervous, as the sphere of light, as it now looked, came nearer. With mounting apprehension, he realized it was on a direct path towards the car. His skin goose-bumped, and he experienced a feeling that 'they knew we were there, watching them.'

As he turned to warn Linda the words froze in his mouth. There was another light, directly ahead of the car, coming round a bend in the lane. It must be a motorcycle headlight, he told himself, it must be . . . but the light was about ten feet off the ground, and if it had been attached to some vehicle, it would have bounced around like crazy in all the potholes. And it was orange, bright orange, measuring about a yard across.

Soon, they would be trapped between the two converging balls of light. Mike lost no more time. He started the engine, slammed the car into reverse, turned so fast the car rocked on its chassis, then sped off back towards the friendly street lights of the Abram roads.

Something had spoken inside his head – *get the hell out of it, time you were gone!*

Linda and Mike arrived home just as *News at Ten* was going off. On the way back Mike had noticed that none of his car lights was working. Andrew, their son, arrived home a few minutes later to find his parents in a highly excitable state. Yet before they could say anything, he blurted out a story of his own.

At around 10 p.m., while his parents were parked in Park Lane, Andrew was half a mile away on a canal bridge with a group of friends. One boy drew the attention of the others over towards Crankwood. Something funny was happening there. Coloured lights and sparks were showing through the trees.

Three miles to the north-west of Abram lies the small community of Bryn. Earlier in the evening a Mrs Heyworth was preparing to go and play her weekly game of bingo in the town. Friday the thirteenth, she thought, will it be unlucky for me? She didn't really care too much. It was the fun of playing and the company of her friend which counted most. When Mr Heyworth picked her up a couple of hours later, she had enjoyed a nice evening, and the last thing on her mind were unidentified flying objects.

At about the time the Meadows family were exchanging stories, Mr and Mrs Heyworth were driving home.

The short journey took them out of the town and across some open country known as The Three Sisters. Co-incidentally, *three* very bright lights hovered over it. Mrs

Heyworth grew very excited, and her husband speculated whether or not they might be military helicopters on a training flight, although neither noticed any sound.

The Heyworths live on the edge of Bryn, overlooking a broad sweep of countryside which merges with the steep slopes of Winter Hill. They climbed out of the car and noticed that the strange lights were still there. They were in a triangular configuration, moving slowly and silently towards the Hill. Definite shapes were now discernible, and Mrs Heyworth realized that her husband's explanation just did not fit.

The two bringing up the rear of the formation were large, brightly lit white spheres, and the silver-coloured leading object was cigar-shaped. The couple watched silently until the odd trio was out of sight, swallowed up by the southern slopes of the dark hills.

Mrs Heyworth's mind was too alive to allow her any sleep. When her husband retired she stayed up, wondering what to do. Finally, she switched on her CB set and spent a long time talking to other breakers about her unusual sighting. Then, for no apparent reason, a loud burst of noise hit the set sending her off the air.

To the south, just inside the Merseyside border, Pamela and Stephen Tate could not sleep either. Pamela was watching a late-night film on television and her husband was reading a book. Stephen sat with his back to the large picture-frame window, while Pamela sat facing it, curled up on the settee. It was a beautiful, clear warm night, and the venetian blind was open, allowing them a view of the starlit sky.

It was now 1.10 a.m. on Saturday, 14 August.

Pamela suddenly let out a cry of disbelief and leapt from the settee to the window, hands gripping the sill tightly. Opposite, across the road, are two houses with a thirty-foot gap between them. *What had caused her to cry out was the impossible sight of something large and brilliantly lit, sliding into view from behind the roof of the house to the left.*

Stephen was now at her side as the entire object came into view. It was a huge cigar-shaped craft bathed in brilliant white light, although, oddly, none of this light illuminated either the nearby houses or the sky behind it. Stephen wanted an even better view, so he ran upstairs to look for his telescope.

Pamela recollected later, the near hysterical effect it had on her. 'It was so huge, so close, I felt it was going to take up the house opposite!'

By the time Stephen returned, the object filled the entire gap between the two houses. If it was *that* near, it was at least thirty feet in length. Pamela rushed to the back of the room, now thoroughly afraid. Her husband watched as the object tilted upwards, a row of 'portholes' evident along its side, climbing, drifting out of sight, travelling west to east ...

The high-pitched electronic screeching noise lasted about five minutes, then abruptly stopped. Mrs Heyworth went back on the air again to find that other breakers had experienced the same period of interference. By chance she contacted some people operating from Matchmoor Lane, up on Winter Hill. After listening to what they said, she rushed upstairs and woke her husband. The time was 1.30 a.m.

The Hill is a favourite location for CB operators. Its high elevation allows the signals to travel much further than down in the valleys.

Excitedly, she told her husband of the conversation, and described how the other breakers sounded on edge, even afraid.

According to them, a large lighted object had come over the Hill and seemed to land in one of the quarries, before taking off again, heading south, in the direction of Frodsham. Others reported seeing it, or something like it, travelling towards Buxton, in the Peak District of Derbyshire ...

What was it that descended on Abram during the night of Friday the Thirteenth? UFO investigators, mainly from the Manchester UFO Research Association, looked for an answer. According to astronomers, there were several meteors recorded in the sky that night, but these were all seen in the early hours of the morning. And the brief flash of a meteor does not compare with the detailed observations of so many independent witnesses. In the wake of that night there were other people who observed the same phenomenon, and several hard-to-pin-down rumours promising something *more*.

At the time the four witnesses were in the fields on the edge of the Abram estate, a Mr Barker was in his upstairs flat, passing from the bedroom to the kitchen, when something caught his eye through the landing window. When an investigator interviewed him, Mr Barker had this to say:

'I'm not saying I saw a UFO, but then again I can't explain it away as a conventional aircraft. For one thing it seemed much larger than an airliner.'

He too described a brilliant white 'fuselage' with a line of oval-shaped 'windows'. The rear was shaped like a fin which glowed an orange/red colour. During the ten minutes of observation, he also saw two bright lights which disappeared behind or inside the main object.

But what of the rumours?

Mike Meadows, himself a CB enthusiast, managed to speak on the air to one of the Matchmoor Lane witnesses, bearing the handle of 'Meatloaf'.

Meatloaf confirmed that a brightly lit object appeared to land in a quarry some distance away. A message was sent to the police and a car arrived from Farnworth. The officer in the car ordered Meatloaf and his friends to 'get off the Hill'. Rumours later circulated that the authorities were 'clearing up for some time'. According to the story, where the object had landed a lot of residue ash was found and taken away for tests.

Intriguing though this sounds, Meatloaf would not

divulge his real identity, and the exact location of the quarry could not be found. Also, enquiries to the police were met only with denials – no record of such an incident existed, they said. Investigators also wrote to the Ministry of Defence for their comment on the theory that it was some sort of military exercise. They chose not to reply at all.

Whatever it was, it was something very unusual, which acted and looked unlike anything anyone had seen before.

Friday the thirteenth – unlucky for whom?

SEPTEMBER

1st Jack the Ripper's first victim was murdered on this date in 1888. Over the next few weeks he went on to claim four more victims and then mysteriously vanished. He was never caught.

9th Snippy the horse was discovered dead and badly mutilated in Colorado in 1967. Many of his internal organs, including the brain, had been removed in a surgical manner – rather like Jack the Ripper treated his victims. This was the starting point for what became known as the 'Cattle Mutilation' mystery, which continues to this day. Thousands of animals, mostly cattle and mainly throughout the American mid-west, have died in similarly bizarre circumstances. Reports also exist from other nations, including Spain, Puerto Rico and Canada.

10th A girl in Plymouth, Devon, claimed that she was attacked by a UFO in 1981. A greenish beam emerged and left severe burn markings on her hand.

19th A photograph of the phantom 'brown lady' of Raynham Hall in Norfolk was taken in 1936 and is one of the most fascinating ghost photographs that are still considered unexplained.

On the same day in 1961 Betty and Barney Hill, became the first reported victims of a UFO kidnap when they allege that they were taken from their car crossing the White Mountains of New Hampshire, USA. Most of the memory of their adventures at the hands of Oriental looking aliens emerged under later hypnosis. A book – *The Interrupted Journey* – and a later TV movie – *The UFO Incident* – were produced about the episode.

23rd A group of children claim that they saw some tiny people – i.e. fairies – riding around Wollaton Park, Nottingham, on this day in 1979. They were reputedly travelling in miniature cars. The children's headmaster investigated the matter and regarded the youngsters as sincere. Other strange apparitions have been reported in the Wollaton area in the past.

24th Dr Jacques Vallee was born in Pontoise, France, in 1939. He has written extensively about the paranormal and the concept of 'Magonia' – a land where a parallel form of evolutionary life might exist – and was the first to draw comparisons between fairy folk-stories and UFO entity reports. Vallee was the model for the scientist, Lacombe, in the movie *Close Encounters of the Third Kind*. He is a computer expert from California and author of successful science-fiction novels in French.

The September Siren

◆

Thank you for your letter. I've been under a bit of stress recently, and on Friday and Saturday something funny happened. I've tried to puzzle it out in my head a million times, and it was only last night that I could tell Brian, my hubby.

At about ten minutes to four on Friday afternoon, I went upstairs out of the way of the kids to get some peace and quiet. I casually glanced out of my bedroom window and noticed a little boy who lives nearby. He was running down a path which leads from the close opposite into ours. I watched him run across the road to his house. In his hand he clutched a piece of green paper. I presume he must have been on an errand for his mum. He reached the pavement, and as there was nothing else to keep my attention, I walked away from the window, looked at the dressing table, and screwed the lid back onto my jar of moisturizer.

I just happened to look back out of the window. I couldn't believe it! *I saw the same little boy with the green paper in his hand, running across the road onto the pavement of our road. It was only seconds before that I had witnessed exactly the same scene.* I stood dazed for a minute feeling very peculiar. Then the kids started calling me, so I went downstairs and forgot about the incident.

The following day, Brian, the kids and I went shopping in Launceston. We were walking through the town when I spotted up ahead and coming towards us a couple – friends of ours. I wanted to avoid them as I wasn't in the mood to stand chatting for ages (you know what I mean?). So I did a quick dive into a café doorway without telling Brian why. Instead I said I wanted to read through the 'for sale' cards on the notice board. We stood there for about two minutes; long enough for our friends to have walked right past the café. I thought, they'll be gone by now, as we came out of the doorway and continued along the street, through an archway and up Race Hill.

I froze. *The couple were there in the same position where I had seen them before diving into the café doorway. Walking down the hill towards us.*

I was trying all day to puzzle it out. They were definitely there the first time. They had on exactly the same clothes both times. I hadn't mistaken them for someone else. I don't think they could have had time to turn around, or go back into the market, or could they? It was all just very strange. Was it coincidence that I saw them at the same spot twice? I hope you can understand this, and you don't think I'm flipping my lid!

There's just one more thing before I go, and again, I hope you'll tell me you've heard of it happening to other people.

I was drifting off to sleep one night about two weeks ago. It was quiet and peaceful outside, and I wasn't thinking about anything much. Suddenly I heard what seemed like fifty voices all trying to talk at once. It didn't sound like it was from outside, but *inside* my head. One voice – a young man's – was the loudest. It repeated just one word: JOHN! I couldn't stand it, and said to myself, Oh shut up! I'm tired, I want to go to sleep ... The voices stopped immediately. I told Brian the next morning, but he hadn't heard anything.

Please tell me you've come across things like this before! I'm sorry to go on but I feel better telling someone I can trust ...'

Gail slipped the letter into an envelope. It was addressed to a paranormal investigator who had been interested in her psychic experiences for some time. The incidents in her letter were the latest in a long list of inexplicable things which had allegedly occurred. Although she had moved to Cornwall only a year earlier, she had fallen in love with the place in the summer of 1978, after leaving home in Warrington to start work in a hotel in Newquay.

But had something intangible, invisible, accompanied her to Newquay which would have been better left behind?

Gail was very happy working at the Carnmarth Hotel in her capacity as a chambermaid. It was there she met her future husband, Brian. Brian shared a room with another waiter called Steve. But Brian and Gail fell so much in love they sometimes shared his bed while Steve slept across the other side of the room.

The hotel was several hundred years old. As with most buildings steeped in history it has its fair share of alleged 'hauntings' and tragedies. Whether these have any bearing on what subsequently terrified Gail Kegan is open to debate. There is a former chef who drowned, an attic room where an apparition was seen by one of the staff, and another room which is icy cold, even in summer.

The night before, Gail had been working late, and was glad to get to bed and feel Brian's warm arms around her. But the boys were on a different shift to her, and were up early the next morning, leaving the room without disturbing the young woman. When Gail did eventually wake up, she glanced at the bedside clock and saw it was 10.45 a.m.

Immediately she was wide awake, sat up, and stared unbelievingly at Steve's bed ...

A pair of feet were moving beneath the sheets. *She could make out the outline of legs but there was no body and no head on the pillow, just feet moving, side to side, together, apart, together ... Where was the head?* her mind demanded. *WHERE WAS THE HEAD?*

At the same time a tapping sound began reverberating through her own bed frame, as if someone was underneath. Gail began pinching and slapping her face making sure it was not a nightmare. But she *was* awake, and another thought occurred to her. Could it be the boys? Had they crept back while she was asleep to play a practical joke on her? That was it. They were hidden under the beds, working the effects from there, probably smiling to themselves. Before long they would crawl out and someone would make a pot of tea, and they would all laugh about it.

She called out their names nervously. It's going to stop in a minute, she told herself, it *must* stop! But she was wrong. The feet in the bed opposite were now becoming frantic, and the tapping beneath her own bed became a loud knocking which she could feel through the mattress. It became louder, heavier and *angrier*. She put her hands over her ears and screwed up her eyes but it was no use.

Suddenly she screamed. The entire bed she was lying in tipped over violently so that she was squeezed between it and the wall. Then there was another knocking – a different knocking – and the bed fall back onto its legs, suddenly released from whatever power had been holding it. The maniacal feet, too, were gone. Just a faint impression beneath the sheets remained.

The knocking continued and Gail realized this time it was coming from the door. But the young woman sat petrified in the jumbled sheets of the bed, immobile with shock. The knocking became louder, and with it came Steve's muffled voice calling her name. Why doesn't he use his key? she thought. He was sounding very worried now, and Gail realized she had to do something. She tried answering the boy but it was no good; her vocal chords just would not work. *She would have to cross the room and open the door.*

Gail had to fight hard to overcome all her fears. It was quiet in the room now. Too quiet? What if her bed started rocking again? What if those feet, that were attached to legs which led nowhere, started their frenzied side-to-side movement again? *What if, as she leapt off the bed, hands shot out from beneath the bed frame and snatched at her ankles?* What if . . .

Steve had stopped his loud knocking. He was shouting something.

'Gail, I know you must be in there. If you don't open the door I'll fetch Brian and we'll have to break it down. Gail?'

She made her move. The bedclothes were flung back, her feet hardly touching the floor as she bounced across the room in terror to the door. She turned the Yale latch. The door would not open! Then she saw why. There were four bolts on the old door, and every one of them was closed . . . In near-panic, she frantically tried to pull back the bolts, tearing with her nails, but they were very stiff with age. At last it was done, and Steve burst into the room. He held Gail in his arms and comforted her until Brian arrived a few minutes later.

Gail stuck down the flap of the envelope. There was a stamp somewhere in her purse. Yes, that time in the hotel ... But that was not where it all started, was it? What was wrong with her? Or, as the paranormal investigators who had interviewed her preferred it, what was so *special* that she should hear disembodied voices and experience other strange things? Or was she mad? But she was no Joan of Arc. No one would burn *her* at the stake!

No, what had started it all lay way back almost twelve years ago. That madness in the hotel was terrifying enough, but what had happened then was more physical and infinitely more frightening.

1976 was a memorable year. Britons recall it because it was the year of The Drought. Rain was scarce that summer, so scarce that hundreds of acres of grass and woodland went up in flames, and rivers and whole reservoirs lost millions of gallons of water to the burning heat of the sun, exposing dry, cracked beds of mud.

It was the year of water restrictions; of bricks placed in toilet cisterns, shared baths, water hoarding and cars driving around covered in coats of dirt. There was plenty to remember about 1976, but Gail Kegan remembers it for none of these things. She remembers it because it was the year she was almost raped.

At seventeen, the blonde-haired teenager, just out of school, had no worries, no commitments. She lived with her parents, had a job of sorts which brought in some spending money, and enjoyed a normal carefree life.

Both Gail and her mother worked at a bakery in Warrington, near the Cheshire border. The family lived on a new housing estate which was well within walking distance of the women's place of work.

September arrived, and Mrs Kegan and her daughter were going to work as usual. It was an early start, and this day they left the house just after 5.30 a.m. At the top of the estate they followed a short-cut along a dirt track, where some houses were still being built. As they drew level with a bungalow, something very strange occurred.

Along the front of the bungalow was a brick wall, and at the top of a short drive, a garage was under construction. It was dark. The two women were talking to one another when Gail stopped. There was a voice, *and it was calling her name.*

...Gail...GAIL... So clear, so *definite.*

'Did you hear that, Mother?'

Mrs Kegan stopped and looked at her daughter, quizzically.

'Hear what?'

'Someone –'

But there it was again.

Gail...Gail...

'Someone calling my name.'

Gail looked around but there was no one about. The voice had seemed to come from behind the wall.

'I can't hear anything.'

Gail...

It was a woman's voice, a little bit like her own, but sweet, so sweet, and with an echoing quality, as if it was coming from the far end of a tunnel. Nevertheless, it *did* seem to emanate from behind the wall. Gail was so sure of it that she walked up the drive to take a look. No one was there.

Over the next two weeks the same thing happened regularly. And every time it did, her mother heard nothing. But to Gail it was as pure and clear as day. Calling her name in that lovely sweet voice, the sort of voice you might obey just because it sounded so *good.* It called her, it drew her behind that wall. But when she looked, there was never anyone around.

She told some friends at work and they just laughed. Her mother blamed it on lack of sleep, preferring that explanation to the more sinister one that Gail was 'hearing voices' because there was something psychologically wrong with her.

But she did not hear the voice at any other time. Only at that spot −coming from behind the wall of the newly built bungalow with its unfinished garage. Because there was no explanation, she became afraid.

She was somewhat relieved later in the month, when she was informed that her job application to another company had been successful. She could start her new job as a cook straightaway. This meant she no longer had to walk past the bungalow on her way to work . . .

The new job was a good excuse for celebration. Gail and a group of friends from the bakery decided to go out for a drink. Nothing special, a town-centre pub then on to a club. It was a great night. Although she was happy about the new job, she felt a little sad to be leaving the bakery, for she was going to miss her friends. Finally it was time to go home. She ordered a taxi and it dropped her off on the new road near to the estate. Gail would take the short-cut down the dirt track.

It was dark and very quiet. As her shoes crunched lightly on the ashes filling the pot-holes, it seemed she was the only person alive in the world. There was no traffic noise and the nearby buildings loomed like sightless monoliths of another time. She felt relaxed, easy. She was the only person about, wasn't she?

This tiny voice of doubt in her mind caused her to quicken her step a little. She was nearing the bungalow now, and thought of the voice that had sweetly called out her name during the past few weeks. Just then she felt hot beer-laden breath on the nape of her neck, and an arm close like a clamp under her chin making her jaws grind and her tongue hurt where it caught between her teeth. The man breathed heavily as he dragged the struggling teenager past the wall at the front of the bungalow then onto the drive, where he fell on top of her.

Gail had no doubts about what was going to happen next. She had read about women being raped, heard stories from her friends and been warned by her parents many times about being out late at night on her own. Now it was going to happen to her, if she let it ...

She managed to let out a scream before a spade-sized hand slapped tight across her mouth. He was struggling with his trousers, her skirt, he was *heavy*, squashing the breath out of her. She had to do something quick. One hand was free, and she tried to prise his fingers away from her mouth. This was a mistake. He went for her throat instead and began to squeeze. Gail's hand flailed about – drowning not waving – searching for something, anything which might help her escape. Her voice was rasping, choking, she saw blackness and stars fade in and out as she realized that rape was now not uppermost in his mind. *He meant to kill her first.*

Gail was growing weaker. Then a miracle happened. How else can it be described? She felt a brick in her hand *as if someone had put it there.* She brought it down hard on the back of her assailant's head and he collapsed on top of her. She struggled and managed to push him off, guessing him to be about six feet tall and weighing around sixteen stone. Gail sat for a few moments on the ground getting her breath back. Just then another man appeared, a neighbour who had been awakened by her scream. But her attacker was already climbing to his feet and staggered off into the darkness.

Gail suffered considerable shock, could not talk properly for three months and had severe bruising round her neck.

But questions remain; was the voice she heard a warning of what might happen? Did this explain how the brick found its way into her hand? Or, like the sirens of ancient mariners' tales, did the voice draw her on to the rocks of her own destruction? After all, she could have insisted the taxi-driver drop her off at her door.

That voice which was so *sweet*, warning her, *or calling her*?

OCTOBER

8th In 1972, at Cairo Mill, near Oldham, a security guard caught a UFO on a chimney, spying. The factory cat was terrified and hid for some days after the experience.

13th At Fatima, Portugal, in 1917, from May until October, ten-year-old Lucia dos Santos and her two cousins observed various aerial phenomena and a white-robed lady. After the first incident, crowds formed to witness the strange sight. They described a glowing globe which sometimes hovered nearby, emitting a buzzing sound. However, no one but the children could see the figure of the woman within the globe, who successfully predicted a miracle on 13 October. Then, 70,000 people observed two suns in the sky. Although today we see the strong UFO connotations, in 1917 it was interpreted as a religious experience.

14th In Dallas, Scotland, a large black wild cat was shot in 1985. It is thought that this new breed might be the result of mating between wild cats and domestic cats. No doubt this animal explains the sightings of large mystery cats *in that area*.

20th In 1967, colour film was taken in California by Roger Patterson of a large hairy man-like creature. Allegedly, this shows Bigfoot.

21st The first reliable British report of a UFO occupant occurred on this day in 1954, in Staffordshire. Also on this date in 1978, a young Australian pilot called Valentich disappeared with his aircraft over the Bass Straits, after reporting a strange object hovering nearby.

27th In 1974, an entire family travelling home by car were abducted and taken inside a UFO by 'aliens'. This happened near Aveley, Essex.

No Room at the Inn

◆

The lush scenery of southern France unfolded around them as they continued the pleasing and unhurried journey towards the Spanish border.

Len and Cynthia Gisby had invited their friends Geoff and Pauline Simpson to make up a foursome. They all left from their respective homes in Kent to travel the thousand-mile trip across Europe to start a two-week break.

Having crossed the Channel by ferry, they found 3 October 1979 was proving a long and energy-sapping day. While it was warm and sunny as they took the autoroute into Montelimar, this merely added to their exhaustion. As darkness fell, they all sensed it was time to find a resting place for the night.

They had preferred not to book anywhere in advance. The pleasure of this holiday was particularly enhanced by its freedom of movement; although they were just a little worried about the fact that none of them could speak more than the odd word of French.

After nine, as the shadows lengthened, they came upon a likely looking motel.

'This seems perfect,' they mutually agreed, and so pulled in to check out its attributes. Unhappily, an odd-looking man in a delightful plum-coloured uniform met them in the lobby with the news that there were no rooms available. The roadhouse was completely full.

The man spoke English, which was a blessing, and informed Len Gisby that all was not lost; 'If you take the road off the autoroute back there – then you will come to a small hotel. I am sure you will find that they have some rooms.'

Being tired, almost any offer to them would have sufficed, so the four agreed to follow this suggestion and took note of the directions offered. Shortly afterwards they found themselves on a strange little side road.

'Look at those posters!' Pauline remarked with glee, as the two women in the party took great delight in perusing them.

They seemed to tell of a circus that was performing locally, with very old-style acts. It was like a page torn out of a history book.

'It's a shame we can't go,' Cynthia commented. But the men said that they really ought to concentrate on reaching Spain as soon as possible. They were after all only passing through France in order to reach their destination.

Len and Geoff were rather concerned about the road over which they were driving. This had deteriorated badly since they left the main highway and with night closing in it was slightly disconcerting.

They bounced over cobbles that seemed almost like a throwback to the Middle Ages. Doubtless they were charming in the daylight, but with the narrow width of the track and the fear that something might be coming the other way round the darkened bends, the men were anxious to reach the hotel to which they had been directed. They could enjoy the scenery in the morning.

Cynthia spotted lights ahead. 'There it is,' she pointed.

But even as they pulled to a halt in front of the long, thin structure, its façade dotted with brightly lit windows, they knew this was not a hotel.

Cynthia got out for a look, but quickly jumped back in again, shaking her head: 'No – it's just some sort of an inn.'

189

They drove on through a stately avenue of trees that looked somewhat forbidding in the gloom. However, despite the complete desolation of the countryside and total lack of traffic they did ultimately find two other buildings. One seemed to be a police station. The other was surely their destination. The enormously welcoming sign 'Hotel' was caught in their headlight beams.

The car drew to a halt, its passengers finding it slightly odd that there was no hotel car park. But then it was obviously a very old and remote establishment. Len clambered out and went to enquire whether there were rooms available. To everybody's great relief he came back to say there were.

'I don't think I fancied going any further,' Geoff remarked. There was unanimous agreement about that.

It was now about 10 p.m., so they carried their hand baggage from the car, leaving the vehicle parked just off the roadway. Then they all went into the hotel to inspect the available accommodation.

It was wonderful. Everything was made up of heavy wood, with the form of the building resembling a ranch-house. Just two storeys, evidently containing very few rooms, and a definite old-fashioned quaintness about every aspect of the decor. In fact, there were no obvious signs that the modern world had ever caught up with this place at all.

They had great difficulty making the hotel owner understand them as he spoke no English. Resorting to a kind of sign language he led them up the stairs to their rooms, which were just as dramatic as the rest of the hotel. The huge beds had bolsters instead of pillows. The sheets were extremely heavy. And the single bathroom which they had to share had plumbing which appeared to date from the Victorian era.

'Look at this,' Geoff chuckled, and showed them the soap that was embedded in a metal bar that was stuck to the wall.

'Isn't this just great? What a tourist attraction – and

right off the beaten track.'

After unpacking they went down for a meal. There were some very rustic-looking men in rough clothing at the bar drinking beer. They eyed the newcomers curiously. The menu was almost indecipherable, but they recognized one word – *oeuf* – and ordered four portions of the egg dish. It turned out to be eggs with steak and french-fried potatoes, piled up on enormous metal plates, and they washed this down with tankards of lager.

The four thoroughly enjoyed the evening but were so worn out that they went to bed early. The bedroom doors had simple wooden catches – another aspect of the rural ambience. Even so, Pauline felt a little intimidated at not being able to lock herself in, so she jammed a chair up against the door so that she was absolutely satisfied that she had a degree of security.

Not that it really mattered. None of them was disturbed during the night. They slept very soundly and awoke feeling refreshed and quite ready to face the challenge of another lengthy drive.

Downstairs they assembled for breakfast. This was a modest affair, with bread, jam and coffee. None of them felt inclined to quibble, even though the coffee was a rather tasteless, thick black sludge.

As they were still eating, a woman strolled in carrying a little dog under her arm. She was dressed as if she had just stepped out of a ballroom.

Pauline motioned Cynthia to look, saying: 'What a get-up for seven in the morning.'

Then two policemen arrived at the hotel, presumably from the station next door. They had large peaked caps, swirling deep blue capes and looked like characters from an old silent movie.

By now convinced that this was just somewhere that was operating as a living museum, perhaps preserving the customs to attract visitors, the four decided to capture their experience on film. Geoff photographed Pauline in the bedroom against the wooden slatted shutters that acted as windows. Len took a couple of shots from by the car, with Cynthia inside the building and framed at the 'window'.

By now it was time to move on, but they were less than certain they knew the best way back to the autoroute. Len struggled with the language and tried desperately to make the gendarmes understand where they were headed.

The officers looked nonplussed at his pronunciation of the word 'autoroute'.

'You can't be saying it right,' Geoff grinned. 'It's *Auto-route*.'

Eventually, the policemen understood that the travellers were heading for Spain and so directed them towards the old Avignon road. Studying the map in the car, Len and Geoff decided this was too much of a roundabout way.

'I think we'd be much better off going back the way we came and finding that autoroute into Montelimar.'

This plan met with mutual agreement. So they went to pay their bill. The manager scribbled a sum on a piece of paper. It read 19 francs ... Less than £2!

'No. No.' Len gesticulated, trying to make the man see that he wanted the bill for all four of them. The manager merely smiled.

Continuing his comic efforts to make himself under-stood, Len tried to discover the true cost. The manager continued to smile and nod. Finally, Len took the piece of paper to the two policemen and showed it to them. They took it, examined it thoroughly and handed it back, nodding amicably.

Geoff – knowing they were onto a good thing – turned to Len and whispered; 'Hey, come on, let's get out of here before he changes his mind.'

Len pulled out some French currency, put it on the table and they hurried out to the car.

It was another hot and sunny day and their fears about finding their way south proved groundless. They followed the cobbled road easily to the Montelimar autoroute and once more set off for their Spanish destination.

All thought of the delightful hotel went out of their

minds. They had two weeks of glorious sunshine and relaxation ahead of them and they intended soaking it up in preparation for the English winter.

Besides which, if anything, they had merely found a quaint little hotel whose owners enjoyed dressing up the staff in old-fashioned costumes and pretending that it was a hundred years in the past.

Two weeks later, the Gisbys and the Simpsons were heading home. There was never any question in their minds that they should stop en route at anywhere other than that wonderful little hotel near Montelimar. After all, the service was unrivalled and the conditions unlike anything you might find in a modern concrete tower block.

The weather was dismal, with rain pouring out of darkened skies. But they found the turn-off and even saw the circus signs. They knew that they were heading in the right direction.

However, try as hard as they might, they could not find the hotel. It simply wasn't there. They scoured the countryside driving up and down, but nothing even remotely similar turned up.

So they found the motel on the autoroute. They asked to speak to the man in the plum-coloured uniform. 'We have nobody like that working here. Nor do we know of any hotel like the one you refer to,' they were studiously informed.

As they drove away, shaking heads and talking animatedly, Cynthia became very agitated. 'It has to be here! It can't just disappear.'

'At those prices it probably went bust,' someone quipped.

'No,' Geoff said pointedly. 'It wouldn't just disappear without trace. Not in just two weeks.'

Finally, they drove north and found a hotel in Lyon. Here they had bed, breakfast and evening meal and it cost them *fourteen* times as much as they paid at the attractive little place near Montelimar.

The four have been back to France several times since, trying to find the hotel. But despite enquiries with the police and local tourist board, no such accommodation appears to exist.

Even so, they never contemplated a supernatural explanation. Not until they got their holiday snaps back from the processors.

All the photographs from both cameras came out perfectly. But the three shots that were taken of the hotel were never returned. Not only were they not returned – from the unbroken sequence of numbered negatives something even more disturbing was apparent.

Although they all *knew* that they had stayed in that hotel for several hours and captured proof of the event on film, the lack of evidence from the camera and the absence of the photographs showed conclusively that they could not have taken any pictures of the hotel at all!

The Gisbys and the Simpsons had spent a night in a phantom building – an olde worlde hotel which simply doesn't exist.

Halloween: A Stranger Walks at Dawn

◆

When Roy Jones stirred himself awake – on the morning when the ghosts are said to walk – it happened in an instant. Never the sort to come around slowly, his senses were immediately sharp and piercing.

Just a year before, Roy had been in hospital under heavy anaesthetic and could still recall how one moment he was dead to the world, the next he was chatting to nurses. Right now he felt the same. His mind was acute. He was very much alive and almost painfully aware that something unusual was taking place.

The sensation was overwhelming. It was that feeling you get when you know what is occurring even before you experience it.

Of course, it had to be a burglar. Somebody had broken into the room and was even now rummaging through his and Muriel's things.

Twisting around as quietly as possible, mindful of what might happen if he disturbed their intruder, Roy confronted the figure square on.

There was never any doubt that someone would be there – at the foot of the bed and only a few yards from him. But who was it?

Nothing could prevent the horror or the surprise when the truth dawned. The figure which stood there – this person he had assumed to be a petty thief – was like nobody Roy had encountered in his entire life.

And yet it continued to stand there, stooping down slightly. It appeared to be inspecting something; taking a great interest in the radio alarm. Just like a criminal who might be weighing up whether it was worth stealing.

This scene was utterly impossible, Roy realized without hesitation.

My God, what is that thing? ... And in reply to his thought, one image filled his mind. *Whatever it may be – their visitor was certainly not human!*

Outside, the morning was arriving with its customary sloth. The half-light of a north Cheshire autumn was enhanced just a touch by the streetlamp outside their Altrincham semi, making conditions good enough to see in full detail the 'thing' now standing in the room.

It was incredibly frail; almost like a child. Extremely slight and slender as if constructed out of balsa wood. It also appeared to be no taller than a young boy. Perhaps four and a half feet high – no more.

It was wearing what seemed to be a diver's wetsuit – or, at least, a black one-piece uniform that clung to the body so tightly it could well have been sprayed on. Roy saw shadows and reflections off the surface that gave clear indication this was a solid figure.

Hallucinations don't come in three dimensions, he kept repeating in his mind, as if the incantation would exorcize the phantom.

There was also something utterly bizarre about the entity. Despite the amazing lightness of its structure the head was out of all proportion. Stuck on a tiny neck like a swollen pumpkin, it was awful to contemplate. A bala-clava-like extension of the suit covered it and fitted so snugly that Roy could not help wondering how on earth the being ever put it on. Surely, it was impossible to get it over that enormous head.

As he watched in fascination, the figure did not move. It continued to maintain its stooping posture, as if it had frozen in that position when Roy had woken up.

It knows I'm here, he told himself. In fact there was a really strange feeling about the entire situation. Roy knew, even as he watched, that the normal reaction of any person waking to find a stranger in the room would be to shout or to leap out of bed – to *do* something. But he was simply flooded with an overwhelming sense of curiosity. It seemed to be pouring out of the creature, radiating all over him – an unintentional peeping tom.

The strangest part of the stooping figure was its chin. This jutted out like an exaggerated caricature of enter-tainer Bruce Forsyth. Was it the head cover that was causing this effect, or was it really the shape of the creature's face?

Roy, by profession a graphic designer who was trained to look at minute details of form and pattern, was entranced by many little aspects of this weird staring match. The entity was allowing him to observe. That much was very evident. It knew he was there. Yet, as if tantalizing or teasing, it was urging him to drink in all the facts that he could about this waking nightmare.

What shade of black is that? he asked himself about the suit. It seemed jet black, standing out against the greyish/

196

black of the bedroom.

Why does it not look to be in correct proportion? he pondered from his perspective as an artist.

What manner of material composes such a wonderful suit? he thought in admiration, almost wishing he could take out a patent. It reminded him of corduroy, being softly ribbed, but with an almost rubbery texture.

From the second that Roy had set eyes on the 'thing', time had lost all meaning. He was under a magic spell, where nothing else in the universe mattered except for himself and his visitor. Muriel was snoring only inches from his face, but the concept of waking her up to share this profound encounter never even entered the realms of possibility.

And now – something else was occurring to his fine-tuned consciousness. I'm short sighted, he reminded himself. In order to see things, even at such close range as this, he had to screw up his eyes and force the image into alignment.

This was precisely what he had been doing, in a subconscious fashion, from the moment that he first saw the creature. If he relaxed his eye muscles now, the edges of the apparition became fuzzy.

This is important, he told himself in triumph. Surely hallucinations wouldn't go out of focus?

Feeling proud of his rationalization in the face of this drama he concluded that a vision would be routed directly from his brain. It would not test the faults of imperfect vision. To do so, it *must* be real!

By now the figure had stood its ground for possibly three minutes – although time had stretched out like an elasticated fog. Roy was aware that the lower legs of his intruder were hidden by the untidy bedclothes, which had rucked up in the night. So he determined to sit up and move his eye-line to get a fuller view.

As he did so, the 'thing' just disappeared. It did not fade or move. One microsecond it was present, the next instant it was gone. But even as the white background of the wall

197

rushed in to plug the gap where the figure had stood, another awesome thought occurred to Roy. Surely if the thing had been a three-dimensional entity such as a man, then vanishing like this would have meant that a hole would be left where his body space had been. That hole would have been filled by air, rushing in to seal the vacuum. That dramatic flow of air would have led to a noise – which would certainly have been audible in this silent bedroom.

Roy cursed himself – now thoroughly confused. In just a few moments he had proven that the figure had to be real ... and now, also, that it had to be unreal!

That was impossible ... As was the entire last few minutes of his life.

Roy had lain there mulling over all these thoughts. Sleep was out of the question, and so he remained staring at the window and the walls and watching the daylight gradually fill in the remaining pockets of darkness.

He looked at the radio alarm – which his visitor had found so intriguing. It read 06.04 – four minutes past six in the morning. At least he knew the precise hour of his close encounter – even if he did not have the faintest idea what he had closely encountered.

At the half hour the man who lived opposite started up his diesel truck and chugged away to work. It was another normal day for most people.

But not for Roy. His universe had changed for ever.

There had been some other strange events in Roy's past. At the time they had not seemed exceptional, but now he wondered what they meant.

That remarkably vivid dream of being in a trench during World War One – a conflict which occurred long before he was born. It was not just a picture – more a live-in movie, where he could hear, smell, touch, feel everything that went on. The sticky mud clung to his boots as he tried to escape the German soldier. The bayonet lunged and he knew that he was dead.

198

Or that other weird dream just a couple of years ago when he saw a huge disc of metal slide out from behind a cloud above his garden, and then drift behind another cloud. It was enormous. He pondered on how incredibly advanced any inhabitants must be. But, of course, that was nothing more than an ordinary dream – a science-fiction fantasy born of watching too much TV.

Later, things would happen that might begin to change his mind. There were incessant little happenings around the house that built to such a crescendo that he started keeping a careful log as they went on.

The time he left the bedroom to go out for a drink and returned to find the casually discarded coat hangars all lined up in neat little rows. Muriel swore she had not been in the room during the hour he had been away.

Or those several times when he left his slippers on the floor, averted his eyes for just a moment and turned back to find them stacked up heel to heel or toe to toe as if some modernist sculptor had decided they were works of art which could form fascinating geometric patterns.

Then there was that dream of their live-wire puppy, Fred, chasing two brightly clad cyclists and running out onto the road in their deadly path – followed by an eerily similar real incident days later. Fortunately, the dream had persuaded him to keep Fred on a very short lead. The dog tried to bolt after the bikes, but Roy's precautions had averted a disaster.

There were many electrical problems, too. The light bulbs switched themselves on and off in his presence, and sometimes when playing Scrabble with his computer, the words it displayed answered questions in his mind at the time! On one occasion the screen appeared to chide him for daring to glance idly through a 'girlie' magazine loaned by a friend.

But the most disturbing of all was the time his father had woken one morning to find Roy standing in the bedroom doorway, wearing nothing but his underpants. Puzzled, Mr Jones senior had got out of bed and switched on the light – only to find Roy's form disappearing like a mirage.

What was most astonishing about this was that Roy normally slept in the nude – but that night he *was* indeed wearing underpants.

Life was clearly far deeper and more meaningful than he had ever credited. But the Halloween apparition was the strangest thing of all, and had no logical explanation – at least, not one on this earth.

It continued to plague Roy's mind although he tried very hard to forget it. And then – three weeks afterwards – something more disturbing took place.

He was in the office at his drawing board, grappling with a tricky job. The time was about 3.30 p.m. Suddenly Roy's mind was invaded by the thought-form of that alien figure.

Oh God – I saw it again! He suddenly – inexplicably – knew.

But it was more than a knowing – it was a transportation. Just like his dream of the First World War trenches. Roy left his office as if carried off in a time machine and he was now back in his bedroom and there was the black-garbed figure – only inches from his face. Roy was lying on his side in the bed staring at the face with its pointed chin. The figure was so close it filled his vision.

During the other encounter he had never seen the entity full on, so this experience was adding new details. He could see that the mask was textured and looked a bit like very grainy photographic paper. Yet it was almost impossible to describe; neither dull nor flat, distinctly solid and yet unlike plastic or glass. It was something completely unknown in our world.

Roy stared at the creature and something far more terrifying began to happen ... The 'thing' was talking to him.

It was not talking in any normal way. The words were entering straight into Roy's mind. Yet, while the 'thing' was communicating in English, none of what it spoke made any sense. It was as if the words were being directed into the unconscious, by-passing any conscious understanding. Roy knew they were being force-fed to him for some purpose but was not being allowed to grasp their meaning.

A terrible sense of fear swamped his being – a form of pure horror that made him want to escape; although he did not know from what. Never had he known that such a distillation of raw human emotion was possible. It was numbing and smothered all other considerations.

The voice was still there – and it was an impossible voice. The only comparison was to take the deepest bass sound a human throat can utter, lower it a full octave, slow it right down and add a guttural reverberation. The whole ponderous result echoed within Roy's head.

Then – suddenly – it was all over. The demon voice was fading into distant echoes of its former self and Roy was back in the office, trying to shake the confusion from his mind. He gazed at the metal board in silence.

What *had* happened to him? Was he going insane? And had this new encounter that he had just lived through pre-dated or post-dated the previous episode?

It felt as if a switch had been thrown inside him, making him live through the very first meeting with this creature, when his great fear was that this hypnotic, rhythmic voice was forcing him into submission and preparing him for future encounters.

But future encounters with what? Where was all this leading?

Somewhere inside – locked away and out of reach – Roy knew the truth must lurk. When the time was right it would be released and he would *know*.

Perhaps there was a way to recover those messages – to discover why the entity had come for him. If he went to a doctor and asked to be hypnotized, would the lock gates open and the memories flood out?

He brushed the thought away with a chill.

It would not be easy to forget what had taken place, but he really felt it would be better if he *never* found that truth.

Sometimes what you did *not* know could hurt you less than what you forced yourself to comprehend.

There could be great security in ignorance.

NOVEMBER

5th An Arizona forestry worker, Travis Walton, was allegedly abducted by aliens in front of his colleagues in a forest on this date in 1975. He was 'returned' five days later. If this case is not a hoax, then it is an unusually long time for an abductee to be 'missing'. Hours, not days, is the norm.

8th Arch UFO debunker Philip Klass was born in Des Moines, Iowa, on this date in 1919.

9th On this date in 1934, Carl Sagan, popular science writer, was born in New York. Also, in 1979, a forestry worker in Livingston, Scotland, came across an object on the ground in a clearing. As he left the scene, several small objects, similar in appearance to sea mines, attacked him and dragged him to the ground where he blacked out. When he came to, his trousers were torn and he suffered nausea. Strange marks were left in the snow, and the police cordoned off the area. A plaque to commemorate the event was placed in the clearing in 1990.

15th In 1966, a car carrying four people was followed at speeds of up to 100 mph by a grey creature, tall as a man, with glowing red eyes and wings. This was just one of the many incidents involving the 'mothman' in West Virginia during the 1960s.

16th Travelling salesman Jack Angel woke up on this day in 1974 after sleeping for *four* days in his motorhome parked near a motel, Georgia. There was a burn on his chest, and his right hand was so badly burned it had to be amputated. Angel had no idea how this had happened. Neither the bed sheets nor any of the furnishings were damaged. No solution was ever found despite intensive investigation. Did Jack Angel survive spontaneous human combustion?

22nd In 1896, a 'winged airship' was spotted on this date over Oakland, California. This was just one of many such mystery airships observed over the USA, during a wave in that year. The airships seemed to be a precursor for modern UFO sightings.

26th In 1977, normal television transmission was interrupted in southern England by a message 'from outer space'. Although this was considered to be a hoax, no one was ever caught.

27th The day in 1978, when the United Nations discussed UFOs after pressure from Sir Eric Gairy, the prime minister of Grenada.

29th Todmorden police officer Alan Godfrey was allegedly abducted on this date in 1980, after confronting a hovering object blocking the path of his panda car. Other police officers in the area saw a blue light moving towards the West Yorkshire town.

Vacant Possession

◆

Harry Golding was a CID police officer, a secure job which carried prestige and paid well enough to allow the family to be choosy about where they lived.

They had decided to buy a wonderful house in Yeovil. Harry had loved it so much and it was incredibly cheap. But his wife, Stephanie, seemed to sense a strange atmosphere about the place. She announced that it was just not possible for her to live there and they had to decline the offer.

Then they found the house in Orchard Road.

The Somerset village-cum-town of Street nestles close to Glastonbury, one of the most famous of ancient places in England. Here, Joseph of Arimathea is reputed to have made a thorn bush spring into life from his wooden staff and there are legends going back many centuries that link the area with King Arthur's Knights and the Holy Grail.

But Orchard Road was rather different. The Goldings bought the attractive stone property from an old lady whose husband had died tragically, hanging himself in the outside coal shed. In fact, the residents of Street were full of tales of so-called ill-luck and other deaths in and around this part of the community. There was even talk of a ley – one of those reputed mysterious trackways – running right through the Goldings' house and heading for Glastonbury Tor.

But none of this had worried the Goldings. Stephanie, acutely tuned into such things, felt the house would be a happy one. And it was suitable for their large family.

On 5 November 1971 – the traditional and ritualistic Bonfire Night – they all moved into Orchard Road, blissfully unaware of what lay in wait.

The house was old. Nobody seemed quite sure how old, but it was at least a hundred years of age, and the way in which it appeared to have grown around a basic box-like starting-point, told of successive owners each trying to add their own touch to the original structure.

The stone was grey and the walls very thick. Originally there had just been a simple two-up, two-down cottage with a single entrance door. But there were now two extensions abutting the front, greatly increasing the interior space. Also a room had been built over the original kitchen and perched there somewhat perilously.

That kitchen was itself a joy to behold. Hardly altered in a century, it had bare stone walls and a flagged floor that attracted the damp. The room was not unlike one of those crazy houses you could find at funfairs, with angles juxtaposed in all directions. The heavy ceiling was so low that a very tall person might have to stoop and anybody could reach up and touch it with little effort.

Everywhere the building displayed its antiquity. Outside the rear door was an old-fashioned water pump. It functioned perfectly and the water seemed crystal clear. But since nobody was quite certain from where it originated they did not dare to taste it.

Stephanie had not seen the kitchen before their arrival, and looked at it now with less than wild enthusiasm. There was nothing labour-saving about it!

'If I had seen this before we moved in I would never have come here!' she ventured. But they all knew the die was cast. They just had to make the best of things and settle down to their new life in their country retreat.

They used all the large square rooms downstairs as living accommodation. These were part of the original house, but the hallway had been added later. Leading off this was a downstairs bedroom which was claimed by Stephen. At sixteen he was the eldest child in the family.

Up a short flight of stairs was another hallway with a second bedroom directly above Stephen's. The only girl, Sarah, who was seven, took that.

Next to Sarah's room a bathroom and another small flight of steps leading to the two oldest bedrooms. The parents occupied one of these, with the other two boys (Peter, nine, and little Patrick, just three-and-a-half) sharing the remaining room.

With so many rooms and unconventional spaces to fill the first few days were busy ones, getting through the unpacking process. But it was immediately apparent that there was something special about Orchard Road.

The weekend progressed cheerfully and on the Tuesday, Harry Golding was doing some cleaning when a strange sensation came over him – a strong feeling that he was being observed.

With so many children in the house, it is natural to assume that the observer was merely a member of the family. But as Harry turned he got a terrible shock.

Standing on the stairs, apparently gazing up at the busy worker, was a strange young boy aged around thirteen.

Harry was about to open his mouth to enquire who the visitor might be and how he had got into the house, when in a flash the boy disappeared.

Completely astonished by this, Harry Golding decided that it was either a trick of the light or something equally explicable and determined to say nothing to the others. Besides, all that this would achieve would be to frighten them unnecessarily.

However, later in the week, at about ten at night, Stephen came scurrying into the dining room where Harry and Stephanie were alone.

'Where's Peter?' he asked.

They thought for a moment then decided that he was in bed. It was well past the young boy's bedtime, of course.

'No, he's not,' Stephen told them.

'Well where is he then?'

'I've just seen him in the hall. I came out of my room and he was standing there in the middle of the passage. I turned round to shut my door and when I looked back he'd gone.'

Stephen reminded them that it was perfectly possible to see all this clearly. The lights were on in the hall and on the landing, as always.

'I came straight in here,' he added. 'There's nowhere else that Peter could have gone from the hall.'

'Well he's not here and hasn't been,' Stephanie insisted.

Stephen's father looked perturbed. 'Are you sure it was Peter?' he asked.

'Well – now you mention it he did seem rather tall. I thought, he's a bit big for Peter. But it had to be him, didn't it?'

The logic was impeccable. Aside from Stephen himself, Peter was the oldest and largest child in the house. There was no mistaking him for the petite Sarah or Patrick.

'Ah ...' Harry said quietly. 'I was not going to tell you this ... but ...' And then he reported his experience on the steps.

They discussed the consequences in a hushed manner and mutually agreed that it should remain a matter between the three of them.

'If there is a ghost in this house, it is best not to scare the children,' they all concurred.

Over that coming weekend the thought of their eerie visitor was not far from Stephanie's mind, especially as she worked alone in the kitchen frying chips. Suddenly a strange feeling came over her. That same acute sensation that her husband had described – complete and certain knowledge that somebody was watching.

Should she turn? Stephanie struggled with the decision. If she did not do so then the feeling would persist. She needed to know what was happening, but was wary of the outcome.

Turning softly – there he was. The young boy aged twelve or thirteen, just as the others had described him. He wore a brownish, somewhat old-fashioned suit. But he seemed to be very smart in appearance. Then, as if satisfied that his presence had been detected, the ghostly boy vanished like a light switch being flicked.

The weeks went by and gradually the family adjusted to living with their ghostly tenant. Indeed, Stephanie Golding began to wonder who *were* the tenants. Whilst they had moved in anticipating vacant possession, perhaps there were less corporeal occupants who were reluctant to give up the lease.

One Saturday lunchtime Peter came downstairs and collapsed into a chair looking ashen.

'I just met a boy on the stairs!' he blurted out.

The moment they had feared had now arrived. All their efforts to keep the matter of the ghost from the rest of the family had been to no avail.

Peter explained: 'I was coming down the stairs and this boy was walking up them.' He paused for effect. 'You know, I bet I walked right through him. I must have done.'

Sarah was by now looking very frightened by this revelation, but unflappable Patrick, who was eating,

208

seemed quite unconcerned.

The youngster – still not four years old – smiled and said to his middle brother, 'You don't have to worry, Peter. He's deady.'

Everyone turned to look at Patrick.

'Deady?' asked Peter.

'Yes – deady,' Patrick confirmed. 'Like *they* are.'

The word 'they' was stressed. It sent shivers down Mrs Golding's spine. Just what did their young son seem to know?

Patrick had always been a bright and enthusiastic lad. Just after he started to walk he would take a ruler or stick and hold it under his arm, with the end resting in his hand. His bearing was exactly like an officer in the army.

He must have been an army man in a past life, became a kind of family saying. But this was less of a joke when, soon after moving to Street, Patrick began to display amazing knowledge about the battle of Waterloo.

He was constantly surprising them all with facts and anecdotes belying his three years.

When they asked Patrick to explain his remark about '*they*' being dead, he did so willingly.

'Oh, it's my other mummy.'

'Who?'

'I call her that,' he advised. 'She's in the house. I see quite a lot of her. She's very nice and she tells me all these things.'

This news was disturbing. So far the adults had only contemplated the presence of a single ghostly lodger. Was Patrick claiming there were more of them?

That question was soon to answer itself.

It was 2 a.m. and Harry Golding awoke wanting to visit the bathroom. As he passed Peter and Patrick's bedroom, he saw the figure of a woman coming out of the door.

He knew that he had just left Stephanie in the main bedroom. So this was not her. Besides she looked totally different. Her hair was tied up in a bun, in a very old-fashioned style, and she had a rich-looking yellow dress that swirled down to her ankles.

Without telling anybody about this, and undecided whether to ever do so, Stephen made the decision academic. At breakfast he announced: 'You know, Dad, you went to the bathroom in the night?'

Harry Golding confirmed that he had done so.

'Well, I heard footsteps coming down the stairs and I thought you were going to get a drink. But they stopped at my door and there was this lady there, standing by the foot of my bed.'

Harry knew before Stephen spoke what her description would be, and it was indeed just as he had witnessed. Stephen added: 'I closed my eyes. But I wasn't a bit frightened. In fact, I felt so good and safe. You know what it's like when you are very little and your mum comes in to tuck you up and cover up your shoulders with the blankets? That's just how I felt.'

He hesitated, then included an afterthought. 'Oh yes — and there was this lovely smell of scented flowers. I'd smelt it before and wondered where it was coming from.'

So many strange things were now going on that they became an accepted part of everyday life in the house.

At 9 p.m. most nights the family would catch the scent of a burning candle as if someone was carrying it across the dining room. In the same room there was heard on many occasions the slow ticking of a grandfather clock; although there were no clocks in the room. And frequently one of the children would call out that he or she wanted some toast 'because the little boy is having some' and, sure enough, the delightful odour of hot, buttered toast was filling the room.

However, while Sarah heard the noises and smelt the smells, for some strange reason she never saw any of the spectral family.

Nor did anyone, other than Mrs Golding, ever meet the phantom father.

Once he appeared standing with one arm resting on the old mantelpiece above the now-removed range. He was extremely tall with black hair and wearing a dark suit. Stephanie could see small details of his clothing, including a cloak with many little capes and a white cravat with a pin in it. He seemed almost overdressed for life in a simple country cottage.

From this and the information which Patrick was picking up from his 'other mummy' Mrs Golding concluded that the ghost family had not lived in the house, but had merely stayed there for a time because their child was ill and he needed the country air to recuperate.

One of the best sightings of all was experienced by Stephanie Golding one night when she went to the boys' bedroom because she thought she heard them call out in the early hours.

They seemed fine and were fast asleep, so she left. But as she stepped onto the landing there stood the ghostly woman. She was only feet away, looking just like a real person and seemingly well aware that she had been spotted.

Her dress was primrose yellow and flowed down straight from a relatively high waistline. Her piled-up hair was brown, easily visible in the dim light from the landing.

'Hello!' Stephanie called, at which point the figure vanished just like a reflection shatters when you throw a stone into a pond.

By now, Patrick's knowledge of the Battle of Waterloo had continued to grow and he confidently explained how it came about.

'The lady says I was there. I was on my horse leading the men and I got ahead of them. Then there were these other men all around me. Before anyone could help me I was killed. Now she says I have to start all over again.'

In March 1976 the family had to leave the house and move to another part of the country because of Harry's job. It was a sad day, since they loved the house. Because they had to move before they actually sold Orchard Road, they never had the chance to tell the new owners about the tenants they might be taking on.

The children grew up and the strange events at Street grew dim in their memories. Patrick, for instance, no longer recalls anything about his 'other mummy' or the things that she told him about his death at Waterloo.

Once they travelled back to Somerset to visit their old home as it now is. They did not reveal the secrets of the house and there was no intimation from the new owners of any strange experiences.

Orchard Road had in fact been completely redesigned and refurbished. The inside had been stripped and new floors cut in. It looked nothing like the old-fashioned country homestead that the Goldings remembered.

They returned to their new home convinced that, just as they could not live in Orchard Road as it was now, neither could their ghostly companions. The house might well reflect the comforts of late twentieth-century living, but it had lost the appeal that had kept that spectral family clinging to its echoes across many years of time.

Like the Goldings, they too must have moved on.

A Bonfire Story

———————◆———————

The year 1926 was a watershed in British sociological and political history. It was the year of the Great Strike. Thousands of men and women, tired of working long hours for little pay, went on strike from Monday, 4 May. This was in support of the coal miners who were being asked to work an extended week for less money. For nine whole days the country was virtually on the brink of civil war. Even when the rest of the country went back to work, the miners continued to stay away, right into November of that year . . .

To a five-year-old boy, going on six, this all meant very little. Living in Bolton, the industrial centre of Lancashire, young Henry Thomson was more concerned with playing Cowboys and Indians and winning marbles than with the worries and hardships of the adult world. Like most little boys, Henry was mischievous, but his latest escapade was to land him in more trouble than he could ever have dreamed of, even in his darkest nightmares.

The events of 5 November – Bonfire Night – were still fresh in his mind as he lay in bed, and the memory of the fireworks, the sticky toffee and the baked potatoes was still vivid, although several days had elapsed since. It had been *great* fun. His mum and dad had let him stay up late, and it didn't matter that he had gone to bed all sooty, his hair and clothes smelling (to him) sweetly of bonfire smoke and the acrid fumes of the fireworks.

He lay under the bed covers in the dark room, eyes bright and feeling wide awake. By adult standards it was still early evening, although darkness had fallen around five o'clock. Henry grew envious – outside the terraced house he could hear his little pals still playing. He wanted to be with them, join in the fun, have a good time like the one they had all shared on 5 November. He tossed and turned but sleep was impossible, and an idea formed in his mind. Henry sat up and clasped his knees through the quilt. He knew what he would do.

Henry Thomson was an only child – an unusual situation in a world before the advent of The Pill and other modern birth-control methods. In fact it was normal for large families to fill cramped houses. But Henry was not *normal*, he was *special*, *gifted* even, something which would grow as the child blossomed into the man. As it was, unlike his friends, he had a bedroom to himself, which meant there was no one to know if he just quietly slipped out of the house ...

Stealthily, he climbed out of bed and quickly dressed, finally slipping on his shoes. He held his breath as his foot accidentally knocked against the chamber pot just tucked beneath the bed frame, but no one came to investigate. Heart in mouth, he stepped warily down the creaking stairs and into the scullery. The way was clear. His parents were in the sitting room listening to the radio. Henry slipped out of the back door and into the night.

It was chilly but fresh out there. Henry made his way across the yard and through the gate. It had been raining earlier and the cobbled streets were glistening, and sticky moisture still clung to the walls of the red-brick houses. Now the cloud was breaking up and stars shone like needle points.

The little boy's friends were delighted to see him. They decided to play hide and seek. In this version, half the gang would hide, then, shortly afterwards, the others would go in search. The seekers faced a wall while the others quickly disappeared. One of the older boys counted to fifty then they all turned round. The best plan, they decided, was to separate and search different areas. Henry volunteered to search the backs of Eustace Street and nearby Woodgate Street.

As he split from the others, he noticed bonfire debris littering the streets and numerous spent firework rockets drowning in the shallow puddles of dirty rainwater. He took all this in fleetingly. There were much more important things on his mind. For instance, where were his friends hiding?

The military-like rows of houses looked all the same. Each had a back yard and a gate – perfect hiding places for small boys playing games in the dark. And it *was* dark in the backs except where a sliver of light might escape through a chink in a curtained window. And it was quiet too, very, very quiet . . . Henry felt a moment of guilt as he saw a bedroom light being put out, probably on some small child being tucked up in bed, but the thought was soon gone as he concentrated on the search.

Most of the gates were closed, and he was not brave enough to open them in case he was caught by a grown-up visiting the outside lavatory. He ran past several ash pits, keeping as quiet as a church mouse; suddenly he stopped. *What was that in the yard of number 21?* The gate was ajar and something very strange had caught his eye ... Everything had its place, he knew that intuitively, whether it was his socks which always went in the left-hand drawer of the dressing-chest, or everything in Eustace Street itself, which to his young mind had probably been there ever since God had created the world.

The little boy in short trousers who should have been tucked up safely in bed, crept back to the gateway and peeped around. What he saw was to remain indelibly etched into his memory for ever.

The light from the scullery window spilled out onto the yard, making the zinc bathtub hanging by a nail from the adjacent wall glisten with the moisture from the earlier rain shower. But that was not what had caught his attention. Peering into the sash window were three figures. *And the figures did not look human.*

They were turned away from the boy, who stared in amazement. Two of them were around five foot eight, but the third, the one in the middle, was several inches taller. All three resembled the Michelin Man. They wore helmets and silver-grey suits ridged in thick padded horizontal bands, black boots, and on the back of each was mounted a box-like apparatus. Tubes from this 'box' led into the neck of the helmet.

As Henry peered around the edge of the open gateway, some small noise, or intuition he was unaware of, caused the creatures to turn. Three owl-like faces stared down at the small frightened boy. Their heads – or helmets – were doorknob-shaped, with two black slitted eyes, no mouth, but a vertical slit where the nose would be. It was this latter which gave the impression of an owl. A loud gargling, or mumbling, sound issued from the tall one in the middle, as all three suddenly advanced towards Henry.

The boy had seen enough. He ran home as fast as his little legs could carry him, and to the astonishment of his parents, burst into the house in blind panic. They were not amused. As far as they were aware, Henry should be in bed fast asleep. Now this, and an incredible story to boot about being chased by three strange figures wearing what sounded like diving suits.

Henry babbled out his story, and in reply his mother gave him a good old-fashioned clout about the ears. That was for sneaking out of the house *and* for telling lies! Mr Thomson was not impressed either. A serving police officer, he was used to villains spinning yarns to wriggle out of trouble. But this was a yarn and a half, fuelled, no doubt, by the boy's imagination. Henry was sent back to bed – this time to stay.

Little Henry Thomson never slept that night, and the next day he stuck rigidly to his story, much to the bemusement of his parents. PC Thomson especially was concerned. Any child with half a brain, having pulled the stunt Henry had pulled, would never mention the incident again – unless … Eventually they agreed that their son had indeed experienced something out of the ordinary. Either that, or he was mentally deranged.

Several weeks later, Henry was walking back from his grandma's house with his mother. There, in the crisp starry heavens, they noticed a bright 'star' moving towards them. As it passed overhead, it seemed to go right through the closed upstairs window of a house. Mrs Thomson was convinced it was a portent of death, and gripping her son's hand tightly, hurried on. Whenever Henry's strange encounter came up for discussion in the family, she always referred to it as 'a visitation by the three wise men'. Henry regarded this view as being a million miles from the truth. The strangely garbed creatures had done nothing but instill him with fear!

The boy grew up into the man, and with him developed a great talent which took several forms. An aptitude for drawing that emerged when a youngster developed, and he became a fully fledged artist. Henry left the rugged moorland of Lancashire for the wilder shores of the world. He discovered he possessed a 'photographic memory' which ensured he could recall every scene and every incident in his life in vivid detail.

'I can paint Cairo street scenes, or Tyrolean byways, many years after having visited them,' he said. Or remember as if it was yesterday, a frightening and bizarre incident which occurred one November to a little boy barely six years of age . . .

But Henry's talents developed along esoteric lines too. He began to exhibit all the hallmarks of a 'psychic'. He met a Scottish lass, called Janet, who was a medium, and they were married. The couple went to live in the Highlands, where Henry discovered he had some very strange powers.

I used to go for walks in the evenings and often saw what I became convinced were UFOs – bright moving 'stars' that suddenly stopped and went off at a tangent. Then one night I thought I would experiment. When a bright star came up over Ben Cruachan, I thought very hard for it to stop, go northwards, then zig-zag west and return to where its ballet began. Much to my surprise it did exactly that! I carried out this experiment on two or three occasions and every time the 'star' obeyed my mental command – whatever the pattern I had thought of!

Despite all this, Henry claims that he never took any of these experiences at face value. During his forty-five years of investigation into psychic phenomena he adopted a 'Sherlock Holmes' approach – 'Everything *must* have an explanation.' But nothing could have prepared him for the baffling experience which was to happen in 1956 – thirty years after his confrontation with the three entities. This latest episode had its roots in World War Two.

War broke out in North Africa on 10 June 1940, when Italy declared war on Britain. British forces plunged towards the Italian position on the border between Egypt and Libya, and in no time at all they were facing German forces under the command of Field Marshal Rommel. The conflict was to continue for almost three years, with both forces advancing and retreating a total of four thousand miles. Eventually Rommel was to lose.

Henry Thomson was caught up in that conflict, serving as a sergeant in the 8th Army under Field Marshal Montgomery. Henry describes it as 'a gentleman's war, a war without hatred'. Both sides were in an alien environment; a vast ocean of heat and sand. They shared and suffered the same discomforts: the flies, the dust, the heat ... the same death.

During his time in North Africa, Henry made many friends, but was drawn towards one in particular. This was a corporal named Alfie Hall, a plump-faced sandy-haired young man, six feet tall, and very popular with his comrades. Henry remembers him as 'a pretty good pal – almost like a brother'.

It was towards the end of the conflict, when the Germans were on the run, that Alfie met his death. They were marching through El Faiyum, in the north of Egypt, the sun blazing down, heat waves shimmering the rocky terrain ahead. One moment the two men were chatting together, the next there was an explosion. Corporal Alfred Hall had stepped on a landmine.

'There's no doubt about it,' Henry said, staring in front of him. 'Alfie was blown to smithereens.'

Needless to say, Henry never expected to meet his friend again.

After the war, Henry was demobbed and followed his aptitude for art and his interest in psychic experiences. By 1956, he and his wife were living in Blackpool. Henry had heard that a physic medium, called Jimmy Gardner, was visiting the town. Mr Gardner had a reputation for allegedly bringing about the materialization of spirits into temporary physical form. Henry was curious.

The venue was nothing spectacular. It was just a room over a shop which had been hired for the evening. Henry was one of about fourteen people who each paid two shillings to see the medium.

Materializations are allegedly produced from a substance called ectoplasm, which extrudes from the medium's body. It has been described as white, alive, and sensitive to heat. After it has taken the form of a deceased person it will return to the medium's body or just simply dematerialize. Mediums who can apparently bring about this phenomenon work while hidden behind a curtain. Critics claim this is because it makes trickery very much easier, but spiritualists say it is necessary to confine the ectoplasm to prevent it from drifting around the room before it can take form.

Henry could not imagine Jimmy Gardner capable of anything, much less trickery. The poor man was so riddled with arthritis that his limbs were deformed and twisted. He was seated in a wheelchair, and the most he could manage without it was no more than two shuffling steps. It had been a considerable struggle, getting the medium up the narrow stairs to the dusty room.

A companion manoeuvred the chair into a corner, and a black curtain was placed in front of it. There was barely room for anyone else behind the curtain, and this was not a stage in a theatre – there were no trap-doors, no back exits. Just a corner, in a room, above a shop. The money taken at the door might just about pay the man's travelling expenses.

Henry was not sure what to expect. He sat with several elderly women, a few younger women who had dragged their husbands along, and one or two men like himself. They had just come to *see*.

'It was amazing! During the evening, six or seven figures materialized in the room; "Aunt Alices", little girls – every one of them recognized by someone in the room as a person they had known who had passed away. The figures were not the least bit ethereal. They looked and acted like normal human beings, and even held conversations with their surviving relatives.'

Yet there did not seem to be any way in which trickery could be involved. Apart from the fact that there was barely room for anyone else behind the curtain because of the wheelchair, Jimmy Gardner – or indeed anyone else – could not have known in advance who was going to attend the séance.

Suddenly, a new figure stepped out from behind the curtain. He was six feet tall and wearing an army uniform. As his face turned towards the light Henry let out a gasp. It was his old pal Alfie Hall, looking exactly like he did moments before the bomb blast. Still twenty-two years old, still smiling in a face turned brown by the burning desert sun.

The 'man' who was Corporal Alfred Hall walked towards Henry and held out his hand.

'Hello, Hen,' he said, using the diminutive of Henry's name as he had used it in the army. Henry took the hand and was surprised to find it warm and perfectly normal. Alfie laughed, slammed his stunned friend on the back, and said, 'Are you surprised to see me?'

During the next few minutes, Alfie reminisced about old times, reminding Henry of things even *he* had forgotten.

'Do you remember that time in the Naafi when that fool Evans knocked a cup of hot coffee all down the Colonel?'

Henry did, *he did*!

Finally, Alfie Hall assured his friend that he was very happy where he was; and with that he prepared to leave. Alfie looked perfectly *normal*, perfectly *solid*, indeed he was warm to the touch, and Henry could still feel that slap on the back. But as the soldier walked towards the black curtain, his form became vague, transparent, until it had evaporated into nothing . . .

Henry Thomson talks in a very assured, rational manner. The fact that he is talking about *ir*rational things should not detract from his sincerity nor his ability to distinguish fact from fantasy and wish fulfilment. His wife has earned quite a reputation for herself as a medium, and astrologer Russell Grant is a family friend.

Henry views his childhood confrontation with the strangely garbed figures and his later experience with a dead man as quite separate unconnected events. Yet if the physical materialization of the dead *can* happen, then why not the materialization of alleged extraterrestrials?

'The three of them were quite solid,' he muses. 'They were definitely there, there was no doubt about it. They cast shadows and made a noise when they rushed to grab me. I will never forget it ...'

The burnt-out rockets in the back street of that 1920s Lancashire town were only spent fireworks. The three entities peering through the window of the terraced house may have travelled there by quite a different vehicle.

DECEMBER

4th At 3 p.m. on this day in 1872, the frigate *Mary Celeste* was found abandoned at sea. All ten crew were missing but there was no sign of panic. Indeed, some accounts state that places were set ready for dinner.

7th During this day and the next, in 1968, pennies began bouncing onto the pavement in Ramsgate, Kent. Some forty to fifty coins came in short scattering bursts for about fifteen minutes.

13th In 1868, three reputable gentlemen claimed to have witnessed the famous Victorian medium, D.D. Home, levitate out through one window of a house and float back in through another.

14th The famous seer, Nostradamus, was born in St Remy on this date in 1503. People claim that his verses foresaw the two world wars and the rise of Hitler, and many other world events still to come. Critics, however, point out the ambiguity of much of his material.

16th Scottish nanny Carol Compton, arrested in Italy on charges of arson and attempted murder, was set free in 1983 after a five-day trial. Three villas where she worked suffered mysterious fires, and in one case damage assessed at £5000 occurred. Although Carol was present when all the fires broke out, including one in a child's cot, there was never any evidence to directly link her with them. Was Carol an unwilling medium for a particular type of poltergeist activity?

20th Metal-bender Uri Geller was born on this date in 1946 in Tel Aviv, Israel.

21st On this day in 1955, a family in Hopkinsville, Kentucky, had a shoot-out with some creatures who invaded their farm. The entities reportedly had glowing yellow eyes, large ears and claws.

24th The *British Journal of Photography* exposed the 'Cottingly fairy' photographs as hoaxes, in 1982. These pictures, taken by two Yorkshire girls, just after World War I, fooled such notables as Sir Arthur Conan Doyle for over sixty years.

27th In 1981, a bear was reported on the loose on Hackney Marshes near London. Despite an intense search involving police, the animal remained elusive.

29th Betty Cash, Vickie Landrum and Vickie's seven-year-old grandson, Colby, were driving towards Dayton, Texas, when a diamond-shaped object appeared and hovered over the road. When it flew off again it was escorted by about twenty-three military helicopters. The effect of this experience on the three witnesses was devastating. Among other things, they claimed to have suffered hair loss, cancers and burns. They tried to sue the American government for $20 million, but in August 1986 the case was dismissed on the grounds that the device did not belong to the USA.

The Miracle of Hollywood

◆

The roads of California are choking with cars. In and around the giant metropolis of Greater Los Angeles, which has no subway system and with bus transportation limited by the frantic and sticky climate, it is almost impossible to move unless you drive one of the millions of vehicles that ply the congested roads.

The pride of the over-stuffed highways is the Hollywood Freeway that streams out of the downtown area towards the glamorous suburbs such as Hollywood and Beverly Hills.

A British motorway can occasionally jam in all four lanes, but the Freeway has four lanes heading in either direction and still the traffic clogs as it pours forward at 60 m.p.h. This is close to the maximum speed that the American law or its driving conditions will allow. Yet despite such precautions there can be extremely hairy moments for the unwary traveller.

It was at the turn of 1975–1976 when Jessica L. Bellman and her mother were driving east down the Freeway in particularly heavy traffic.

In LA, 'rush hour' is a relative term, as often the nightmare can last most of the day. But at these peak periods the conditions are even worse than normal.

Such were the circumstances here. Jessica's mother, Anne, was driving their small runaround in the outer 'fast' lane directly behind an enormous van. Jessica monitored the situation warily. It was just like riding in the shadow of a giant wall. But Anne was a good driver. She knew the road. Everything would be all right.

In front of the van, masked and invisible, was a thick sludge of traffic that was almost bumper to bumper and yet moving at speed. This can be the time when conditions are most dangerous, for with no car going faster than another, the unchanging pattern seems to instill a false sense that speeds are much lower than they really are.

But if you run into anything at 60 m.p.h. the outcome is catastrophic.

Conversation was drifting on as Anne half focused on the van and let automatic pilot guide her less conscious movements.

But then – total disaster! In one brief instant the van

ahead gave a sudden lurch. Its wheels were locking and the unseen driver was losing control. Swerving madly it careered over to the left-hand side, dancing a jig as its driver struggled desperately to regain possession of the vehicle.

Luckily for the van driver, being in the fast lane made all the difference. There was nothing bar the hard shoulder to his left and no vehicles blocking the path. Masterfully, he succeeded in bringing the beast to heel and screeched the tons of metal to a halt in almost perfect front-forward posture.

However, in the two seconds that it took for this to happen, the sense of danger became acute within the minds of both Anne and Jessica.

For the road ahead now gaped wide. Where the van had once been there was a small hole, just a few yards long. Beyond that the line of traffic was nose to tail, as it was behind them.

There was just no space in which to manoeuvre. No way in which there was room to brake. Yet, that was the only course of action open to them.

With all the instincts of self-preservation, Anne slammed on the brakes. At such speed that in itself was a highly dangerous thing to do. But it was precisely what anybody *would* choose in the same situation.

Unable to continue dead ahead, unable to swerve left because the van was in that welcoming spot, Anne glanced quickly at the three lanes to her right. Every single one was packed with cars. There was nowhere for her to escape.

Whatever, Anne had braked so hard that the car was sent into a wild spin, wheeling and circling like some crazy circus dancer. Except that this particular side-show had only one certain outcome. The oncoming traffic loomed and, as they flew with the wind and their devastating impetus, both women knew that there was no way to avoid smashing into several other vehicles in lanes two, three and four.

Jessica turned in that moment of extreme panic and

looked at her mother, sitting just inches from her side. The older woman had her eyes fixed firmly on the road as if this simple act would dissolve the enormity of their plight.

Jessica herself gripped the dashboard tight and put her right hand, palm outspread, onto the side window. An eerie silence enveloped the car as they ploughed on towards the other traffic – now forming a blurred stream of colourful metal.

For an instant the two women's eyes met and seemed to exchange a silent prayer.

'Oh, my god, this is it! We are going to die!' The words – either thought or spoken – filled their minds.

And it was not a question, or a possibility. It was an absolute certainty. There was no way out of their predicament.

They were truly doomed.

Earlier in her life, Anne Bellman had experienced something very strange. For many years she had felt herself subjected to a presence.

It started one day when she settled down in bed and suddenly knew with an overpowering awareness that there was someone – or something – in the bedroom alongside her.

Opening her eyes she looked into the darkness, but nothing had been visible. And then she felt the bedclothes being pressed down on her. There was no doubt about it – someone was walking on the bed in a circle round her body!

After that occasion, it would happen often. Whenever Anne lay on a bed or a sofa, the same experience would be repeated. But she never felt frightened or worried by these events. Indeed, it was a very friendly presence.

As if something was protecting her.

Jessica opened her eyes for a moment. They must still be sweeping across the Freeway in their ill-fated vehicle. But what was most peculiar was the total lack of any sound.

226

It was as if they had suddenly been plunged to the bottom of a very deep well. Jessica knew that the traffic always made a rumbling sound, even when you were inside a car. Given their present dilemma, there should be screaming brakes and honking horns and all the other signs of hysteria as the other drivers frantically sought to escape the instrument of death that was spinning uncontrollably across their path.

Yet there was none of this. In fact there was nothing. Not even the car engine or the wheels were making any noise. No sound of tyres bursting under the pressure or metal grinding against metal.

It seemed like they were gliding silently through the air or had slipped into another dimension where the Hollywood Freeway was just a scene that was projected like some backdrop in a movie.

The faces of two men swam past Jessica's vision. They were inside a car; laughing and talking, smiling and changing gears. But how could they not be aware of what was happening?

It was as if Jessica, her mother and their car were totally invisible.

Suddenly, there was a jolt and the car was still.

Jessica sat motionless, breathing deeply and sobbing to herself, 'Oh God! I'm dead!'

But they were not dead. Somehow the car was on the right-hand hard shoulder at an angle to the road, so that the rear jutted out into the oncoming traffic of the slow lane.

With superb reflexes Anne pushed the car into reverse, backed onto the lane and drove down the Freeway for a few hundred yards.

Still the silence washed over them. Neither woman spoke. It was as if they were under a spell – protected by some magic cocoon.

Then Anne pulled the car off the road and parked expertly on the shoulder. As she did so she let out a scream, piercing the silence and breaking all the tension. Jessica gulped hard and swallowed warm air. All the sound was now descending onto them like a deluge of water when the surf hits the beach at Malibu.

Still shaking, they sat there for some minutes recovering a modicum of composure.

'What happened?' Jessica forced out.

'I don't know,' said Anne, shaking her head.

'How did we get here . . .?' Jessica asked as she took in the three lanes piled up with moving traffic. There was the bustling fast lane, from which they had somehow miraculously departed without mishap.

Jessica mentioned the two men in the car that had passed by. 'They didn't even seem to see us,' she noted. 'It was just as if we weren't there.'

They spoke a lot about miracles and a guardian angel 'protecting' them but none of this accounted for the practicalities.

Just *how* could they cross four lanes of dense and swiftly moving traffic without hitting a single vehicle?

Just *how* could they do this without any other driver even noticing that they were spiralling across the Freeway?

Just *what* was that weird silence that swallowed up the whole area as they scythed through the dense traffic on the highway?

There were no answers to any of these questions. The two women were left simply thanking someone – or something – who must remain unknown.

'There must be a logical answer,' Jessica insisted.

But must there?

Perhaps this was just another miracle of Hollywood.

If You Go Down to the Woods

◆

Lieutenant-Colonel Charles Halt surveyed the scene as he walked into the dark interior of Rendlesham Forest. The

Suffolk countryside was very still as he prepared for what promised to be an interesting night.

Several other men were with him, but this was still an unnerving experience. Halt knew why they were out here: to search for evidence of a reported UFO that had come down in the woods. Lumbering motorized 'light-alls' accompanied the party to illuminate the way towards whatever they might find. But there was some sort of infuriating energy drain and they just weren't working properly.

Halt fingered the small office tape recorder he had brought out with him and spoke disdainfully into the microphone:

'Ah – one hundred and fifty feet or more from the initial ... I should say *suspected* ... impact point. Having a little difficulty – we can't get the light-all to work. Seems to be some kind of mechanical problem. Gonna send back and get another light-all.'

He clicked the switch and flipped off the recorder. Best to be methodical and register this expedition by the book.

It was his choice to be out here in the dead of night. He could be back in bed, like those people in the village slumbering peacefully in their post-Christmas stupors.

Looked at rationally, it was a crazy idea. Yet he had a responsibility to find out the truth, and those men who made the report did seem to have been very disturbed by something.

They said it was a UFO – and a UFO near a NATO air base could pose a problem.

The base was actually twin bases housing the 81st Tactical Fighter Wing, with its squadrons of A-10 'Tank-buster' aircraft, screaming noisily over the farms and cottages. The tranquillity of the little population centres such as Hollesley, Sudbourne and the market town of Woodbridge was a fragile thing when any big operation was underway.

Bentwaters was the main centre, with four of the six aircraft squadrons, but it was linked to the smaller unit at

Woodbridge, just a two-mile jaunt through the pine trees. And Woodbridge had its own star attraction: the 78th Aerospace Rescue and Recovery Squadron – trained with giant helicopters to pick up astronauts from the North Sea. Not that such a mission had ever become necessary – so far.

Since Christmas Day all manner of activity had been going on in what was normally a slack time.

First, there had been the huge light in the sky on Christmas night itself. Aircraft over Eastern England had seen it, but the official explanation was that it was just some space junk – part of a Soviet satellite coming back through the atmosphere in spectacular fashion.

And then there had been that report made by a patrolman from the East Gate of Woodbridge that a light had come down into the woodland. An aircraft crashing in flames? A bright meteor? Who knows, but it had to be investigated.

So it was – and three of his men had gone out there and confronted a structured craft about the size of a Mini car which they had chased through the forest. The base was seething with rumours about the incident. That one guy had closed in and tried to climb on top of it, as if he were some cowboy rounding up a steer. That another had been spaced out by the whole experience and was taking some time to be coaxed back home, because he was convinced 'they' were coming back and he wanted to be there.

Now – this incident – the third inside the last couple of days, telling of a glow in the trees that had been radioed through by a security patrol officer.

In charge of the security team that night was Sergeant Alan Benson, a good man. He could be trusted to sort things out.

Benson had been at Woodbridge on business round midnight, near the alleged part of the forest when the sighting occurred. He immediately told his section commander, Lieutenant Bruce Englund, who realized that he needed authorization and so had checked it over with

Halt. The Lieutenant-Colonel was officially deputy base commander for the twin bases, but that night he was in acting charge. This was his baby and he had no intention of screwing it up.

Alan Benson, Bruce Englund and the flight chief went out to the location and met up with Charles Halt. Several other men were there too. Despite the late hour quite a pantomime was unfolding.

Halt inevitably had very definite ideas of who should be allowed into the dense thickets of trees down the little track that was a forestry access road. He set about selecting suitable personnel, some of whom seemed young and fairly inexperienced. The rest had to stay back as the team battled out to the 'suspected impact point' with the defective light-alls and an engine that needed coaxing. The wretched truck at times just wouldn't seem to go.

It was now after 1 a.m. and new light-alls were in position. They seemed to be functioning satisfactorily. The chief of base security, Major Malcolm Zickler, and one of the base disaster-preparedness officers, Sergeant Nevells, were reportedly out there too.

After all, they could not have any idea what they were about to face. If it was a plane that had gone down, then disaster was the right word for it. If it was a UFO – like the earlier reports implied – then there didn't seem to be *any* right word for it!

Charles Halt switched the tape back on. 'Okay – we're now approaching to within about twenty to thirty feet of the area. What kind of readings are we getting? Anything?'

The question was addressed to Sergeant Nevells who was using a form of geiger counter to test for radiation. On a half-a-millirem scale it should be giving a figure of about two or three units – *if* the area was normal.

'Just minor clicks,' the operator confirmed.

'Where are the impressions?' Halt enquired, surveying the tall Scotch pines in their closely packed and soldierly formation. In the dark it was very hard to see anything at all, but some landing traces were supposed to be here.

A hand pointed them out.

'Is that as big as they are?'

'There's a better defined one over here,' someone noted.

Sergeant Nevells reported that they were up to four units on the counter – slightly above what the background level should be.

Halt could now see that there were three indentations in the ground that were marked with stakes in a roughly circular area between trees. The counter was used to check each of the 'pod' marks for level.

At the third spot Nevells picked up. 'Yeah – now I'm getting some residual. The meter's giving off a little pulse.'

Halt nodded. Fine – they must do this right. 'Let's go to the centre of the area next and see what kind of reading we get there ... Ah, are you reading the clicks? I can't hear them ... Is that about the centre, Bruce?'

Bruce Englund confirmed that both answers were affirmative. But the geiger counter was speaking for itself.

'That's about the best deflection needle I've seen yet,' Halt enthused, peering at it. 'Can you give me an estimation – we're on the point five scale and we're getting? ...'

Nevells read off the amount: '... That's about half a millirem.'

They all knew enough to realize this was stronger than it should be. Something was causing the counter to give excessive radiation readings. Suddenly they seemed somewhat vulnerable in that vast wood.

Then a 'blast area' appeared right underneath their noses and the two geiger counters started to screech.

'This thing's about to freak!' Nevells advised.

'Yours too,' cried Halt, looking at the spare.

They were now reading seven-tenths on the scale – seventy per cent of maximum. But the Lieutenant-Colonel, knowing his job, still spoke calmly into the tape: 'We've found a small blast – what looks like a blasted or scruffed-up area here – we're getting very positive readings.'

No sense in taking any chances, they should be prepared in case the area was really hot. '... Okay, I've got the gloves on now. Let's make a sweep of the whole area about ten feet out – make a perimeter run around it. I'm gonna depend on you to count the clicks.'

Gingerly the group of US Air Force officers edged around the three 'pod' marks, which they labelled '1', '2' and '3'. On the trees facing in towards these holes there were some strange abrasions.

'You're right about the abrasions,' Halt acknowledged. 'I've never seen a pine tree that's been damaged react that fast.'

A frantic search for something to capture the evidence followed.

'You got a sample bottle to put that in?' Halt asked. 'Right let's identify that as point number one ... That stake. Got that, Sergeant Nevells?'

'Closest to the Woodbridge base,' the disaster specialist checked.

But before Halt could affirm this the radio jumped into life, with a message from 'Alpha One Security'.

'Ah – we got two other personnel requesting permission to come out to the site.'

The security officer on site flipped the button on the microphone and barked in a no-nonsense voice: 'Tell them *negative* at this time. We'll *tell* them when they can come out here. We *don't* want them out here right now.'

Meanwhile, Charles Halt was proceeding with the sample gathering operation – telling the others to collect some of the sap and include it in sample number one. When satisfied this was progressing successfully, he returned to his dictation into the machine.

'There's a round abrasion on the tree – about three and a half to four inches in diameter. Looks like it might be old – but there's a crystalline sap.' He examined the sap. It looked very peculiar.

Another tree facing the centre of the landing site was found to have similar damage. Halt – with astonishment growing by the minute – saw that further proof was necessary. 'Okay – why don't you take a picture of that. Remember your picture, Neil. I'll be writing it down ... Oh, it's coming out on the tape.' He checked with the recognition, then added: '... Your first picture will be between marks two and three.'

'Anyone got a tape measure?' the Sergeant asked.

Halt proceeded to document matters: 'You're getting readings on the trees you're taking samples from, on the side facing the suspected landing site?'

'Four clicks max,' Nevells agreed.

'Up to four. Interesting ... Make sure where you're taking a sample. That's the strongest part of the tree.'

The officer with the other counter was meandering around the trees away from the landing spot. 'If you go to the back,' he reported in his drawling southern accent, 'there're no clicks whatsoever.'

Halt picked up on that. 'No clicks at all on the back – it's all on the side facing ... the, ah ... interesting.'

The men decided it was time to bring out the 'star-lite' scope which was used to check for heat sources. You could use it to hunt for living bodies buried in dangerous hidden positions, e.g. under rubble, because even a small amount of heat gave off infra-red radiation and was turned into light.

A spotlight was shone onto the area under study and the scope was focused in. Then the beam was switched off. If there was radiation the area would now glow faintly through the excitation of atoms from the light.

'Hey! You're right!' the commander yelled. There was a white streak on the trees and in the various pod marks on the ground. 'This is *eerie* ... A white spot ... this is *strange*.'

At that instant a high-pitched warble began. Some sort of alarm was being triggered.

'Oops!'

'Watch you don't step on it ... Let's step back – don't step all over it,' Halt warned them back from the precious trace marks.

From the new vantage point, Halt spoke into the

machine again: 'There's some type of abrasion on the ground where the pine needles are all pushed back and we get a high radioact ... er, a high *reading* ... You're sure there's a positive after-effect?'

The man using the star-lite scope affirmed: 'Yes – there is, definitely. There *is* an after-effect. It seems that when the lights are turned off and once we are focused in and allow time for the eyes to adjust we are getting an indication of a heat source coming out of that centre spot ... which will show up on the ...'

'Heat or some form of energy,' Halt cut in and reminded. 'It's hardly heat at this stage of the game.'

They all pondered the implications of these 'pods', the radiation readings, the damage to the trees and the gaping holes in the pine canopy overhead – suggesting that something had *indeed come down* from the sky and landed on the ground, just as the eye-witness reports seemed to indicate.

As they were still measuring, great confusion arose in the background. There were calls through the radio about a light being seen. Then the forest erupted into a cacophony of noise. The deer, rabbits and birds were being stirred into life and cows and sheep from a nearby farm were kicking up a rumpus. In the middle of the night this was certainly most unusual.

The commander flipped the switch on his recorder: '01.48 hours – we're getting very strange sounds from a farmer's barnyard animals ... very, very active – making an awful lot of noise.'

But then his words were interrupted by a cry from one of the men.

Halt cut short the excited jabbering: 'You just saw a light – where? ... Calm down ... Where?'

The man who had been taking the samples directed his superior: 'Right on this position – here – straight ahead between the trees ... There it is again ... Straight ahead of my flashlight beam – there it is!'

Halt saw it. All the men saw it. 'What is it?' the commander asked soberly.

'We don't know, sir,' the witness admitted.

Everyone started to talk at once suggesting options. Could it be a house light? A fire? A lantern?

Brushing the suggestions aside, the Lieutenant-Colonel spoke into the recorder: 'It's a strange small red light – maybe a quarter, a half mile out – maybe further – I'm gonna switch off now.'

He turned off the machine and they concentrated on the glow that was pulsating in a slow rhythm through the trees.

The night was misty and this throbbing glow seemed to be cutting through the haze from some distance away. Halt ordered the men to douse all the flashlights so they could see better and then he spoke into the tape again, giving details of the slowly pulsating light.

It had a cycle of four or five seconds on/off and was reddish in colour. It was estimated to be 110 to 120 degrees (i.e. east-south-east) from where they stood on the edge of the forest, and looked to be low down towards the ground.

Remembering to keep the tape going and despite the awesomeness of the situation, Halt proposed that they move out into the open.

As they moved into the field adjoining the wood, he recorded: 'The light is still there and all the barnyard animals have gone quiet now ... I'm through to the clearing. Still getting a reading on the meter.'

Sergeant Nevells confirmed this, and the bearing of the light. Someone noted: 'I think it's something along the ground. It's something very large.' But they could all see that.

With his voice beginning to display the emotion he was surely feeling, Halt reported: 'We're about 150 to 200 yards from the site. Everything else is just deathly calm. There's no doubt about it. There's some type of strange flashing red light ahead.'

'Sir, it's yellow,' one of the men pointed out.

Halt concurred: 'I saw a yellow tinge in it too ...

236

Weird!' He hesitated, uncertain of what he was seeing. Then he felt a growing conviction. 'It appears to be moving a little bit this way. It's brighter than it has been. *It's definitely coming this way*!'

As the trained military officers watched, they could see the large glowing form ahead of them in the trees. It was basically red on top but there was a new and very disturbing effect. It seemed as if it were splitting into rainbow colours that were being thrown all over the place.

'Pieces of it are shooting off!' Halt exclaimed. 'There's no doubt about it – this is *weird*!'

Some members of the little expedition were by now standing in astonishment, gazing at the thing. They had come out here hunting for traces of an object that had reportedly come down on a previous occasion – a mystery plane or a UFO. The last thing they expected was to confront something like this.

And they were out in the heart of the country, at least a mile from any reinforcements.

Two other lights were now visible. Halt kept repeating phrases like: 'There's something very, very strange,' as if this might help.

Suddenly one of the men called out: 'It just moved to the right.'

'Yeah – strange – whew!' Halt agreed. Then proposed: 'Let's approach the edge of the woods up there. Want to do it without lights?'

Nobody was going to argue with their commander. He seemed remarkably in control of things; although his words were showing increased inflexions as he gave his running commentary on tape.

'We're looking at this thing and we're probably about two to three hundred yards away. It's kind of like an eye looking at you, winking. It's still moving from side to side and when you put the star-lite scope on it, it sort of has a hollow centre – a dark centre – like the pupil of an eye and through the star-lite scope the flashes are so bright it almost hurts your eye.'

Undaunted, they crossed the little road that separates the clearing from the farmer's land – actually a large family homestead owned by gamekeeper Vic Boast. A second field lies beyond with a tiny stream running towards the coast, where the Orford Ness Lighthouse lay winking just four miles east-south-east.

Halt continued: 'We've passed the farmer's house and crossed into the next field and now we have multiple sightings of up to five lights with similar orbits.'

Everywhere they looked in the sky there seemed to be strange forms.

The recorder was now switched off more than it was on. It was difficult concentrating on anything but the events unfolding about them.

'Just crossed the creek,' Halt remembered to report. Then he asked for readings. The meter was still giving three clicks – indicating more or less normal levels.

An hour had now passed since they first saw the object and then set off on this quest from the landing site amidst the trees. They had no real idea where they were in the misty darkness, except that it was somewhere between the forest and the coast south of Orford. By now the glow appeared to be more distant and Halt recorded: 'Looks like it's clear out towards the coast – right on the horizon. Moves about a bit and flashes from time to time. Still steady and red in colour.'

Although they had now been out in the cold of the December night for several hours, nobody was eager to leave. At 3.05 a.m. two half-moon shapes had suddenly appeared in the distant sky to their north and seemed to be jigging about. After a minute or so they turned into complete circles, as if part of them had been obscured by a dark and lightless surface for a time. All these events amazed the officers. Standing in the trees hemmed in by UFOs was a new experience for them and they could do little but watch in quiet stupefaction.

At 3.15 a.m. things began to happen quicker and more intensely than any of them anticipated.

'Now we've got an object about ten degrees directly south,' Halt commented. But the moon shapes were still visible too. Indeed ... 'The ones to the north are moving away from us,' he pointed out.

The officer with the southern accent cried agreement: 'It's moving out fast.'

Nevells added: 'This one on the right is heading away too.'

The commander mulled this over, but then split the night with a warning: 'Mmm. They're both heading north ... *Hey!* ... Here he comes from the south. He's coming toward us now ...'

There was no doubt in the minds of these men that Charles Halt was right. The reddish glow was sweeping across the forest as if deciding that the game was over and it was coming to get them.

Alan Benson, who had been quiet throughout much of the proceedings, now saw from his location that after a long period of observing just lights they were about to experience a very close encounter.

A roughly plate-like shape was coming at them, with a red light on top and a bank of blue lights around the rim. Beneath it was a curtain of yellowish mist and rainbow colours as if diffused by a prism.

Halt, his voice breaking up, croaked into the recorder: 'Now we observe what appears to be a beam coming down towards the ground ... *This is unreal.*'

The 'thing' came down into the clearing where Benson stood. In terror and disbelief he watched it begin to close in. Then it shot away at such an amazing speed that it almost seemed to vanish in a flash. As it did so a cold blast of wind hit the men.

Sergeant Benson, in his terror, saw scenes from his past life rush through his mind. Perhaps this was going to be the end.

Minutes went by, during which nobody was in a fit state to have spoken anything into the recorder. Slowly, Halt flipped the switch again to report that the lights to the north were still in the sky. He added, in tones of disbelief and finality: 'We're turning round and heading back towards the base.'

Two weeks later, after discussion with Squadron Leader Donald Moreland, the British base commander acting as a sort of caretaker over the American occupants, Charles Halt decided to set down an official memo on the fantastic episode. He then despatched it to the Ministry of Defence in Whitehall.

An RAF base at Watton in Norfolk had reputedly recorded some of the incidents on radar and US intelligence staff had already taken the tapes for analysis. But it was the Lieutenant-Colonel's duty to inform his British allies, from whom the Americans merely leased the twin bases.

Halt headed his memo 'Unexplained Lights' and described the first encounter with the plate-like object that had landed in the clearing. Then he spoke of the discovery of the traces and the radiation readings and the subsequent sighting made by himself, and others, of various lights.

He did not mention many details, including those of the close encounter, as he was not sure how the sceptical British Defence Ministry would react to such information. Halt was understandably careful, knowing that the MoD might not look too kindly on an officer who saw strange things. He was inevitably forced to be cautious without the reassurance that they would take him seriously.

He also did not mention that he had put all the events on tape, 'live', as they occurred, or that the group had taken plaster casts of the traces and photographs of some of the incidents. Some of the pictures were fogged, but others were not.

Halt signed the report and sent it to London. Neither he nor Squadron Leader Moreland heard anything further about the matter.

Later the American officer *was* promoted to full Colonel and appointed base commander. After several more years at Bentwaters he was sent back to the USA. Most of the other men who had witnessed the encounters were re-assigned within a few weeks of the events.

About a month after the encounters, on orders from the Forestry Commission, the area where the traces were discovered was cleared. Before any hint of the events leaked out to the public the site had become just a wasteland of tree stumps.

When news did filter out that something mighty strange had happened in that forest, the British government denied any knowledge and continued to do so for over two years.

In April 1983 the Ministry of Defence wrote to Jenny Randles at the third request and confirmed that 'USAF personnel did see unusual lights ...' and that '... no explanation for the occurrence was ever forthcoming.'

In June 1983 the memo sent by Halt to the British government was released under the Freedom of Information Act in the USA to UFO researchers who had been approached by a now retired airman.

In August 1983 Jenny Randles took this memo to the Ministry of Defence, admitting possession of a document whose existence had been denied since December 1980, knowing that she might be contravening the Official Secrets Act by having possession of it.

The MoD accepted the report as genuine, were satisfied by the way in which it had been obtained and said they had no further evidence on the case because they considered that the events had *not* been a security threat.

In October 1983 Questions were asked in the House by Conservative MP and NATO Defence Committee member, Major Sir Patrick Wall. The then Armed Forces Minister, John Stanley, agreed that he had seen the Halt memo but saw nothing of defence relevance in it.

In 1984 similar sentiments were expressed, with a comment of 'nothing further to add' when former chief of staff at the ministry, Lord Hill-Norton, former head of the relevant MoD department, Ralph Noyes, Alliance MP, David Alton, and several other influential sources all tried to crack the secrecy surrounding this case.

At the same time the British government denied that there was any substance to claims of radar tracking, or that any photographs, samples or tapes of the incident had been obtained. These claims were also denied under the US Freedom of Information Act.

Shortly afterwards the tape on which the foregoing *true* story was based was released to investigators by Colonel Sam Morgan, former commander at Bentwaters.

Morgan stated that he believed the tape was genuine and the men involved in the encounters that it reported were apparently sincere.

So it is up to you to make up your own mind what *really* happened when a group of trained and fearless US servicemen dared to go down to the woods one night . . .

DEATH

The Man on the Stairs

———————— ◆ ————————

Linda Pall's father was dead. After a long and fruitful life he had contracted the terrible disease of asbestosis, and with the poison building up in his lungs he had finally succumbed to the pain and suffering.

It was now August 1988, two months after his passing, and the family were preparing for the placing of the headstone above his grave.

The night before the ceremony, Linda could not help but think about the coming event. For comfort she shared her bed with her husband and with beautiful Lisa, their six-year-old daughter. The girl's long auburn hair lay about her face as she slept, and Linda remembered just how proud her father had been of his beautiful one and only grandchild.

As Linda sat upright watching her family's sleeping forms, a sudden heavy weight pressed down onto the bed beside her feet. *Someone was sitting there.* A weight of about ten stone was crushing the bedclothes – but there was nothing whatso-ever to be seen!

Oh God, it's Dad, she thought. He's come to see Lisa one last time!

She gently nudged her husband, desperately trying to wake him up. A nudge to his shoulders did the trick. As he surfaced from his slumber, Linda felt the weight lift and disappear. Her father had finally gone home.

She told her husband the story but he was rather sceptical. However, he agreed to the suggestion that they move the bed around into a new position. Just as Father might want his headstone moved.

Linda felt calmer the next day, but could not help casting her mind back a couple of years – *was it happening all over again?*

She had come from a Liverpool family where psychics were not simply tolerated, they were accepted. Both her mother and grandmother had often reported strange little anecdotes. Things that had happened in their lives which they claimed defied all rational explanation.

To Linda they suggested an over-active imagination; nothing like that had ever happened to her. If being psychic was a family trait then it seemed to have skipped one generation. Although those occasions when she sensed certain things about others – or about Lisa – were odd.

Lisa was a lovely child, born in the early spring of 1982 and soon toddling along the banks of the Mersey near their new home by the Runcorn–Widnes suspension bridge. What a picture she made in her 'We love ET' top, bought more to reflect the interests of her mother than anything else.

One Saturday night in late January 1986, Linda was on her own, which was not unusual at that time. She was in the open-plan living room watching television. It was about 9.30 p.m. and Lisa – who was still only three – was asleep upstairs.

Or, at least, she should have been ... but Linda could now hear the child's voice.

Baffled, she went to see what her daughter was up to and found Lisa at the foot of the stairs, gazing into empty space and talking to thin air.

What was she witnessing? Did Lisa have an imaginary friend that her mother had not been aware of before? If so, it seemed to be someone quite big who, from the angle of her daughter's vision, was presumably sitting or crouched on about the third stair.

'She's there,' Lisa spoke suddenly, half turning and pointing to her mother.

Linda was shaken, but stood her ground as the child continued to talk to the invisible presence. Her daughter's cheeks were flushed red, as they often were when she conversed with adults – especially male adults.

'No,' the child continued. 'He's gone with the band.'

Obviously, she was referring to her father who was a drummer with a group and who had gone out to do a live 'gig' as was usual at weekends.

Linda was paralysed with surprise and fear as this unearthly conversation continued. Lisa was doing more listening than talking herself, but her mother could see that to the girl it was a perfectly normal discourse that was taking place. The only thing which made the whole situation in any way puzzling was that the other party in this two-way communication simply wasn't there.

'Lisa – come on now!' Linda said softly. But the girl ignored her and continued with the conversation.

'Come on – it's late,' Linda tried again. But her daughter was beginning to show a trace of tetchiness and merely grunted.

Linda Pall was feeling very cold by this point. Whether this was a real chill or just the shock of what was taking place was not yet clear.

Finally, Lisa said 'Bye' and turned away from the stairs. Linda made a quick grab for the youngster and took her to the settee where she sat her on her knee.

Holding her, Linda tried hard to get the child to focus on the TV set. But she could not even concentrate on this herself.

Every so often Lisa would turn and look at the stairs and giggle.

'He's still there,' she told her mother, whose heart was racing by this time.

After half an hour or so, the girl suddenly said, 'He's gone now' and returned her full attention to her mother. Then she drifted off to sleep.

When Lisa was once more settled in bed, Linda went out and sat on the front doorstep, with an overcoat to protect her against the cold. It was some time before her husband returned, but she needed his reassurance desperately.

About three months later, on another Saturday night, Lisa's father was again on a gig and Lisa was in bed with her mother waiting for him to return. Her fourth birthday had now passed and the mother and daughter often spent these evenings reading together.

Suddenly the girl sat up straight and looked at the bedroom door.

'He's here, Mum,' she said.

Thinking it was her husband, Linda glanced up. But there was nobody there. The house was silent.

'Who's here?'

'The man. He's peeping through the door. I can see his eyes.'

A clammy coldness began to creep over Linda at these words. Just what was going on here?

'What does he look like?' she asked the child.

'I don't know. He's got white hair. He's nice. He talks to me.'

If this was just a game that Lisa was making up, she was very good at it.

'What does he say to you?' her mother probed.

'He wants to know where you and Daddy are.'

'Can't he see us?'

'I don't know. But you can't see him. Only I can. He calls me "Chuck".'

This revelation startled Linda. 'Chuck' was a pet name that she had been called as a child. As far as she was aware, Lisa could not have known that fact.

'Why is he coming here, Lisa? What does he want?'

The girl smiled, as if the man had said something

246

pleasant to her. 'He says that I have to be nice. He told me, "You have a good mummy".'

Linda Pall watched her daughter as she settled down again. Of course, many youngsters have invisible friends whom they invent so that they can have joint adventures. But this seemed different somehow. Lisa was reacting to 'the man with the white hair' as if he were a real person.

At times it was rather uncanny. Lisa seemed such an intelligent girl, wise for her age. She had a burning intensity of knowledge beneath the surface, as if she were destined for great things and was being directed from afar by someone else.

A mother's hope for her only child? Linda wondered. But no, it seemed to be more than hope. It was a conviction. Almost a premonition.

There had been a recent sadness in the family. Linda was cut off from her grandfather, who had shunned them after a silly family row.

It was all very trivial and Linda and her husband had tried for nearly three years to patch things up and bring the family back together. But the old man was simply returning their letters unread and unanswered. By the winter of 1985–1986 this meant that they had not seen him since Lisa had started to walk.

And then he died. A massive heart attack struck the seventy-year-old and he was gone before there was time to say goodbye.

As usual with such matters there was great cause for regret. Why had they allowed a petty squabble to keep them apart? If only they had said what they really felt and been able to have one last chance to tell him that they loved him.

They were eventually informed of the tragedy in a roundabout way through family connections and learnt that the funeral had taken place on the Monday after that first Saturday – the night when Lisa had first started to talk to 'the man on the stairs'.

There was a famous nonsense rhyme Linda remembered from childhood. How did it go now?

As I was walking down the stair,
I met a man who wasn't there.
He wasn't there again today,
Oh how I wish he'd go away.

The morning after the second incident, Linda brought out her wedding album. Lisa had not seen the photographs before, all showing a time when the family had been happy and united.

As Linda turned the pages her daughter watched idly. Suddenly the little girl's eyes lit up and focused on one particular photograph.

'There's the man!' she cried with delight.

'What man?'

'The man with the white hair. The one who comes to talk to me . . . My friend.'

It was the man whom Lisa could barely know and whom she had never seen since taking her first steps.

It was Linda's grandfather.

SOURCES AND ACKNOWLEDGMENTS

The stories which comprise the various chapters of this book are mostly based upon either personal communications and/or interviews between the authors and the witnesses. Some conversations are reconstructed by the author.

Additional sources of information, or in cases where direct contact is not the major reference point for the story, are noted as follows.

January: *The Bi-centennial Terror.* We are very grateful to Keith Basterfield, Ray Brooke, Pony and Vladimir Godic of UFO Research Australia for their extensive assistance to us and their on-site investigation. Also Bill Chalker for supplying his first-hand observations on the matter.

February: *The February Fire.* Useful data can be gleaned from *The End of Borley Rectory,* H. Price, published by Harrap; *Poltergeist,* C. Wilson, published by NEL; and the Purnell part-work *Man, Myth & Magic.*

May: *The Whit Monday Mystery.* Useful information can be obtained from *The Complete Works of Charles Fort,* C. Fort, published by Dover Press; and the Orbis part-work *The Unexplained* (see issues 49 and 51).

June: *In Broad Daylight.* See *UFOs: 1947–1987,* edited by H. Evans and J. Spencer, published by Fortean Tomes; and Kenneth Arnold's own – but very rare – book telling the story, privately published with Ray Palmer in 1952.

July: *When the Lights Go Out.* See the detailed investigation report by Dr Berthold Schwarz, published by FSR May/June 1971.

249

August: *Terror in the House of the Dolls.* See UFOIN investigation case file by John Watson and re-appraisal of the case published by Albert Budden in BUFORA Bulletin No 26, 1988.

December: *If You go down to the Woods.* This was a five-year personal investigation by Jenny Randles, with East Anglian researchers Brenda Butler and Dot Street, as recounted in their 400-page book *Sky Crash* published by Grafton Books. However, this chapter contains later documentation procured under the Freedom of Information Act by US researchers with CAUS (Citizens Against UFO Secrecy), acknowledged below, and the precise wording comes from the actual 18-minute 'edited' tape of the events recorded live by Colonel Charles Halt as events unfolded in the forest. This was released to the British investigators in August 1984 and is now in the possession of the authors of this present book.

It should be stressed that this chapter is as accurate a reconstruction of the dialogue on the tape as is currently possible. If any errors are made in transcribing or ascribing certain words to certain people, we apologise.

Special thanks must go to Ray Boeche, David Clarke, Barry Greenwood and all at CAUS, Ralph Knutt and Roy Sandbach.

FURTHER INFORMATION

It may well be that you have experienced a paranormal happening in your life. The purpose of this section is to offer you assistance. Under each heading you will find notes about what to do and where to go for more information about a particular type of experience. We hope this guide may help.

Appearances and disappearances

The book *Into Thin Air* by Paul Begg (NEL) deals with this mystery and is one of the few available titles on this subject. Clairvoyant Robert Cracknell has written about his own experiences as a sort of psychic detective, hunting for missing persons, in *Clues to the Unknown* (Hamlyn). Also the present authors have a book which looks in some depth at half a dozen cases of recent mysterious disappearances or similar tragedies. The title is *Death by Supernatural Causes?* (Grafton).

Bedroom Visitors

Probably the most scholarly examination dealing with this field can be found in *The Terror that comes in the Night* by David J. Hufford (University of Pennsylvania) – an excellent research into traditions of what he calls the 'Old Hag' type of bedroom visitor. You can also find material about states of consciousness on the sleep/wake interface which some people believe to be related to these phenomena, in *UFOs: The Image Hypothesis* by Australian Keith Basterfield (Reed). Don't be put off by its UFO title as its scope is much wider. If you can gain access to the material of the Society for Psychical Research don't miss the superb 1886 survey 'Phantasms of the living' by Edmund Gurney, F.W. Myers and Frank Podmore. Old but good.

Children and ESP

You can find material from a psychologist's point of view in *The Radiant Child* by Thomas Armstrong (Quest). This is a deep look at the reasons why children may have psychic experiences. From a personal perspective you could read the experiences of Matthew Manning in his books – see for example *The Link* (Corgi). These describe how as a child and a teenager he underwent numerous strange experiences. Indeed he was barely an adult when he wrote this book – although he is now a perceptive and highly regarded healing medium, who shuns stage shows and psychic stardom.

Dreams

There are more books about the meaning of dreams than almost any other subject. Most offer you very conflicting views. Just read (or try to read – it's not easy!) the books by psychologists such as Freud (who interprets them sexually), and Jung (who sees archetypal imagery there) and the late science writer Chris Evans (who has a computer-based version). Ann Farraday is a good, modern, serious and professional writer on dream theory and offers useful practical experiments in her books. But for a general and objective look at dreaming and its possible paranormal associations you can do much worse than read *Dreamers* by John Grant (Ashgrove).

Entities

Undoubtedly the book to read in this field is by Hilary Evans and entitled *Visions–Apparitions–Alien Visitors* (Aquarian Press). Its original (and in our view superior) title was *The Entity Enigma*. As this suggests, it surveys the inter-relationship between every type of non-human figure you can imagine. It seeks a psychological perspective, but even if you do not agree with that conclusion, its sensibility and wealth of case material makes it indispensable when hunting for clues. Also worth looking at for more unusual perspectives are books by Jacques Vallée and John Keel, for example, Keel's *Disneyland of the Gods* (Amok Press).

Ghosts

There are probably more bad books about ghosts than there are good ones and the general reader, or witness to an apparition, will struggle when faced with making the distinction. A very good scholarly work is *Apparitions* by Celia Green and Charles McCreery (Hamish Hamilton). This reviews the factual results of their modern survey of apparitions, giving a whole range of hard data. Otherwise the two best popular writers are Peter Underwood, President of the Ghost Club – see, for example, his *Hauntings* (Dent) and, a little more analytical, Andrew MacKenzie. The latter's *Hauntings and Apparitions* (Heinemann) is a good general introduction and the more recent *The Seen and the Unseen* (Weidenfeld and Nicolson) really shows you how ghost stories can be investigated in this rigorous day and age.

Guardian Angels

Not content with writing the book discussed above, Hilary Evans penned a sequel in 1987 entitled *Gods – Spirits – Cosmic Guardians* (also from Aquarian Press). This is equally worthy and contains material about guardian spirits. A useful little book from Aquarian (the Evans books in contrast are weighty tomes) is by Kevin McClure and entitled *The Evidence for Visions of the Virgin*. As the title suggests, it brings a paranormal researcher's eyes to the tricky subject of modern religious-entity visions.

Haunted Houses

You can purchase books that tell you about every manner of haunted establishment you may visit (including a haunted pub guide from Guy Playfair!) For a gazetteer-style approach to the most haunted country in the world, try *Our Haunted Kingdom* (Fontana) by Andrew Green, another lively ghost hunter/writer, or the more recent *This Haunted Isle* by Peter Underwood (Harrap, Javelin).

Mediums

You have probably heard of the many books by the late Doris Stokes (ghost written by Linda Dearsley). Her Christian namesake Doris Collins now seems to have taken over the role with her own autobiographies. But if you want two very contrasting studies, then try Anthony Borgia's *Life in the World Unseen* (Corgi), which professes to give you a chapter-by-chapter travel guide to the place you will move to after death; also David Lorimer's scientific and scholarly examination of the life-after-death question, *Survival?* (Routledge and Kegan Paul).

Near-death Experiences

Doctor Raymond Moody started this trend with his international best-seller of précis case studies. Now thousands of people claim to recall visionary experiences when they temporarily 'died' and were brought back to life. Of course, they had not really died or they would never have come back. So we don't know if these are reports from the final stages of this existence or the first steps into another. The best books to give you a broad review come from an American psychologist, Dr Kenneth Ring – *Life at Death* (Coward, McCann and Geoghagan); a British psychologist, Dr Margot Grey – *Return from Death* (Arkana); and Dr Michael Sabom, an American cardiologist, giving the medical perspective – *Recollections of Death* (Harper and Row, Corgi).

Out-of-body Experiences

For those who have visionary experiences of seeing themselves outside their physical body (i.e. floating or flying in a 'spirit body' sense), you should be comforted to know this is a surprisingly common experience. Virtually every near-death experience starts in this way. There are some pretty trashy books on how to project yourself into the spirit world and fly through mountains or fall through the floorboards. However, the two most responsible studies come from Celia Green, whose Institute of Psychophysical Research in Oxford has done some invaluable research into many phenomena and has collated results on these cases into *Out of the Body Experiences*; and a book by Bristol psychologist, Dr Sue Blackmore, who has had out-of-body experiences and began as a believer. She now feels there is a psychological explanation – see her *Beyond the Body* (Heinemann).

Poltergeists

Poltergeists can allegedly do many things, from throwing rocks to upturning beds. Usually the physical manifestations are fairly minor. Theories range widely from ghostly apparitions to some energy connected with the witness. You can read a general study by Colin Wilson in *Poltergeist* (NEL), or a more in-depth report from leading experts and theorists Alan Gauld and A.D. Cornell in *Poltergeists* (Routledge and Kegan Paul). A fascinating book is *Conjuring up Philip* by Iris Owen and Margaret Sparrow (Harper and Row, Pocket Books), which describes a wonderful Canadian experiment carried out by a group of people who developed an artificial poltergeist and even named it Philip! Extremely illuminating about the nature of the poltergeist phenomenon.

Premonitions

If you have a vision of the future which comes true then

you are probably just one of millions who will never experience such a thing again. The question is where does coincidence end and precognition begin? But for some, having premonitions becomes a regular occurrence. Arthur Koestler, the philosopher, examined the question from a point of view of the laws of chance, see *The Roots of Coincidence* (Hutchinson, Picador). Aeronautical engineer J.W. Dunne tried a 'dream diary' experiment many years ago which can still be useful today if you fancy trying to provoke premonitions in your life, see *An Experiment With Time* (Faber). Of the many general books about the subject, describing case histories, one of the least pretentious is *Premonitions* by American Herbert Greenhouse (Turnstone, Pan). But probably the most scientific attempt to understand the question comes from researcher Danah Zohar who looks at the phenomenon in relation to modern physics in *Through the Time Barrier* (Heinemann).

Reincarnation

The belief that we live through a cycle of lives in differing bodies is a basis of many leading religions. Modern studies began in the Fifties when a woman under hypnosis recalled a life as 'Bridey Murphy' more than a century earlier – although that case has its drawbacks. The leading researcher is Dr Ian Stevenson, who has published many huge volumes detailing his investigations (although no popularized books). You could try to find his *20 Cases Suggestive of Reincarnation* (University Press of Virginia). In Britain, Joe Keeton has used hypnosis to retrieve more 'past lives' than almost anyone and has two books that describe his work, *Encounters with the Past*, written with Peter Moss (Sidgwick and Jackson), and *The Power of the Mind*, with Simon Petherick (Robert Hale). However, the best book on the subject is Ian Wilson's masterful – and critical – review of all the evidence, which throws many spanners in the works, entitled *Mind Out of Time* (Gollancz). Watch out for the more crudely titled paperback,

Reincarnation? (Sphere), because it has an update at the end with more damning information demolishing some 'real past life' cases.

Telepathy

Dr J.B. Rhine was for many years the scientist who put most effort into the question of whether mind-to-mind communication was possible. He conducted years of laboratory tests and you should look out for his books. Today Dr Carl Sargent has taken up the gauntlet with modern techniques and his work is worth a look also; see, for example, *Explaining the Unexplained*, with psychologist Hans Eysenck. Psychic Rosalind Heywood writes expertly and very lucidly about her personal telepathic experiences in her books – and they are well worth finding, e.g. *The Infinitive Hive* (Chatto and Windus). Jenny Randles has also written a book trying to relate ESP experiences to the five *known* senses to see what we can learn from current scientific knowledge. This is entitled *Sixth Sense* (Robert Hale).

Timeslips

There are few studies of cases where people claim to have literally entered a different time and lived within it. However, there is fortunately a very good book from Joan Forman, not very helpfully entitled *The Mask of Time* (MacDonald and Jane, Corgi). Aquarian Press have also released a 1989 annotated version of *An Adventure* – a classic book from nearly a century ago, describing the alleged visit by two English gentlewomen to the Palace of Versailles in France, where they then apparently slipped into a past age and met Marie Antoinette.

UFOs

Like ghosts, there are books about so-called 'visitors from space' overfilling the bookshops or libraries. Many are awful and reinforce this media-inspired stereotype. However, if you look hard enough you will find that there are almost as many theories to explain UFOs as there are sighting reports. Authors to look out for and ensure you are getting a good synthesis of the problem are Dr J Allen Hynek, Dr Jacques Vallée, D. Scott Rogo and John Keel (whose books are wonderfully eccentric but provoking). Also watch out for Hilary Evans' nice little primer *The Evidence for UFOs* (Aquarian Press). Jenny Randles has published ten books on the subject. She recommends her *UFO Study* and *UFO Reality* (Robert Hale) as starters. Jenny has also published *Abduction* (Robert Hale, Headline, Inner Light), reviewing cases where witnesses claim to have had close encounters with UFO occupants. As to cases of military cover-up, you can read Timothy Good's *Above Top Secret* (Sidgwick and Jackson, Grafton, Morrow), which crams in a great deal of evidence, although it is heavily orientated towards a belief in UFOs as spaceships and needs a modicum of caution. For an overall review of the subject, your best source has to be *Phenomenon*, edited by Hilary Evans and John Spencer (McDonald/Futura), which consists of a series of three dozen papers by many of the leading researchers in the world, surveying the entire field as it stands in the Nineties.

Weather Phenomena

The best known book in this field is *Circular Evidence* by Colin Andrews and Pat Delgado (Bloomsbury). Wonderful colour photographs but a thin and possibly misleading text. Dr Terence Meader has published numerous papers in the *Journal of Meteorology* and his theoretical work is summarized in *The Circles Effect and its Mysteries* from Artech (i.e. the Journal publishers). The social side is well covered in BUFORA's 112-page booklet *Controversy of the Circles*, from Paul Fuller and Jenny Randles, who have also claimed to have the answer in *Crop Circles: A Mystery Solved* (Hale). However, the debate rages on.

USEFUL ADDRESSES

Fortean (i.e. all sorts of unexplained mysteries)

ASSAP (Association for the Scientific Study of Anomalous Phenomena).
Has an open membership and publishes journals, runs libraries etc.
56 Telemann Square, London, SE3 9YS, England.

CSAR (Center for Scientific Anomalies Research)
A team of scientists studying anomalies. Ordinary members can join as subscribers to their excellent book-length magazine, *Zetetic Scholar.*
PO Box 1052, Ann Arbor, Michigan, MI 48106, USA.

Fortean Times
The best magazine in the field, issued approximately quarterly, packed with reports.
96 Mansfield Road, London, NW3 2HX, England.

FORTEAN RESEARCH CENTER
An American group that has similarities to ASSAP but is smaller.
PO Box 94627, Lincoln, Nebraska, NE 68509, USA.

Strange
An American version of *Fortean Times*. A new and worthwhile addition.
PO Box 2246, Rockville, Maryland, MD 20852, USA.

Psychic Phenomena

Fate
An excellent monthly magazine – the world's only serious news-stand supernatural offering. Always full of personal accounts and investigations.
PO Box 64383, St Paul, Minnesota, MN 55164–0383, USA.

Psychic News
The newspaper of the Spiritualist movement, with news about mediums and clairvoyants. Highly committed, but always interesting.
20 Earlham Street, London, WC2H 9LW, England.

SPR (Society for Psychical Research)
The grandfather of all psychic research. Over 100 years old and with a past members' list reading like a Who's-Who. Demanding standards, but very serious.
1, Adam and Eve Mews, London, W8 6UG, England.

UFOs

BUFORA (British UFO Research Association)
The oldest and major national group in Britain. Open membership. Stages monthly lectures in London and has libraries, investigation teams etc.
16 South Way, Burgess Hill, Sussex, RH15 9ST, England.

CAUS (Citizens Against UFO Secrecy)
A serious movement dedicated to extracting 'the truth' from governments.
PO Box 218, Coventry, Connecticut, CT 06238, USA.

CUFOS (Center for UFO Studies)
America's scientific research group formed by the late Dr J Allen Hynek. Has first-class publications, including *International UFO Reporter*.
2457, West Peterson Ave, Chicago, Illinois, IL 60659, USA.

FSR (Flying Saucer Review)
Once the best-respected publication in the field. Currently rather patchy in its presentation, but still has good case material from time to time.
FSR Publications, Snodland, Kent, ME6 5HJ, England.

MUFON (Mutual UFO Network)
America's main investigatory team. Open membership, lectures, monthly journal etc.
103 Oldtowne Road, Seguin, Texas, TX 78155, USA.

NUFON (Northern UFO Network)
Publishes *Northern UFO News*, listing British sightings, and (from affiliates IUN) *UFO Brigantia* – an in-depth analytical magazine. Reduced joint costs.
37 Heathbank Rd, Cheadle Heath, Stockport, Cheshire, SK3 0UP, England.

UFO CALL
A regular updated news and information service from BUFORA, written by Jenny Randles. Available at set rates by phoning 0898-121886 in the UK.

UFORA (UFO Research Australia)
The main UFO investigation/research team, with publications, membership etc.
PO Box 229, Prospect, Western Australia, WA 5082, Australia.

GHOST HUNTERS
True Stories from the World's Most Famous Demonologists

Ed and Lorraine Warren
with
Robert David Chase

In over three thousand investigations in the last forty years, Ed and Lorraine Warren have been helping people to understand, cope with and overcome terrifying experiences from the supernatural. Here, some of their incredible encounters are detailed:

– A 16-year-old girl suffers repeated sexual attacks from one of the most feared types of demons, the incubus.

– The entire population of a village is driven from its homes by satanic forces.

– Frequent sightings of the legendary Bigfoot are reported by an impoverished hillside community.

– In a psychic vision, three men are identified as the murderers of a beautiful young woman.

GHOST HUNTERS offers concrete proof that the demonic underworld exists and is much closer to home than most of us realize. This collection of baffling and bloodcurdling cases will have you sleeping with the lights on.

"These down-to-earth and otherworldly snippets of 'demonic infestation' will interest ghost watchers everywhere"
Booklist

FUTURA PUBLICATIONS
NON-FICTION
0 7088 4837 0

WOULD YOU BELIEVE IT?
Odd Tales from a Weird World

Philip Mason

MADNESS, MARVELS AND MIRACLES . . .

Enter a freakish world of horror and humour in stories so
perverse, so macabre, so madly improbable that no fiction
writer would dare present them . . .

- In January 1984, Ainsley Huskisson wrote The Lord's
  Prayer four times on the back of a 12½p stamp.

- Jailed for seven years for polygamy, Indonesian Ali
  Nasution's plea for mitigation rested on the fact that he
  had already divorced 93 of his 121 wives.

- 28-year-old Asif Mohammed from Dundee, suffering
  from depression in November 1984, chopped both his
  feet off. Surgeons later sewed them back on.

- A 14-stone Californian woman was acquitted by a San
  José court in March 1983 of killing her son. She had sat
  on him for two hours as a punishment.

WOULD YOU BELIEVE IT?

These breathtaking, mindboggling, stomach-turning facts
are guaranteed to hold you spellbound. Now read on . . .
the world out there is even stranger than your wildest
imaginings . . .

FUTURA PUBLICATIONS
NON-FICTION
0 7088 4780 3

All Futura Books are available at your bookshop or newsagent, or can be ordered from the following address:
Futura Books, Cash Sales Department,
P.O. Box 11, Falmouth, Cornwall TR10 9EN.

Please send cheque or postal order (no currency), and allow 60p for postage and packing for the first book plus 25p for the second book and 15p for each additional book ordered up to a maximum charge of £1.90 in U.K.

B.F.P.O. customers please allow 60p for the first book, 25p for the second book plus 15p per copy for the next 7 books, thereafter 9p per book

Overseas customers, including Eire, please allow £1.25 for postage and packing for the first book, 75p for the second book and 28p for each subsequent title ordered.